VERTIGINOUS LIFE

Series Editors:
Michael Herzfeld, *Harvard University*
Melissa L. Caldwell, *UC Santa Cruz*

The anthropology of Europe has dramatically shifted ground from its emergence in descriptive ethnography to the exploration of innovative theoretical and methodological approaches today. This well-established series, relaunched by Berghahn Books with a new subtitle, invites proposals that speak to contemporary social and cultural theory through innovative ethnography and vivid description. Topics range from migration, human rights and humanitarianism to historical, visual and material anthropology to the neoliberal and audit-culture politics of Schengen and the European Union.

VERTIGINOUS LIFE

An Anthropology of Time and the Unforeseen

Daniel M. Knight

berghahn
NEW YORK · OXFORD
www.berghahnbooks.com

First published in 2021 by

Berghahn Books

www.berghahnbooks.com

© 2021, 2023 Daniel M. Knight
First paperback edition published in 2023

Library of Congress Cataloging-in-Publication Data

Names: Knight, Daniel M., author.
Title: Vertiginous life : an anthropology of time and the unforeseen / Daniel M.
    Knight.
Description: New York : Berghahn, 2021. | Series: New anthropologies of Europe
    | Includes bibliographical references and index.
Identifiers: LCCN 2021017479 (print) | LCCN 2021017480 (ebook) |
    ISBN 9781800731936 (hardback) | ISBN 9781800731943 (ebook)
Subjects: LCSH: Crises—Greece—Psychological aspects. | Time perception—
    Social aspects—Greece. | Vertigo—Greece. | Greece—Social conditions—1974–
Classification: LCC HN650.5.A8 K64 2021 (print) | LCC HN650.5.A8 (ebook) |
    DDC 303.409495—dc23
LC record available at https://lccn.loc.gov/2021017479
LC ebook record available at https://lccn.loc.gov/2021017480

British Library Cataloguing in Publication Data

A catalogue record for this book is available from the British Library

ISBN 978-1-80073-193-6 hardback
ISBN 978-1-80073-910-9 paperback
ISBN 978-1-80073-194-3 ebook

https://doi.org/10.3167/9781800731936

For
Charles Stewart
and
Debbora Battaglia

Με αγάπη και θαυμασμό

Vertiginous

'Vertiginous', from the Latin *vertiginosus,* is the adjective form of 'vertigo', a disordered state characterized by whirling dizziness. In Latin, vertiginous means *a turning or whirling action.* Both vertigo and vertiginous descend from the Latin verb *vertere,* meaning 'to turn'. Vertiginous and vertigo are just two of an almost dizzying array of *vertere* offspring, from 'adverse' to 'vortex'. The 'dizzying' sense of vertiginous is often used figuratively. Vertiginous is also used to describe being unstable or unsettled in opinions; inconstant; apt to change quickly; marked by inconstancy, instability or rapid change (Merriam-Webster Dictionary 2021).

Linked to: Vertiginate
Intransitive. To turn round, spin, or rush dizzily.

Synonyms for Vertiginous
Aswoon; dizzy; giddy; light-headed; reeling; spinning; swimmy; whirling; woozy.

CONTENTS

❦

PREFACE

⤳⤳

Unlike the phenomenon it describes, the development of vertigo as a concept to further our understanding of lives caught in the reverberations of chronic crisis has a distinct trajectory. The term was first brought to my attention by Charles Stewart, who was at the time providing written comment on the then unpublished manuscript that would become *History, Time, and Economic Crisis in Central Greece*. He suggested that the proximate pasts (Ottoman landlords, Axis occupation, the Great Famine, dictatorship and the millennium stock market crash) that I was describing as returning to haunt the lives of people in Greece at the onset of the 2008/2009 global financial crisis could be characterized as 'temporal vertigo' – intense confusion as to where and when one belonged on the usually unquestioned linear timeline of temporal and material progression – a 'spin-cycle on repeat', Charles would add when revealed to be a reviewer on a later paper. Indeed, 'temporal vertigo' first appears in Charles' blurb on the back cover of *History, Time, and Economic Crisis in Central Greece* and aptly captures the sense of free-falling through time. In the graceful, understated, yet masterly manner that maketh the man, with those two words my mentor rocked my world. Palpitations of potentiality rushed through my veins: 'Temporal vertigo ... yes, this is exhilarating!' Temporal vertigo described the everyday experience of topological time I had been at pains to illustrate, effortlessly seizing the textures of affect and embodiment, the ricochets people felt as they lived precariously between rapidly onrushing pasts, the entrapment of the present and the cliff-edge of failing futures. Not knowing where to turn, questioning *when* they were living. It was lives being knocked off-balance by the crisis juggernaut, protracted Proustian stories of veering and floundering, the dolly zoom of perspective distortion creating the falling-away-from-oneself feeling as James Stewart chases Kim Novak up the bell tower, the frenetic disorienting paranoia of Scorsese's *Goodfellas*, of the shuddering camera closing in on Jack Lord on the balcony in the opening credits to *Hawaii Five-O*. It was the life of a Greek farmer investing in promises of the future while falling through history, an Athenian businesswoman detached from the Self having lost it all, a migrant suspended in emptiness, trying to escape one crisis but crashing head-on into the next.

After expressing to Charles my desire to run with the term to try to build some initial epistemological layers into what seemed like such a powerful concept – something he generously and wholeheartedly encouraged – I developed a paper on the vertigo caused by cyclical political promises of emergence for discussions I convened with Rebecca Bryant and Joyce Dalsheim in 2015 in San Diego. Playing to the American Ethnological Society theme, the paper considered how Greeks were feeling seasick with constant promises of emerging from a state of crisis into prosperous futures while the immediate social environment suggested they were being plunged back through history to material conditions last witnessed by the wartime generation. In the audience that scorching March afternoon was Debbora Battaglia. Those few days in San Diego would go a long way towards shaping my scholarship for years to come, with my hanging on every word of Debbora's incisive, sharp and beautifully articulated interjections. In just a few sentences, a phrase here or there, a knowing sparkle in the eye and tilt of the brow, Debbora is inspiration for so much of my intellectual musings on vertigo, particularly in providing confidence to travel beyond the mundane, to embrace the literary and speculative, and leave all shades of the Self on the page without bowing to pressures to conform. Her commentaries on my work, many of which have gone towards figuring out the nuances of vertigo, are innumerable and priceless.

The San Diego paper became an article in a special issue of the *Cambridge Journal of Anthropology* (*CJA*) on 'Time-Tricking', edited by Felix Ringel and Roxana Moroşanu. The collection had its roots in an Association of Social Anthropologists of the UK and the Commonwealth (ASA) session we convened in Exeter in 2015. Grounded in reflections on the first two incarnations of *Star Trek*, in the *CJA* piece vertigo is framed as a vortex through which local people feel they are being sucked. In the concentric spirals of space-time, they discuss repetition, stagnation, déjà vu, exhaustion and that infamous *Star Trek* bad-guy line 'resistance is futile'. Although the content of the article is not reproduced in this book, it does represent the first significant public airing of the temporal vertigo concept.

At this stage, temporal vertigo still existed at the level of abstraction, a theoretical tool to think through everyday experiences of topological time, but not especially well substantiated in detailed ethnography. It was at the 'Orientations: The Anthropology of the Future' gathering I convened with Rebecca Bryant at the University of St Andrews in 2018 that Nigel Rapport brought home the need to, as he put it, 'populate' the category of vertigo with affect, emotions and everyday practice. How did people actually *live* vertigo on a daily basis? 'Tell me more about how this effects their daily being', he pleaded. Nausea, he had picked up from my presentation, might be a good place to start, since there were numerous references to feeling sick and giddy in the narratives of my research participants. As the Master Storyteller of individual human experience, Nigel's words set me on the next phase of the challenge to better formulate precisely what this vertigo was for my interlocutors by way of thick description, and this subsequently led to another round of ethnographic research in Greece.

Participants at the 'Orientations' event were generous with their critical interventions; conversations with Jan Bock, Kristin Loftsdóttir, Felix Ringel (again) and Raluca Roman were provocative. Our keynote speakers Rebecca Bryant and David Valentine brought new energy and magnificent vertiginous disturbances to our days together in St Andrews and to subsequent exchanges. My work with Rebecca has its roots in shared time spent at the London School of Economics and Political Science in 2012–13 and she has been relentless in pushing me to dig deeper into how futures are constituted in crisis contexts. With expertise on temporality that far surpasses my own, Rebecca has brought new, often staggeringly philosophical (to my eyes) angles to a project that had originally focused on the proximity of disparate pasts at a time of crisis. Our collaboration came to a head with a coauthored book *The Anthropology of the Future*, which in peripheral ways speaks to vertiginous lives fashioned by the intricate and ever-changing ways in which the future influences action in the present. Working with Rebecca made me, I would like to think, a more critical thinker and encouraged me to pay even closer attention to how ideas take form on paper. With a thesis on how timespaces are structured by teleoaffects and include common vernaculars that orient life towards the future, on completing the book I found myself dissatisfied with how I had 'populated' (to use Rapport's term) the 'Time of Crisis' epoch. Working with the same terminology, this book goes some way towards addressing my concerns.

The impetus to devote a book-length manuscript to unpacking vertigo came from a keynote lecture I delivered in Beer Sheva, Israel, in May 2019. After talking on the subject of 'Futural Orientations in a Time of Technology', which mentioned in passing a few ideas glossed as temporal vertigo, conversations with Nir Avieli and Fran Markowitz convinced me that I needed to pause longer on a phrase that had by now become my go-to to capture both my ethnographic and theoretical understanding of life in twenty-first-century Greece and much of the Western world (for I was by now becoming a citizen of Brexit Britain). Stepping from the lecture theatre stage, a wide-eyed Fran greeted me with: 'The Vertiginous. I want more!' Our discussions expanded to include Martin Frederiksen, who brought new perspectives to a rapidly accelerating exchange.

The desire to grapple with the affects and vernaculars of a Time of Crisis inevitably led to an expansion of the concept of vertigo beyond merely the temporal. As will become apparent, the *Vertiginous Life* project now has three key pins – temporal, material and existential – entwined with the everyday uncertainties associated with indebtedness and financial precarity, and far more besides. Going further than the concept of precarity that has received much attention in economic anthropology in accounting for vulnerability and dispossession in late neoliberalism, vertigo captures the multilayered experiences of life in chronic crisis, as people meld existential questions about being in the world with material loss and physical displacement, and suffer the psychological consequences of being permanently imprisoned while interrogating once-undisputed notions of linear temporal progression.

The temporal, spatial and existential characteristics of vertigo come together in a section of Chapter 4 on 'Emptiness', which was the theme of discussions with Dace Dzenovska in 2018 and again in 2019 at the University of Oxford under the auspices of the Centre on Migration, Policy and Society (COMPAS, Oxford) and the Centre for Cosmopolitan Studies (St Andrews). Long a subject of ethnographic and analytical enquiry for Dace, I was invited to think through emptiness as an emic category of crisis Greece that marked a transitional moment after the destruction of the old world order and before the full emergence of the new. I am profoundly grateful to Dace for sharing her intellectual baby and continually challenging me to better understand what precisely the numerous iterations of empty/emptiness/emptying mean when used in common parlance. It was when writing our coauthored Introduction to a special collection of *Cultural Anthropology*'s *Theorizing the Contemporary* (2020) that vertigo, for me, moved beyond purely the temporal and I began to incorporate spatial displacement (Rubble, Chapter 2) and wider existential concerns (Unknowingness, Chapter 1) into a theory of crisis in European late modernity that transcended the borders of Greece.

Beyond those already mentioned, ongoing conversations with Nicolas Argenti, Laura Bear, Elisabeth Kirtsoglou, Andrea Muehlebach, David Sutton and Dimitrios Theodossopoulos have contributed to expanding parts of this book. As well as being generous in engaging with vertigo and captivity, the extraordinary literary talent Susan Lepselter has guided the way in which I have structured this book and provided me with the confidence to embrace stories that overlap with, interweave in and run parallel to a resonant *something* that helps people make sense of their world. David Henig, my longtime friend and long-suffering coeditor of the journal *History and Anthropology*, is always a willing and incredibly able sounding board quite literally twenty-four hours a day. He is unique and a foundational rock in this adventure. At St Andrews, I am fortunate to count among my colleagues Christos Lynteris and Ana Gutiérrez Garza, two of the sharpest minds and most generous people one is ever likely to encounter. Their companionship and critical input continue to shape my work. In the School of Art History, José Ramón Marcaida Lopez has provided friendship and a listening ear, offering alternative readings of the intersection of history, science and existential quandaries. Two of my marvellous doctoral students, Kate Fredricks (Eritrean migrants in Italy) and Gabriela Manley (Scotland's political futures), have offered boundless energy and exciting new perspectives on temporality, futures and political subjectivity. Gabriela's research into the Scottish National Party's promises of an independent Scotland where the future is empty, allowing a creative timespace for collaborative emergent potentiality, has been particularly influential and, I believe, poignant in our times. Supervising her challenging thesis that tests analytic boundaries on utopias, the anthropology of time and future-pasts, while remaining grounded in a highly politicized ethnographic field, has led to innumerable conversations and exchanges that have shaped large sections of this book. Under Gabriela's stewardship and with Felix Ringel's collaboration, in 2020 we founded the ASA's Anthropology of Time Network (ATN). Stimulating discussions with my wonderful students on the modules 'Anthropology of Crisis', 'Global Capitalism' and 'Anthropology of Connections' have enlivened this project.

Special acknowledgement must be reserved for Michael Herzfeld, whose starlight I travel towards. Particularly for young (and no longer quite so young) scholars of the Mediterranean, Michael is the exemplar of how robust ethnography and theoretical nous can have an impact on the wider anthropological discipline, transcending continents and fluctuating intellectual fashions. He launched an endeavour to further anthropological knowledge from an obscure corner of the Eastern Mediterranean and built ethnographic theory from Europe that has stood the test of time and continues to lead global debates. He has provided unwavering support for more than a decade and it is a privilege to publish in the *New Anthropologies of Europe* series he edits with Melissa Caldwell.

Following my research participants on their trials and tribulations has been a vertiginous experience in its own right. Some of the research presented herein began in 2003; nearly two decades encountering friends, colleagues, family and informants all over the country. At times, research has been funded by the Leverhulme Trust, the Economic and Social Research Council (ESRC), the Engineering and Physical Sciences Research Council (EPSRC), the British School at Athens, the École française d'Athènes and the National Bank of Greece. Sections of the material contained here have been discussed with colleagues in Canada, France, Greece, Italy, Israel, Luxembourg, Norway, the United Kingdom and the United States. Parts of this manuscript have benefited from close reading and detailed feedback provided by Nir Avieli, Debbora Battaglia, Rebecca Bryant, Dace Dzenovska, David Henig, Susan Lepselter, Fran Markowitz, Marek Pawlak, Stavroula Pipyrou, Nigel Rapport, Charles Stewart and Marilyn Strathern. Elisabeth Kirtsoglou, Felix Ringel and Dimitrios Theodossopoulos have also passed comment on an unpublished article that became a section of this book. For all their critical insights and interventions, I am extremely thankful.

To end, an unusual but heartfelt acknowledgement. I am sincerely grateful to Marjory Finlay at St Andrews Tennis Club for providing me the sanctuary of the clubhouse to write substantial sections of this book. Without kids summer camp 2020, it is unlikely that this manuscript would have been completed. A little peace and quiet, accompanied by the soothing repetitive pop of ball on racket, goes a long way. To my family, Stavroula Pipyrou and Bella Eugenia Pipyrou-Knight, I say, simply, 'thank you'. Stavroula provides inspiration for so much of my person and this is reflected in my writing. Always, she is the creative spark. Her elegant anthropological flair and inimitable imagination are far superior to mine.

Vertiginous Life offers an alternative reading of vulnerability and intense affective strife against a backdrop of economic precarity. It is dedicated to those who have loved, lost, fought and conquered the tumultuous decade. I hope that herein lies a compassionate account that begins to tell their tales.

Daniel M. Knight
St Andrews, 2020

Map of Greece. Source: Library of Congress

INTRODUCTION

Vertigo
Temporalities and Inconstancies

❧

Vertigo. The first time. That first experience. Who could ever forget it? Mine was on the deck of a Brittany Ferries service from Plymouth to Roscoff. On stormy seas in gale-force winds, the 160-metre vessel being thrust back and forth by pounding waves, sea spray moistening the brow. Even my grandfather, a weathered old seadog born and raised in the fishing villages gracing the south coast of England, was feeling it. I was nine years old and this was hellish. But more than the overpowering urge to projectile vomit, I had found from the moment I had stepped on board in Plymouth harbour – on waters my grandfather ominously described as 'a millpond' – that I could not bear to look over the side railings. A terrifying compulsion to jump was mixed with a sincere dread of falling, a fear not so much of height, but of giving in to the desire to launch myself overboard. The then-gentle rhythmic rocking of the in-port ferry combined with the pulsating proximity / distance of the water below – something akin to the dolly zoom effect employed in Alfred Hitchcock's *Vertigo* (1958) and later in films such as *Jaws* (1975) and *Goodfellas* (1990) – provided a cocktail of motions that induced a surreal sensation. Over the years, I would come to understand this perspective distortion as a form of motion sickness – nausea, dizziness, blurriness as I tried to maintain focus on an ever-shifting horizon.

The next occasion on which I encountered vertigo was far more intense. This was no variety of motion sickness, but a loss of a sense of historical trajectory – an unnerving disorientation in temporal perspective. I was fifteen years old when I returned from school one crisp and sunny December afternoon. A note, written in my mother's hand, was taped to our front door. It directed me to check in with our neighbours on the opposite side of the road on the run-of-the-mill suburban estate in Somerset where I grew up. I read that my brother, three years my junior, had been taken to hospital by ambulance earlier that day after returning home from a clarinet recital. This struck me as odd but probably nothing too much to worry about, given my mother's reassuring tone. After all, we had walked to school together that Monday morning, planning after-school activities and chatting about soccer (the relative virtues of Chelsea and Newcastle United, and our upcoming road trip to watch local side Taunton Town in the latter stages of the FA Vase competition). Without thinking much about it, I dutifully called on the neighbours, who told me that my brother, who had no history of the condition, had suffered a mild epileptic fit. I strolled back across the road and unlocked the front door. As I stepped into our garishly carpeted hallway, something simply did not feel right. An eerie sensation engulfed me and I shuddered to the core. In a time before mobile phones, I spent the next three hours in the house by myself, trying not to pay attention to the uncanny emptiness of the space I was in, which normally was alive at this time with noise from computer games and rustling packets of biscuits. At the same time, I was aware of an existential emptiness like the bottom had just dropped out of my world. Those three hours seemed like days, and twenty years on I can still recount the details of my minute-by-minute activities. Later, I would relate this episode to Ernesto de Martino's (2012) crisis of presence: a sense of detachment from time and space, suspension outside the Self, looking down from an outer-body perspective as from the top corner of the room; a period of hyperconsciousness where the background had been blurred out, bringing one's own existence into sharp relief. It is difficult to describe the combination of disorientation and clarity that this was a critical point in my life. The house was spiralling and I was the central point of inertia for its centrifugal force.

In an attempt to maintain my footing and reimmerse myself into the standard timeline, I tried to engage with the familiar. A popular children's television programme, *Blue Peter*; my father's oversized armchair that carried the unmistakable scent of a life of physical labour; a glass of supermarket-bought orange squash – all pivots holding in place the remnants of normality. But I still could not shake the feeling that the house was spinning around me, my stomach torn to shreds as though I had swallowed a box of razor blades. The chill of a haunting winter breeze gently rattled the back door, my ear honed in on the incessant squeaking of the family pet guinea pig. I was on pause, in a state of arrest, and the world around me was careening.

Suddenly the unnerving stillness was broken when the headlights of a car swung into the front driveway, piercing the darkness of the living room (to this day, I do not recall why I had not switched on the lights, for it was 6.30 PM in December), obscuring the faces of the presenters as the beams reflected off the television screen. I turned my head sharply to see my grandparents' mauve Renault Espace people carrier. This was weird. Why my grandparents? They lived in another town an hour away. The world came flooding back in high-speed, breaking the exhausting stasis of the past hours, a pulsating zoom accompanied by a cinematic whooshing sound clicked me back to reality. From slow motion to fast forward. My brother was dead, aged twelve, after suffering a massive brain haemorrhage while in the bathroom after his music exam.

My grandmother, gasping for breath, spluttered: We had to rush to Frenchay Hospital in Bristol to make a final decision on continued life-support. So that was why the lock on the bathroom door was hanging from a single thread of a precariously bent screw. I had noticed it there when I went upstairs to change out of my school uniform, following routine, but I had not *seen* it. That was the stain on the carpet. All these were signs that the old world order had perished, that my childhood had been abruptly ruptured and that I had fallen into *a new time*. My time home alone was the transitional gap where vertigo had made itself known, unannounced. It was a timespace between orders where I could physically feel my former Self fragmenting and flittering away, as if on the currents of the evening wind. I knew myself as a suspenseful condition of incoherence. I had been trying to pivot on the familiar while pasts and futures rushed to a point of convergence. Three, two, one, fingers snap, you're back in the room.

On reflection, what I find striking is that it was those three hours, the minutes and seconds, that transformed my being, not the aftermath of coping with a tragic loss. A mature and well-grounded teenager, in the coming months and years I would find direction relatively easy to establish, focusing as I did on education, my partner at university and building a career. The story has been narrativized over the years, retold to loved ones, a social worker searching for trauma who identified me as cold and emotionally disengaged, even at times to a class of Master's students. Yet I am never fully able to capture the vertiginous atmosphere at home during those intermitting hours. I also question aspects of my recollection – was it really a sunny day, for I remember short-sleeve shirts in December? Surely not. Why did the neighbours seem so sure my brother had suffered an epileptic fit? Did they not see his condition on admittance to the ambulance? They were eyewitnesses, weren't they? Did my parents really not try to call me during those hours, even from a hospital phone? Did the welfare of their other son at a time of peril not cross their mind? Did they call and it was me who whitewashed this from history? How selfish of me to even raise this here. What is more, *Blue Peter* finishes at 5.30 PM – always has done, always will do. Why then, in my mind's eye, does it still provide the background sights and sounds when my family pulled into the driveway at 6.30 PM? I swear it was still on TV. Were my brother and I discussing soccer that morning or were we engaged in a bitter argument over the most endearing qualities of Sabrina Johnson, a girl in his class? Actually, I seem to remember him running on ahead. Was that because he saw a friend beckoning down the alley or, maybe, was I taunting him about his portly figure? Of course, despite being there, I shall never know. In affinity with literary great W.G. Sebald (1990), my manic and feverish musings on the mingling of personal facts and fictions leave me entranced by the tenacity and fallibility of memory. To this day, my parents' small upstairs bathroom sends my head into a spin, provoking flashbacks to episodes past and leaving me to ponder the what-might-have-been. *Blue Peter*, launched in 1958 and still running today, shall always be on air that December afternoon in the year 2000, locked into a timespace of eternal, shattering, eerie vertigo.

*****

Indulgent though this initial intervention might seem, this book is constructed around such character-centric leads, building from individual experiences of vertigo to offer a broader framework for contemplating the affective structure of a Time of Crisis. I hope that the reader can relate to some aspects of my story, occasions when time becomes elastic, the world is spinning, there is an apparent shift in temporal rhythms, and material objects, sights and sounds become uncanny. There might be the sense, the feeling or atmosphere of epochal change, *nothing will ever be the same* ... Out with the old and in with the *something else*. Over the course of many years, friends and colleagues have related stories that resonate with the vertigo I felt during those three hours in December 2000. Of being caught in an earthquake that lasted just seconds of clock time, leaving behind not only the rubble of buildings but also the destruction of the Self, an indelible mark that led to a reassessment of person in the world.[1] Or perhaps the situation of living beside a loved one with terminal illness, stretching over many years. Reconsidering the temporal horizons of 'the future' as onrushing, expecting an imminent rupture and not knowing what comes after the hyperconscious present. With each new dawn, the carer might awake with a smack to the stomach that leaves them gasping for breath, head pounding, or perhaps they dully return to a moment of time held blessedly in abeyance. A student at an elite higher education institution recalling their experience of life in an East African refugee camp, their home destroyed by international conflict, the toil of existence during ten years spent in spatiotemporal limbo, now left second-guessing the vertiginous anguish of childhood interrupted.

My project here is to follow the trail of people who express having experienced vertigo as a profoundly personalized shift in sociality. My hope is to provide a better ethnographic and analytic picture of that *something* that seems essential to understanding the affective structure of a Time of Crisis. As I approach it, a Time of Crisis may be individual, shared, societal or even global. It may last seconds, days, years – indeed, it may remain immeasurable partly or wholly in duration. Time maps are not my primary concern. The Greek economic crisis from which my ethnography is drawn stretches over more than a decade; within this period, there are, inevitably, innumerable bubbles of interrelated crises. Of course, people die outside wider societal crises such as austerity, war or pandemics (I do not compare their qualitative attributes or subjective takes on 'severity'). Unemployment rises and falls and may touch one family multiple times before knocking on the door of their neighbours. A Time of Crisis welcomes and elaborates the discourse of fate, chance, luck – the roll of the dice into time and space. One person's crisis is another's opportunity, as evinced by international investment in Greece's energy sector and foreign (particularly Russian) interest in buying up Greek property, including islands. Sharks will always circle. I do not claim to provide a smooth omniscient picture that can account for the experiences of all within the calendrical decade of Greek crisis and its 'fallout' (Masco 2015); timespaces overlap and interweave, and their constitutive stories may converge or meander down different alleyways. My contention is that a Time of Crisis, regardless of duration or scale, is a transformative epoch where things feel different, lives take on strange and unexpected trajectories, folds and loops, and there is often the sense of stuckedness or hyperconsciousness.[2] Nausea, dizziness, falling, a sense of splitting from the former Self. The affects that populate a Time of Crisis can peramble across the individual to the collective without contradiction[3] – indeed, this is its definitive modus operandi as a structuring device that calls forth the necessity of naming it.

EPOCHS

A Time is Crisis in the context of Greece refers to a period that transcends the calendrical decade 2009–19. My primary focus throughout the 'crisis years' in Greece has been on temporality, or how everyday people have reconsidered and utilized their pasts, presents and futures to make sense of crisis. This forms the basis for my current thinking on vertigo as elemental to the affective structure of a Time of Crisis, so it is worth pausing to momentarily review. What I have termed 'culturally proximate' pasts as disparate as the era of Ottoman landlords in the 1800s, the Great Famine of 1941, the Second World War occupation, the 1967–74 dictatorship and the late 1990s stock market crash inform everyday coping strategies, the contextualization of increased social suffering and poverty, and facilitate futural planning, hopes and expectations in crisis Greece (Knight 2012a, 2015; on repetition of past events, see Bandak (2019)). One of the profoundest effects of the ongoing crisis, I have argued, has been the way in which it has stimulated people to rethink their relationship to time. Borrowing poignant metaphors from my long-term muse, philosopher of science Michel Serres, one can imagine fragments of time getting caught in the filtration process of a percolator, thus remaining present and relevant, or people living among the usually unseen sediment being tossed and turned in the countercurrents beneath the deceivingly placid flow of a powerful river (Serres and Latour 1995; Knight 2015: 8–9). The social topology of the past, present and future helps us make sense of how people live a period of rupture and social change (Knight 2016). As Charles Stewart and I have argued in our coauthored introduction to a collection entitled *Ethnographies of Austerity: Temporality, Crisis and Affect in Southern Europe*: 'Modern linear historicism is often overridden (and overwritten) in such moments by other historicities showing that in crises, not only time, but history itself as an organizing structure and set of expectations, is up for grabs and can be refashioned according to new rules' (Knight and Stewart 2016: 13).

In the same publication, Charles Stewart riffs on how moments of crisis invite critical reflection on commonly held assumptions of temporal (and historical) succession, which I believe illustrates my thinking on how crisis transforms perspectives on time and leads nicely into the concept of vertigo presented in this book.[4] Referring to a scene in Lee Katzin's 1971 film *Le Mans*, Stewart recites how the race car driver played by Steve McQueen realizes he has to avoid a slow-moving car. The scene of the car careening, skidding and crashing into the guardrail is shot in a mixture of slow motion and regular speed, flashing back and forth to close-ups of McQueen's face. Lying stunned, in a state of shock and spiralling confusion, his mind flits back and forth from the present to the moment he first perceived danger, through all the stages of the event. At this point, the past, present and future are simultaneously caught in processes of re-evaluation and projection, a dizziness of swimming, perhaps drowning, in the fluidity of time (Knight and Stewart 2016: 3). McQueen's character is searching the archives of time to make sense of the vertiginous event that just smashed his world, yet his head is still spinning from the impact and it is impossible to focus long enough to establish a sequence of happenings. The current project on vertigo goes beyond previous concerns with temporal topologies with markedly historical trajectories and is intended as more than simply another ethnographic analysis of the financial crisis. The venture, I hope, is far more ambitious in accounting for the existential, material and temporal qualities of disorientation that I call 'vertigo' that, after a *Le Mans*-style smash to shake the world, form an intricate and inalienable part of the affective structure of an epochal Time of Crisis.

In a recent publication, Rebecca Bryant and I have argued for under-standing everyday temporalities through the notion of timespaces that pro-vide actors with common vernaculars, affective structures and aims in how they orient their lives (Bryant and Knight 2019). At the communal level, timespaces and their affects are often described in the vernacular in epochal terms – a Time of War, a Time of Prosperity, a Time of Brexit. For instance, living in the Time of Brexit may evoke nausea, panic and apocalyptic spec-ulation for the Remainer. A Time of Peace in the Middle East may be eaten into by the anticipation of imminent displacement and violence (Hermez 2012, 2017). Epochal thinking may transcend boundaries of cities and na-tions, as in the collective sense that the Time of Trump has beckoned in a new era of politics with global consequences and a new set of catchwords and imaginaries, or the shared hope expressed by people across austerity-ravished Europe when the radical left came to power in Greece in early 2015.

A Time of Crisis, then, has a set of shareable vernaculars, affects and ori-entations that shape everyday action, giving the timespace its own rhythm, atmosphere and *feel*. The affective structure presents people with projects, recommended paths and futures, guiding or informing practice within the timespace without forgoing novelty. Vertigo, I propose, is an integral ele-ment of the affective structure of a Time of Crisis. In Greece, the Time of Crisis is marked by existential ambiguity, multiple forms of emptiness, nau-sea and anxiety, and eerie feelings of life suspended in captivity. Paralysis, stasis, what Henrik Vigh (2008: 17) terms 'progressless motion', mark the temporal rhythm and speed, somewhat paradoxically surrounded by on-rushing pasts and futures that are both intensely proximate and always just over the horizon, out of reach. It is partially this condition of permanent 'not-quite' and 'almostness' that gives this timespace its vertiginous edge, proliferating as it does in the transitional gap between the destruction of the old world order and the not-quite emergence of the new (Dzenovska 2020; Shir-Vertesh and Markowitz 2015).

Going back to popular culture to elucidate, the movement towards a the-ory of vertigo is captured nicely in the opening credits to the original series of the American television series *Hawaii Five-O* (1968–80), where the cam-era shudders as it approaches a cityscape from above the crashing waves of the Pacific Ocean. The camera switches between flashing images (the rele-vant 'bits' or 'events' caught in Serres' percolation) before juddering, almost pulsating towards an apartment block where, on a lofty balcony, stands the striking figure of protagonist Steve McGarrett (played by Jack Lord). Mc-Garrett swings round to a pause, staring straight down the barrel of the cam-era. After such a vertiginous ride, the viewer is captivated by the stillness of the shot, an elongated and somewhat uncanny present, before the dizzy-ing camerawork starts again, frantically clicking away at images of varying relevance until the next freeze-frame. A Time of Crisis is Steve McGarrett pinned down on either side by vertiginous camera shots of events that form plotlines of past and future episodes, travelling at different speeds. For a moment everything makes sense, but the ride has been sickening and no two successive images bear logical connection.

Epochal thinking frames perceived differences in the temporalizing of human activity, expressing an apparent shortening or lengthening of the relationship between past, present and future in our own lives. Learning to live with drastically decreased household income, policy attacks on healthcare, energy and property rights has impacted people in different ways. The Time of Crisis in Greece and beyond has become a timespace of trying to cope with unknowingness, attempting to familiarize the unforeseen, and reconciling broken dreams of futures past. 'Crisis time' has burst through the boundaries of the event itself (the 2009–19 economic crisis) and the fallout continues to order everyday life. As such, crisis has become both a form of governance (Dole et al. 2015) and a rhetorical narrative characterizing and driving our times (Roitman 2014; cf. Vigh 2008). As Christopher Dole, Robert Hayashi, Andrew Poe, Austin Sarat and Boris Wolfson have argued in their landmark multidisciplinary book *The Time of Catastrophe* (2015), the temporality of crisis should not be confined to solely the 'rupturing of the temporal continuity of history that heralds a destructive and unexpected ending' (Dole et al. 2015: 7; see also Holbraad, Kapferer and Sauma 2019). Instead, the timespace of crisis continues to order the mundane far beyond the event, providing what Serres (1995) might term the 'background noise' of everyday life that parasitically preys on its subjects, inducing vertigo at every turn. Populating the affective structure of a Time of Crisis, of which vertigo is a fundamental constitutive, is a central aim of this book.

WHIRLPOOLS

A crisis of presence in de Martino's sense goes some way towards accounting for the vertigo of a Time of Crisis, in that individuals are detached from normalized rhythms of time and history. The loss of established historical and cultural reference points through displacement and distress undermine the presence of the Self, leading to a growing sense of disorientation, as I recall experiencing while waiting for news on my brother's condition. De Martino's 'deep anthropological perspective on precarity' relates to social and existential experiences of subjugation, migration and alienation, crises that undermine the foundations of intersubjective personhood (Farnetti and Stewart 2012: 432). A timespace of crisis, momentary or chronic, is a disorienting place precisely because of the stagnation of the 'dynamic power that ordinarily propels the individual toward the future'. Trajectories are lost, temporal rhythms change. De Martino explains:

> The reality of the world appears strange, mechanical, sordid, simulated, inconsistent, perverse, dead; and presence is felt as lost, dreamy, estranged from itself, and so forth … [the individual is] detached from the present, precisely because he cannot fully 'be-there' … in the present, being still anchored or polarized in an undecided critical moment of his own personal history. (2012 [1956]: 435)

In my opening narrative vignette, I reflect on the uncanny timespace enveloping a critical event, the vertiginous atmosphere, and feeling that the world around is operating at a different speed. Not fully 'being there' is something most of us can relate to at certain times in our lives, where we become numb to the world and to ourselves. The losing of Self and world, for de Martino, signals existential precariousness where the movement outside of historical becoming is marked by an overpowering sense of anguish. The risk of radical alienation from history and society, and all familiar reference points, is a theme that comes up throughout this book, where unknowingness of Self and world creates anguish, described in narrative as anxiety, emptiness, yearning and entrapment. For my interlocutors, the Time of Crisis has a sense of detachment where normal rhythms of historical becoming are under scrutiny; 'the givens of the past and present *should* become something novel in the future' but instead forge messy trajectories or are indefinitely ruptured (Farnetti and Stewart 2012: 432). A Time of Crisis fractures timelines of anticipated historical succession and the consuming anguish incites the dizziness, nausea and assorted affects associated with vertigo. On anguish, de Martino elaborates:

> crisis of presence is the ultimate risk of losing the human accompanied by anguish … that anguish is a reaction of presence in the face of the risk of not being able to overcome critical contents, and of feeling oneself headed for supreme abdication … Anguish signposts the attack on the very roots of human presence, the alienation of oneself from oneself. (2012 [1956]: 439)

The anguish of not being able to overcome crisis – subsequently creating an existential crisis – and of the future apparently never emerging as once expected or planned leads to feelings of being trapped in a temporal spin-cycle or of falling through the cracks in time. Increased anxiety towards Self and society based on the vertigo of captivity, of never emerging, is a recurrent theme in crisis narratives. There is a constant belief that other worlds and other futures are passing by, are inaccessible and are defeated by entrapment in chronic crisis. As will become apparent in the subsequent chapters, there is regular reference to how crisis is indexed by alienation from Self and society; a Time of Crisis oversees the destruction of cultural life and human history as it *should* be written (de Martino 2012 [1956]: 440).

The anguish of dehistoricization, or removal from normalized temporal and historical succession, triggers the affects of vertigo. Historical discontinuity stimulates vertiginous movement into a sublimely new timespace. Concerned with both presence and historical discontinuity, philosopher of history Eelco Runia (2010: 1) explicitly identifies the relation between transitional timespaces and vertigo, arguing that discontinuity is primarily a human creation marked by a double-edged fear of falling and a wish to jump. In my reading, Runia makes two key points. First, at moments of historical rupture, where we may claim a radical new timespace has opened up, people find themselves standing on the edge of time. Teetering on the verge of a new era, they are consumed by vertigo, a dizzying confusion of whether to resist the widening vortex or to embrace the unknown. Having taken leave of their presence in the present, 'to stand on the brink of time' cultivates a sensation of struggle between the wish to step down and the desire to throw oneself off the cliff-edge (Runia 2010: 15). The analogy of the cliff-edge is similar to Marcel Proust's (1992) description of the giddiness experienced when balancing on high slits that never stop growing, year upon year, as time accumulates. The sensation of being 'miles high' makes walking in the world dangerous with the ever-increasing potential to fall, perched on the vertiginous summit of time, peering down at personal and collective pasts. At such heights, 'certain people claim to have felt the coldness of death' (1992: 106). Point two of Runia's thesis contends that some people may embrace vertigo, and this is a decision to be applauded. Indeed, giving in to the vertiginous is a positive choice, since these pioneers will forge ahead in creating a new era of distinct history. The destruction of vertigo, and the emptiness of the vortex, also holds latent possibility (Dzenovska 2020; Dzenovska and Knight 2020). Runia's ideas on 'the vertiginous urge to commit history' are highly thought-provoking and ultimately helpful in building a theory of vertigo and crisis. But they are not wholly unproblematic. Let us pause to consider them here.

Like de Martino, Runia is interested in the connection between historical rupture and loss of presence, and sees vertigo as a state of possession that stalks this transitional landscape. It is productive to take the basis of his argument from an observation he makes on French philosopher and sociologist Roger Caillois' thesis on games. Here, the destruction/possibility duality is at its clearest. *Ilinx* (the Greek for 'whirlpool') is a genre of gaming (such as racing videogames) that deliberately distorts perception by pursuing vertigo and incorporates an element of creative inevitability that vertigo will eventually consume the player. Caillois explains these games as being:

based on the pursuit of vertigo and which consist of an attempt to momentarily destroy the stability of perception and inflict a kind of voluptuous panic upon an otherwise lucid mind. In all cases, it is a question of surrendering to a kind of spasm,
seizure, or shock which destroys reality and sovereign brusqueness. (2001: 23)

More than the feeling of dizziness and nausea found in the existentialism
of Søren Kierkegaard and Jean-Paul Sartre respectively, for Runia, vertigo
involves the inclination to surrender and the dual-aspect destruction/pos-
sibility of the vertiginous jump into the *ilinx*, whirlpool, created by physical
or metaphorical movement (Caillois 2001: 24). My initial vertigo onboard
Brittany Ferries was caused by the multiple motions of the voyage – up and
down, port to starboard – provoking physical sickness that was multiplied
when I looked over the side of the boat to the depths of the ocean below.
At that moment, another form of vertigo kicked in, an internal battle over
whether to jump based on surrendering to an overpowering sensation that
devoured body and mind. It is the multiplier effect, the fear of not being able
to resist, the wish to overcome the fear, the fear that fear itself may not be
enough to deter that causes the sensation of *ilinx*, a maelstrom or vortex that
manifests itself as dizziness.

Vertigo in this incarnation entails the annihilation of the stability of perception linked to timespaces of 'disorder and destruction' (Runia 2010: 14;
see also Runia 2014: 107). The inherent destructive order of vertigo distinguishes it from the fear of heights and the fear of falling. Runia suggests that
perception distortion – perhaps, for the purposes of our argument, crisis
rupturing the unquestioned continuity between past, present and future –
triggers the wish to jump and the desire to destroy. The sense that the emptiness has to be filled may mushroom into something so overwhelming,
so oppressive that people begin to fear that they will not be able to resist
(Runia 2014: 114–15; Caillois 2001: 23–26). Vertigo is, then, indicative of
violent suspense. This approach resonates with a key argument on vertigo
and emptiness that is the subject of Chapter 4 of this book, namely that at
a Time of Crisis, lives are held in suspension, positioned in the transitional
timespace between the destruction of old world orders and the emergence
of new, something I experienced in the vertiginous three hours waiting for
news on my brother's hospitalization. The timespace of emptiness and suspension, as scholars such as Dace Dzenovska (2019, 2020) have argued, simultaneously holds the ruins of futures past and innumerable possibilities of
the not-yet. When looking over the cliff-edge into the emptiness, or vortex,
of uncertain and unexpected futures, the vertiginous possesses both creative
and destructive potentiality (Manley 2019a).

The second of Runia's contentions relates to vertigo as a positive state,
for he argues that the truly courageous take the jump and create history,

leaving behind the familiar to selflessly cross the frontier of time. His stance is linked to an approach to presence that he describes as follows: 'Presence is the desire to share in the awesome reality of people, things, events, and feelings, coupled to a vertiginous urge to taste the fact that awesomely real people, things, events, and feelings can awesomely suddenly cease to exist' (2014: 53–54). The human condition is perverse in its desire for continuity and familiarity alongside discontinuity and surprise. This line of argument resonates with Serres' reflections in his aptly titled *Times of Crisis*. Serres borrows from medicine when declaring the crisis moment to be a point where existence is endangered as a person or organism confronts a growing infection. At this critical 'fork in the road', a life-or-death decision must be made (2014: xii). If the crisis moment is survived, then the person should establish a new path since reverting to the previous condition would imply a loop-like return to the original course leading to crisis. The choice of reverting to past trajectories or forging anew is the vertiginous cliff-top scenario that propels the person either towards death or something innovatively new. Many fear the obligation to invent, says Serres, yet others have the audacity to delight in the life-altering challenges of crisis. For Runia, the pursuit of the awesomely new is enabled by stepping off the cliff-edge into the vortex of the unforeseen. He ultimately states that if people fail to embrace vertigo, the future will always have the 'same blank implacable face; in reality everything ultimately has its way if just left alone' (2014: 115). The future will be unending cyclical crisis without emergent novelty.

It is at this point where our paths diverge. I could – actually I have – (co)written a whole other book that would contest Runia's forgoing of agency and subjectivity in future formation, an argument that appears to support fate as the primary orientation of future-making (Bryant and Knight 2019). In fact, I find Søren Kierkegaard's reading of destruction/creativity in the vertiginous moment helpful here, although his own preoccupation with freedom of choice – to stand ground or fall – is somewhat distracting for our context of chronic crisis.[5] In the pursuit of better defining dizziness, in *The Concept of Anxiety*, Kierkegaard first distinguishes anxiety from fear:

> [Anxiety] is altogether different from fear and similar concepts that refer to something definite, whereas anxiety is freedom's actuality as the possibility of possibility. Anxiety may be compared with dizziness. (1980: 42)

Kierkegaard exemplifies his understanding of dizziness as anxiety founded in freedom, which he illustrates with a story that, once again, is staged on the edge of a tall building or cliff. We find ourselves in familiar territory – a man looks over the edge, experiences the focused fear of falling, but also a simultaneous and terrifying impulse to throw himself intentionally into the abyss. The vertiginous moment is one of possibilities. For Kierkegaard, this experience is anxiety caused by freedom of choice. The potential to choose even the most self-destructive of possibilities, prospective suicide, triggers vertigo. This anxiety over possibilities and realizing the freedom of choice in the *possibility of possibility* manifests as dizziness:

> He whose eye happens to look down the yawning abyss becomes dizzy. But what is the reason for this? It is just as much in his own eye as in the abyss, for suppose he had not looked down. Hence, anxiety is the dizziness of freedom, which emerges when ... freedom looks down into its own possibility ... Freedom succumbs to dizziness. (1980: 61)

Kierkegaard insists that the possible creativity of vertigo depends on how the condition is navigated and upon educating the Self to find originality on the frontier of destruction. The terrifying assaults of anxiety are fraught with danger, but can also awaken the senses to potentiality beyond; vertigo *can* be both destructive and generative *if* navigated appropriately and only in certain intersubjective interactions. This takes us back from the do-or-die ledge that Runia proposes, where the courageous leap to create history almost comes across as an obligation, the next logical step, to create history for some form of collective good. However, Kierkegaard levels the playing field slightly, acknowledging that for many people, the danger of dizziness is experienced as overpowering, as something that can overwhelm and seize the individual – this seems to be Serres' stance when saying some people fear the precariousness of crisis, while others delight in the challenge to invent. The more creative the individual, the more anxiety they feel and the more creative potentiality they possess. If people can navigate vertigo 'correctly', Kierkegaard postulates, they will be able to destroy the status quo to create 'new and original forms of living' (May 2015: 40).

Kierkegaard answers the question of agency and intersubjectivity that is silenced by Runia, who deems the future blank and inevitable if the leap into the *ilinx* is not embraced. But in turn he places too much emphasis on freedoms that are not always available or clearly evident in a timespace of chronic crisis. In a Time of Crisis, individual freedom is often curtailed through structural violence, deep economic reform, increased targeted political exploitation, xenophobia and so on. In broad brushstrokes, throughout this book, the stories of vertiginous life are ones of struggle, some of conquest, nearly all with the underlying premise that people are being forced to search for alternatives to once-familiar livelihoods. It is rare to find accounts where vertigo could be construed as a positive or even a creative state of existence. At times, people may give in to vertigo, accepting or resigning themselves to the uncomfortable comfort of the crisis status quo, as in Chapter 5, where we meet people who could be said to identify with their captors in a form of societal Stockholm Syndrome. A creative engagement with vertigo is perhaps most evident on occasions where people have relocated to once-abandoned ancestral homes in search of stability in the simplicity of 'village life', as discussed in Chapter 2, but this would still be rendered as a 'return to pasts' in Runia's (or indeed Proust's) terms, thus tempering novelty. Still further, the fleeing from crisis Greece evinced in the so-called 'brain-drain', a topic covered in Chapter 4, could be construed as a leap into the vortex of the unknown to create new life through a clean break, in Runia's words, 'a strategy for escaping from an unbearable tension by doing something – by breaking apart from what one used to cherish, by eating the apple, by committing an "original sin"' (2010: 14). There is individual freedom to run, to relocate, but people themselves would usually class this as an attempt to escape the vertiginous state of crisis Greece. The leap of faith here is to distance oneself from dizziness, to sooth anxiety, the creation of a new life in a new place where emergent possibility is a side-effect of absconding from crisis. Real life and the motives behind such decisions in a Time of Crisis are far murkier than portrayed in the philosophies of Runia or Kierkegaard. Succumbing to the vertiginous struggle is, for me, more a sign of exhaustion with a decade of crisis or a coping mechanism rather than a courageous leap into the abyss to forge new history or an awesome step beyond the status quo towards a historical *mutation* (Runia 2014: 111). Vertigo is something far more grounded and mundane, taking hold as people come to reconcile the destruction of past lives (expectations, hopes and beliefs) with the choppy emergence of new social, political and aesthetic orders. This is not to do a disservice to the research participants; rather, it is to acknowledge the idealism of philosophies that propagate how vertiginous struggle should be embraced. Kierkegaard seems to concede this when noting that vertigo can be expressed in muteness as well as a scream, meaning that the subtle everyday struggles with vertigo are as intense and significant as sublime statements and grand gestures of history-making.[6] In my reading of vertiginous lives, loss is not generally regarded as positive or perceived as a pioneering leap benefiting the collective. The abyss people are staring into is one of deep, dark, incredibly daunting loss.

Loss is central to the all-encompassing power of vertigo in Richard Goodkin's (1987: 1173) comparative reading of Proust and Hitchcock, 'the incongruity of feeling one's finite being, limited in time and space, in the dizzying presence of the infinite, the abyss'.[7] Vertigo surfaces in the hidden, unexpected and lost elements of pasts and futures, in the gaps between orders and while searching for meaning in the limits of the unforeseen ('surprise' in Runia's terms). Obsession with the temporal in Goodkin's interpretation of Proust is in extracting its riches, operating at what Goodkin (1987: 1173) considers the 'highest expression of [the] mortal state'. The many years of temporal baggage – what Serres (1995) calls the 'cartload of bricks' being dragged into the future – creates a sense that freedom can only be found when cutting loose historical burden, yet this is accompanied by the fear of forgetting and deleting the past (Proust 1992: 1047). Hitchcock's *Vertigo* also explores the limits of mortal existence and the experience of the infinite, the sensation that the mortal and the timeless, or perhaps man and God, belong to two radically incompatible worlds. The protagonist's vertigo ceases when he surrenders any ambition of joining his love interests in the world of immortality (death) and mortality (together in 'the real world') by letting go of any future attempt to bridge the finite and the infinite (Goodkin 1987: 1176). In layperson's terms, vertigo ceases upon the acceptance of loss, being primarily evident at the point of contest, of coming to terms, and in moments of (in)decision while balanced on the edge of the *ilinx*.

Proust's giddiness, the dizziness of Kierkegaard, the nausea of Sartre, de Martino's anguish, Runia's falling – in all, vertigo signals the struggle between person and world, between the freedom of action and suppression of the Self, between irreparable loss and creative potentialities, taking place in a transitional timespace of unforeseen rupture and change. In the local vernaculars contained in this manuscript, people tend to shift between these terms of affect interchangeably, identifying little difference at an experiential level. Yet in the pages of philosophical debate, scholars go to great lengths to establish heuristic distinction. It has not been, and will not be, my intention here to present each and every one in turn, since the purpose here is to provide ethnographically led theory on a timespace of vertiginous precarity and change. At points in this book, the analysis turns to nausea, loss, dizziness and the vertigo of existential and material emptiness, which are treated according to the core writings on these themes. Perhaps Caillois' observations on amusement park rides are a revealing place to conclude for now, since he scales up vertigo to the point of being a potential long-term social structure. While Runia and Kierkegaard emphasize the creative possibilities of destruction and applaud the courageous individuals who 'take the plunge', Caillois urges caution in embracing vertigo as primarily a positive, creative threshold. Vertigo, he says, is an assault on every organ, a fear often only counterbalanced by the observation that everyone else around is enduring the same. People turn pale and dizzy to the point of nausea. 'They shriek with fright, gasp for breath, and have the terrifying impression of visceral fear and shrinking as if to escape a horrible attack' (Caillois 2001: 26). If this is to be scaled up to societies enduring a Time of Crisis in which vertigo is a crucial constitutive of the affective structure, then we need to detail the fine-grained existential consequences and affective nuances of this complex social-political-historical milieu. 'The faithful do not agree to be entirely captivated', nor do they deem to be without danger the vertiginous seizure.

There should be, he assumes, a precaution against vertigo, if people take the decisive and difficult leap to jump through 'the narrow door that gives access to civilization and history [to progress and to a future] then this 'basis for collective existence' (Caillois 2001: 141) can lead to a dangerous vicious circle of vertigo, life inside the *ilinx*, clawing away at body and mind, from which there is no escape.

SCALES

The following chapters aim to provide standalone theoretical insights on the affects and resonances of vertigo, while producing an overarching framework to better understand lives in crisis. As such, the chapters work on multiple scales, each focusing on an individual whose life I have encountered at various stages throughout nearly two decades of ethnographic and archival research in Greece. It is my intention to build on the thick ethnographic description of these individuals in order to draw out key conceptual points on how people experience multiple forms of vertigo at the heart of their lives in chronic crisis. The topics tackled may seem disparate – unknowingness, ruination, the elsewhen, emptiness and suspension, and captivity – each forming as they do the backbone of individual chapters that can be read as a commentary on vertigo and crisis in their own right. Rather than adopting (and thus being tied to) a single approach from a specific school, I draw on literature from fields as diverse as existentialism, the philosophy of time, speculative fiction, film studies and material culture to unpack these themes. This epistemological diversity is essential to best account for the nuances of vertigo being portrayed by each person in my story.

Throughout the book three pins of vertigo become apparent: the existential (exemplified in Chapter 1), the material (Chapter 2) and the temporal (Chapter 3). Although not mutually exclusive and often becoming indistinguishable from one another, each chapter foregrounds one of these essential nodes in the delicate intricacy of vertiginous life. As one might expect, the existential depicts struggles with the Self, the fissures created in personhood as lives are ruptured, torn apart, scattered in the wind and stitched back together. The loss of dreams, livelihoods and loved ones to the violence of crisis has left an indelible mark on the essence of being and becoming. Trying to reconcile with former Selves is an undercurrent churning up the sediment underlying many narratives in this book. Taken to the extreme, on occasion the question 'what is the point of existence?' is posed as people grapple with a sense of futility in a world of unforeseen violence that has decimated public and private domains.

Materiality takes centre stage in the vertigo felt by people forced to re-locate to unknown or unfamiliar physical environments, including villages abandoned since the Greek Civil War in the 1940s. Displacement fosters vertigo engrained in stone walls, derelict homes, and objects and environments drenched in occasionally uneasy historicity. Displacement is at once spatial and temporal. Simply resting a hand on the cold stone of a crumbling schoolhouse transports one on a journey of intense and unexpected topological connectivity, events and lives frantically grasping through the fog of decades of displaced space and time. The extraordinary is often embedded in the materiality of the mundane, confusing trajectories of the ultramodern and traditional, providing a gateway to entangled pasts and catapulting into futures of accelerating global abstraction (Avieli and Sermoneta 2020).

In some instances, the forced relocation is across national borders where families are divided and careers are remade in far-off lands. Further, interaction with changing technological landscapes triggers questions about temporal trajectories. Photovoltaic panels have become a common sight in the crisis years as part of a 'saviour' economic programme and reference futuristic, ultramodern, European, clean, green sustainability. Yet the engineers who install the infrastructure heat their own homes with wood-burning stoves, which speak to traditional, pre-modern pasts, reminiscent of village life and peasantry. For me, the materiality of my parents' bathroom still triggers vertigo, a portal to the affective past and a timespace of dizzying personal inquisition.

Underpinning all thematics and theoretical excursions is my original concern with temporal disorientation, or how crisis muddles trajectories that would have once been undisputed. Time's arrow, so often taken for granted as the engine house driving social and material progression in the post-Enlightenment West, has become noticeably skewed. The cartoon cuckoo clock has been smacked with an Acme Corporation crisis-branded mallet and the springs are well and truly hanging out, on display for all to see. Temporal vertigo ducks and dives its way throughout the forthcoming pages , weaving together discussions on personal unknowingness, changes to physical and material environment, concepts of emptiness and suspension, and more overarching concerns about the affective structure of a Time of Crisis. People reflect on how crisis has sparked feelings of falling back through the past to a timespace once lost to history, of being trapped in an elongated inescapable present, of being written out of futures once seen as birthrights. Time may be said to be inverted, spiralling, repeating or standing still.[8] Often, pasts are onrushing as spatiotemporal arrangements considered to be constitutive of bygone eras resurface. Future-oriented desires and expectations are put on hold. As the rupture of crisis becomes a chronic

state, the uncanny present transforms from a timespace of suffocating captivity into one of uncomfortable comfort with the recognizable status quo.
In an era of crisis, as Carol Greenhouse (2019: 86–87) proposes, the move
away from inevitability associated with uninterrupted linear progression delivers heat to time.

The richness of ethnographic description on display calls for a somewhat
messy analysis that follows the intricate narrative strands and attempts to do
justice to the fifty shades of vertigo. There is no single model that captures all
local nuances and 'modes of knowing' vertigo (Masco 2006: 37). Yet the final
two body chapters go some way towards drawing things together in producing an ethnographic theory of vertigo that forms part of the predominant
affective structure of chronic crisis beyond the borders of Greece. First by
presenting the case of lives suspended in the transitional emptiness between
multiple crises (Greece and Brexit Britain), something I propose is a feature
of European late modernity, and then through a theory of societal Stockholm Syndrome where people ultimately become accustomed to the vertigo
of crisis, I argue for the vertiginous as a marker of our times. Ultimately, it
is my contention that vertigo crosses and weaves through domains of life to
become one of the foremost ways through which people experience not only
crisis but also the everyday axioms of violence to which we have been ex-
posed in the early part of the twenty-first century (Pipyrou and Sorge n.d.).

The analytical and epistemological angles are punctuated by vertigo as
affect or, more precisely, the multiple affects of vertigo. Nausea, dizziness,
the sense of falling or spiralling out of control, loss, déjà vu and repetition,
confusion as to where and when one is living, and entrapment and captivity all surface at regular intervals. Vertigo is sometimes easy to pin down
linguistically and through local vernaculars. People talk about 'feelings' and
describe the textures of vertigo ('it is like …'). Particularly striking are the innumerable occasions when people describe nausea and dizziness when being hit by the often-unforeseen microruptures to everyday life constitutive
in the small-print of crisis – when discovering that the pension pot is running low, when an employer announces pending redundancies or when political decisions, such as those regarding citizens' rights or capital controls,
scupper the most carefully made plans. These utterances feed directly from
a more generic atmosphere of anxiety about the curtailing of personal freedoms at the hands of an Other beyond accountability, as well as the height-
ened uncertainty concerning the form and substance of a society emerging
from chronic crisis. As such, vertigo transcends easily identifiable words and
phrases, experienced as an atmosphere, or in Gernot Böhme's words, 'an
aesthetic that contains inescapable affective and emotional resonances', a
timespace 'with a certain tone of feeling' (Böhme 2017: 12). Vertigo is that

'something in the air', a cluster of 'free floating' intense affects, identifiable through association with a repetitive narrative trend (Lepselter 2016: 2).

Inspiration for an approach that foregrounds the atmosphere or at times intangible *something* running through individual narratives of the uncanny comes from the quite masterful work of Susan Lepselter. Exploring the resonance of stories of abduction and captivity in various genres of American culture, Lepselter frames her project as follows:

> Though it is never a one-to-one kind of symbol, the accumulated stories that point to a forgotten *something* do suggest what that something might be. There are stories of ... multiple ways that a life is disappointed by master narratives of progress and success. There are stories ... resonating in scattered and displaced effects within everyday life. (2016: 19)

Lepselter advocates the reading of parallels between stories, some spoken and others seeming to affectively resonate with master narratives (or inversions) of daily life in a specific timespace (a similar approach is taken by Joseph Masco (2006) on drawing together diverse narratives of the nuclear uncanny). For Lepselter, the timespace is that of post-Cold War US society that is still coming to terms with nuclear fear, federal government conspiracy, medical developments such as cloning and surrogacy, and the hauntings of slavery. For me, the timespace is crisis Greece, where the fallout of over a decade of economic and political reform has infiltrated almost every area of life. Master narratives of progression, European belonging and mythistories of civilization have been challenged, perhaps defeated, and an overpowering feeling of disorientation prevails. It is the parallels and resemblances between stories of diverse realms of human experience that, accumulated over an extended period, must be recognized as pointing towards the same *something* (Lepselter 2016: 19). Put simply, in crisis Greece, people regularly seem to talk of the same *thing*, a life in an uncanny timespace where they experience a sense of vertigo. Sometimes the researcher must make the connections themselves, based on a combination of conjecture and long-term field experience; the reading of an atmosphere or aesthetic of vertigo that runs through individual stories that leaves one gasping for breath and clutching at straws to piece together the significance of the unsaid (on beyond-verbal communication of critical events, see Pipyrou (2020) and Kidron (2020)). At other times, people directly verbalize the vertiginous, most readily through everyday affects of nausea, dizziness, anxiety and a sense of life spiralling out of control. This book examines the intense elaboration of vertigo as it moves from a fleeting sensation to the centre of life in chronic crisis.

In framing my exploration of vertigo and crisis, it would be easy to simply replace Lepselter's 'resonance' with 'vertigo' in the following passage. For a moment, I ask the reader to indulge me, for I believe it helps clarify my intentions:

> And, I argue, the resonance [vertigo] itself becomes another story. The sense of uncanny resonance [vertigo] becomes an expressive modality, a vernacular theory, a way of seeing the world, a intimation of the way *it all makes sense* ... [it is] the intensification produced by overlapping, back and forth call signs from various discourses. The uncanny narratives here acquire affect, intensity, and meaning through their resonance and dissonance with other more familiar cultural narratives ... Resonance [vertigo] describes the social, affective, and aesthetic dimension of a perspective based on apophenia, finding connections between signs, and often understanding that process as political. Here those connections are based on resemblance and repetition. (Lepselter 2016: 4)

In the field of critical literature, an excellent example of the disorienting narrative technique can be found in the writing of W.G. Sebald. Particularly in his 1990 work *Vertigo*, Sebald combines history and travelogue, memoir and fiction to take the audience on a disarming and perplexing literary journey. The reader is left second-guessing the connections between narratives while knowing that *something* is holding the story together. Searching in the gaps of Sebald's haunted ramblings, one is left wallowing in the nauseating uncertainty of how the prose *should* be read and where one might next be flung. Crisis Greece reads as a Sebald novel filled with expressive resonances where vertigo has become a storyline in its own right through the multiple criss-crossing of affects, aesthetics and political processes that produce an atmosphere of that *something* that repetitively surfaces in life narratives. The topological connections may sometimes be neatly on display and other times seemingly distant from each other, and in constant distorted movement vis-à-vis the emergent master narratives of progression and consolidation. The multiple shades, rhythms and forms of vertigo express what it is to live in a Time of Crisis. As a marker of the timespace of chronic crisis, vertigo is, for me, *the* vernacular that runs through cultural arenas as diverse as political association, workplace precarity, migration and displacement, environmental ethics, relations with extended family, inheritance practice and so much more. The resemblance and repetition of words, decisions, feelings and tones of interaction point to vertigo as the expressive modality of seeing and making sense of a world in crisis. It is the themes that echo and multiply within this modality that make up this book.

It is getting late and the sun is rising below the horizon on this English summer morning in December. I adorn myself in a short-sleeve shirt and step out into the snow. I can hear my telephone ringing vociferously on silent mode as my mother tries *not* to contact me. I see my brother walking next to me way off in the distance. You join me. We ride in the back of an NHS ambulance aboard the mid-morning 7 PM Brittany Ferries service from Plymouth to Sto'Vo'Kor that left port in 1994 and continues its eternal crossing. On tempestuous seas, our voyage scythes its way through the thickening haze of contradiction, paradox and perplexity that is vertigo. The nauseating motions – pulsating, shuddering, falling, treading water and screeching to a halt – distort our perception of time, materiality and existence itself. The reflections off the shimmering black ocean blind us, leading us to question what we really saw back there, ahead in the haunting ghostly abyss. *Titanic*. What is known is that the unknown out here is familiar, the unforeseen expected.

NOTES

1. Dimitris Papanikolaou (2011) has noted how the Greek economic crisis has been likened to an 'earthquake', a writer telling him 'we are in the middle of an earthquake; there is no time to pause and think how we scream about it'. He uses this analogy to discuss how the crisis is a critical point in the 'disturbance' of linear genealogies of the past.

2. Unthinkable events often proliferate narratives of unthinkability, meaning that people cannot think about anything else (Masco 2006: 4).

3. Writing on crisis as an endemic condition, Vigh (2008: 13) suggests that crisis can be divided into two interrelated dimensions, namely social and personal crisis. In fact, he argues that understanding crisis as context allows us to see 'the contexts in crisis' and to analyse 'crisis embedded in crisis'.

4. Although the article is coauthored, this addition should rightly be attributed to Stewart.

5. Michael Jackson (1998: 171) suggests that when struck by crisis, people feel unable to control the exterior forces influencing their possibilities and choices – they lose control of their lives and struggle to regain and re-establish social order.

6. The 'unthinkability' of events, Joseph Masco (2006: 3) tells us, takes them outside of language and comprehensibility, placing them 'into the realm of the sublime'.

7. Loss takes centre stage in Katalin Makkai's (2013) prominent commentary on *Vertigo*. For Makkai, one of the internal workings of the film is to awaken an uncanny sense of loss alongside desire. The first viewing reaches into the future. The second is not a simple re-viewing of the first object. The film is lost on both occasions despite the viewer's desire to both comprehend and maintain the temporal mystique of the storyline. When the audience realizes that there will never be another first-time viewing of the film, hence the trickery of the plotline will never again be in the realm of the unknown, there is a lingering disturbing feeling of never having had possession of the lost object (the film) in the first place. There opens 'a blank, a hole, or an abyss' and a sense that the film eludes possession. The film also eludes presentness, she continues, 'it is, or I am, always too late or too early … always ahead or behind [the storyline]'. And this is the feeling that the film thematizes (2013: 140). The film will always remain irrevocably lost in time, out of reach.

8. In an argument calling attention to repetition and return, Andreas Bandak looks beyond the singular event. He discusses how some events are not left in the past, but tie together landscapes of imagination, fear and haunting, as well as of resilience and responsibility, for futural purposes. The recurrence of events at different scales has the 'potential to tie down whole communities' (Bandak 2019: 190). Events thus play out in history, in memory, and as an ongoing and recurring possibility. His paper is part of a special collection on repetition (Bandak and Coleman 2019).

CHAPTER 1

MAIRI

The Nausea of Unknowingness

I had formed an intimacy with her voice, worn to a gravel by 10,000 cigarettes. Two, sometimes three times a month, she would call to speak to my grandfather with whom, after they met on a business trip in the early 1990s, she had formed an endearing friendship over the course of two decades. Years would pass before I met Mairi in person, but the charisma, strength of will and aura of someone secure with her place in the world effortlessly transcended the 2,000 miles from Greece. To my mind, she was a mythological being, the topic of dinner table reminiscence, an iconic example of how one should *become* in the world. Athenian born and raised, the daughter of a successful international businessman and his professional wife, Mairi knew who she was, where she came from, and was confident about her destiny. As a child, all I knew was that Mairi, born in the elite neighbourhood of Kolonaki, was educated at the University of Oxford before marrying an aspiring politician, Grigoris. She was the CEO of the family business importing high-end Italian clothing, a venture through which she met my grandfather in around 1994. This, she once assured me without a hint of irony, was not her dream job, for she only ever really wanted to be a philosopher. She was a mother to three children of high expectations, and purportedly moved with such grace and elegance as to knock an unsuspecting man off his feet from the other side of the room. She was, I was told, a striking brunette with unusually piercing blue eyes, a heroine straight out of the *Finos Film* genre of movies made famous in the 1960s and still a central part of Greek popular culture. Clever, confident, astute, poised. Despite the distance, Mairi supported my grandfather – and by extension my family – through tough times. Not in any monetary sense, not even through a physical presence and not, to my knowledge, romantically, but simply by his knowing that she existed. She was on his team in business and in life. He once told me that this made him feel 'invincible', that 'any deal could be done', and helped him 'believe in the ability to be successful without hurting anyone'.

It was with this vision that I anticipated Mairi's arrival at my home in central Greece one sweltering August day in 2009. She had offered to take me the 200 miles to the capital as she was 'just passing through' returning from a business event in northern Italy, for which she had taken the ferry crossing to the northwestern Greek port of Igoumenitsa. This was the type of thing she would do. Of course, she was closing another international deal. Obviously, she was travelling again. Sure, she would collect me on a last-minute whim in 45°C heat and I could stay with her for a few nights in Athens, without prior notice, to take care of some bureaucracy in the capital. This was the indefatigable Mairi: powerful businesswoman, homemaker, star of her own life-as-movie. I must say, I was a little nervous, for I had, by this point, fifteen years of stories and intercepted phone calls playing on my imagination. On the drive south I was taken in. Her beauty, her charm, the way that nothing could faze her. She discussed her retirement, which was planned for 2012. Her pension plan set up by her late father would provide a substantial payout. Mairi found a sense of security in this safety net that would facilitate more ambitious investment projects in her retirement years. Not that she was in any particular need of money (she did not flaunt it, for she was driving a mid-range Nissan). I was reliably informed that she owned three homes – one in a suburb of Athens, another on a nearby island and a grand villa on a hilltop overlooking the bay to the south of the city. The latter doubled up as a side-business hosting wedding receptions and holiday retreats for paying customers and her vast network of friends and acquaintances. It was also once used as a setting in a popular 1990s Greek soap opera. While on the topic of possessions, she was contemplating purchasing an established vineyard for her husband's seventieth birthday.

Besides material success, Mairi had freedom – physical and psychological, moving in the highest circles of the city, hosting a regular card-playing club, always with houseguests, trips to London and New York, and invitations to fashionable events. Mairi's one regret in life was that she could not quit smoking. Something I recall from my childhood was the voice of my grandfather booming from his study chastising her for this 'dirty habit' that she must not let 'beat her', while himself puffing away on an aromatic fat Cuban. She promised him that when one of her children married, she would quit once and for all. Smoking, it turned out, was a major part of Mairi's persona of a powerful businesswoman, cigarette in hand, twirling around as she gesticulated and remonstrated to make the hard-nosed deal. As the sun set on the sweltering evening of our first encounter that summer's day, I reflected on my impressions of her as the pillar of strength I had heard a hundred times over the telephone or talked about with my grandfather on long walks over Exmoor – I recall him using her as an exemplar in a lesson on how to purchase property one bleak day as we strolled over the hills overlooking the Bristol Channel when I was aged ten. What was it that made her so remarkable? I concluded that she knew precisely who she was and the role she had to play in life. She was comfortable with her being, her existence in the elite circles of Athenian society. She was the film star of her own black-and-white romance. She seemed so sure of herself, as if life could pose no question that would unsettle her world.

The crisis years would erode Mairi's life piece by piece, sometimes as violent slow-motion drip-dripping, other times as chaotic rupture. In this chapter we drop into Mairi's life over the course of a decade to experience the vertigo of crisis in the form of unknowingness (Pippin 2017). Mairi has become unknown to her Self, detached and distant from everything she thought defined her. She lives a tense anxiety-inducing, vertiginous condition, suspended between who she believes she is, what the world has taught her for sixty years, and a life in freefall brought on by a Time of Crisis. Her person being eroded in the crisis years has created what Robert Pippin, writing on the philosophy of vertigo and the anxieties of suspension, has termed 'profound unknowingness' (2017: 14), a form of everyday vertigo primarily manifested as inescapable nausea. By 2020, Mairi is broken and housebound. Her remaining one home has been divided into three and she sleeps in the former cellar. Her savings are lost and her pension is in tatters. One child is divorced, one unemployed and the other six feet under. With quivering hands, she still promises to quit smoking. Mairi's story also shows how crisis has touched the highest echelons of society, disregarding class and status, tearing apart those who were once deemed untouchable.

By following Mairi, we also unearth the polytemporal speeds of vertigo and touch upon the multidimensional imprisonment or 'captivity' of crisis that will be explored in detail in Chapter 5. At once rapid and in slow motion, each event has taken its toll separately, but only when one takes a step back can the cumulative impact of a decade of toil be truly surveyed. The narrative that follows plugs into the spiralling events of the crisis years to develop a theory of vertigo as unknowingness, which Mairi describes as manifesting itself as physical nausea. Akin to Jean-Paul Sartre's protagonist Antonine Roquentin in the novel *Nausea* (1965 [1938]), she is experiencing an existential crisis where her essence of being used to mean something, but now, through layers of detachment and tragedy, she is nothing to herself. She does not recognize herself in her own image and it is this unknowingness of the Self that creates vertiginous nausea.

NAUSEA

'There are two things that remain with me during the crisis: nausea and the sense that I no longer know myself. I am detached from who I once was.' Mairi breaks the silence of the luncheon table. She has been toiling over the oven for the past three hours, preparing separate dishes for her children, husband and the anthropologist who is in town to present a paper at the British School. 'The main thing is that I have this constant nausea it the pit of my stomach. A feeling of sickness at what I have become, what this country is going through. I cannot usually pin it to any one activity, but just being alive makes me feel sick. I carry it everywhere, all day, every day.' The nausea Mairi describes first set in when, after many years of planning her retirement, her pension fund collapsed in 2011. She had been banking (quite literally) on taking early retirement with a private pension that would not only help to sustain her own livelihood but would also allow her to contribute more financially to her children – ultimately leading to lavish marriages, she hoped. Planning up to three years in advance, she had already invited friends to stay at her island home and in Athens, and had embarked on a substantial renovation of the villa with the aim of attracting wealthier clientele and maybe host more television productions. Speaking in 2015, she said that 'the nausea is suffocating. I feel trapped. It is inescapable. Sometimes so physical that I end up gagging, but most of the time a dull humming that pinnacles when I feel that I am no longer in control of my life, I have been stripped of what it is to be "Mairi"'.

With her business nosediving following the onset of increasing austerity measures – it was to eventually close in 2015, strangled in a messy entanglement of debt and regulatory bureaucracy – Mairi only received one-third of her pension lump sum upon retirement. Her husband suffered similarly with his state pension. The renovations at the villa had to be put on hold. Not only could the loan repayments not be met, but the demand for lavish ceremonies was also in decline, even among the Athenian upper classes. Her eldest child had lost her job when the retail outlet she part-owned went into liquidation, her middle child lived in the city and was relatively stable in a middle management post, while her youngest went through a series of painful relationships and separations. Two children had moved back into the family home, giving Mairi no alternative but to divide the house into three separate apartments. After selling a small plot of land to fund the building work, she converted the upstairs into a one-bedroom flat for her eldest and the middle floor into a one-bedroom dwelling for her youngest, moving herself and her husband Grigoris into the basement. 'Suddenly my life was flipped upside down. It is one thing to not be able to afford things financially, but quite another not to be able to live. I mean, to be who you are with the freedom you are so accustomed to.' As well as now 'returning to the chores of being a housewife', including cooking and cleaning for her children, she no longer had space to host her friends, either on long-term visits or for the twice-weekly card-playing evenings. 'I became a housewife, and then not even that. I wasn't Mairi anymore. It was sudden and indescribably disorienting. One day I was my own person, with freedom, a sense of direction and self-worth. Then I am in captivity, a slave in my own home and in my own country and I have done nothing wrong ... What have I become? I have nothing. I am nothing.'

Mairi's existential crisis within the wider context of 'crisis Greece' was experienced in two interrelated ways, she suggested. From the moment the realization dawned that she would not be receiving the expected pension, thus throwing all anticipated futures of retirement life into disarray, she felt a nausea that she could not shake. The crisis knocked her off her futural trajectory – the plans, expectations and aspirations for the latter years of her life (cf. Bryant and Knight 2019) – and triggered a suffocating, anxiety-inducing sickness felt in the 'pit of [her] stomach'. The nausea came from a sense of losing control of her identity, a distance and detachment from the Self that Pippin (2017) has termed the 'unknowingness' of vertigo. It was the unknowingness of the Self, the unrecognizable shell of 'Mairi', that was the cause of the persistent nausea. Mairi interjects: 'objects conjure memories of the past, but that was another person back then. Mundane, everyday objects make me feel sick. I cannot sit on the sofa without feeling disoriented, like my head is spinning, for this is not the place my sofa should be'. Mairi's life has been reconfigured, spatially, temporally and in essence. 'When driving down the motorway [the road that bypasses the city centre] I turn my eyes away from the mountain where my villa is located. If I looked up there, I would lose control of the car. I would become dizzy, sick, spin off the road.' She now experiences objects and relations as nausea-inducing (cf. Serres and Latour 1995)[1] and has a numbness to materiality and to social relationships. 'It is also the little things, things that were once ordinary and now seem like they belong to another lifetime or like they never really ever happened.' Mairi questions her own recollection; are these events just figments of her imagination, her mind playing tricks? 'I mean, this house was alive and hosting the card-playing evenings and having people to stay ... that was me ... but I don't recognize myself anymore. I can't associate that these people [herself before and after crisis] are one and the same.' The 'little things' that were once 'ordinary' are reflective of the everyday slow-motion erosive violence of crisis that eats away at the person (Ahmann 2018).

The 'gradual brutalities' of slow violence operate at multiple temporalities and may not at first glance be considered particularly destructive (Davies 2019: 1). Yet it is the repetitive erosive nature of their accumulative force that wears down the person. Drawing popular attention to the term, Rob Nixon contends that:

> Violence is customarily conceived as an event that is immediate in time, explosive and spectacular in space, and as erupting into instant sensational visibility. We need, I believe, to engage a different kind of violence ... incremental and accretive, its calamitous repercussions playing out across a range of temporal scales. (2011: 4)

Mairi took the initial violent rupture of the economic crisis in her stride, expecting it to be 'just another "thriller" that the media like to make a storm about'. Rather than simply blowing over, gradually, piece by piece, everything she had built up, all that she had lived for disintegrated. Before she knew it, before she even had chance to notice it was happening, her past toils and future plans had gone up in flames, lost to the winds of austerity and structural reform. The explosive, sensational event of 2009 continues to have repercussions on her everyday life, like the residue shockwaves of the Big Bang still shaping the extremities of our universe 14 billion years later, or what, inciting terminologies of the nuclear age, Joseph Masco (2015) calls the 'fallout' of world-shaping events. This violent ordinariness of accumulation (Povinelli 2011), Lauren Berlant (2011: 95) suggests, leads to a general wearing out whereby 'deterioration' becomes 'a defining condition of ... historical existence'.

This certainly seems to be the case for Mairi. The accumulative wearing-down of the Self has left her head spinning and she is facing the sickening realization that *this is life*. More of the same and not finished yet. The division of the home, the return to cooking for her children that was a task once confined to the past, the inability to host houseguests – these 'little things' are not insignificant at all, but are rather central to Mairi's sense of unknowingness, detachment and disorientation. She now lives in suspension, in a hazy alternate reality away from the certainty of both her person and her future that she had constructed in the pre-crisis years. She walks in the world in a zombified state, accompanied by an all-encompassing soundtrack of melancholy loss that she cannot wholly grasp. She knows that she can never return to her past Self, she does not recognize the present and she has lost all futural momentum. There is an affective stillness to her existence in the here-and-now, she is left motionless while the hurricane-force winds of a traumatized life consume her (Stewart 2011).

Many aspects of Mairi's story correlate with themes explored in Jean-Paul Sartre's now classic existentialist novel *Nausea* (1965 [1938]). Indeed, Mairi's language and metaphors resonate with those expressed by Sartre's lead character, Antoine Roquentin, as he loses his grip on his own essence, culminating in an overpowering and inescapable nausea. In an account mapped by Mairi's descriptions of her life stripped back to its unrecognizable bare bones by the everyday violence of crisis, inanimate objects and situations encroach upon Roquentin's ability to define himself and his intellectual and spiritual freedom, evoking a deep sickness. 'The faces of others have some sense', he explains, 'some direction. Not mine' (1965 [1938]: 16). Roquentin exists in disorientation, strangeness and powerlessness that he finds overwhelming, leading to him becoming convinced of his own uselessness. Whoever he talks to about this nausea, it does not seem to work. In existential crisis, he begins to think that he might not even exist.

Roquentin concludes that everything happens without reason (as in Mairi's declaration 'I've done nothing wrong'), so he is superfluous, provoking nausea in interactions with subjects and objects. At the point of this vertiginous revelation when a person comes to understand that 'every existent is born without reason, prolongs itself out of weakness and dies by chance', we are seized by a 'sort of nausea', Sartre suggests. Then there is no longer living, just surviving (Sartre 1965 [1938]: 191). A striking parallel between the accounts can be identified in Mairi's explanation of how she no longer recognizes herself in the mirror: 'I sit at my boudoir to brush my hair in front of the mirror and emptiness stares back. Blankness. Nothing. The person there, the thing, is not me. It is a shell, quite hollow. I ceased to exist many years ago, when life was taken from me.' In Sartre's *Nausea*, Roquentin speaks of his disgust of his own reflection to express his loss of essence, the freedom to fashion his own identity; the face in the mirror has become 'an animated image of [his own] existence' (Nelissen and Coullet 2016: 8). His reflection captures a world that has become strange, unrecognizable – uncanny objects, persons and Self. Mairi also feels stripped of her essence, the being that makes her unique. In her own words, she merely 'exists'.

In 2020, Mairi casts a forlorn figure that simply exists, pressing on with everyday activities that provide her with no direction and no satisfaction. In 2017, she lost her daughter in a freak car accident, the vehicle leaving the road on the hilltop not far from the grand villa she once owned. The official story is one of heavy rain, poor visibility and slippery tarmac, but with her child secretly in debt, without a job and rarely venturing from her room in the family home, there is more than an undertone that perhaps she became another victim taken by crisis (cf. Davis 2015; Knight 2012b; Pipyrou 2014b). A year later, her youngest child divorced after less than two years of marriage, his wife citing his supposed inability to look after their family owing to his precarious employment situation and increasing arguments over money. These episodes were abrupt extra ruptures within the timespace of crisis, major incidences in their own right that punctuated ongoing everyday struggles like spikes on a bar graph. They were also sources of potential shame on Mairi and Grigoris' family and were most certainly the catalyst for an increased sense of personal failure for Mairi. 'You simply don't expect it.

To outlive your own child. You cannot anticipate it, imagine it, or ever over-come it. And then another child lives through their own catastrophe with its own inescapable pain.' Mairi believes that she 'should have done better' by them, providing a successful business, their own homes and more emotional support – all aspects of her being that were devastated by outside forces during the early years of the financial crisis. Her (in)ability to provide on ma-terial and affective levels tore her further from her sense of worth: 'when you realize that your children have no future and there is so little that you can do about it you wonder what the point is in all of this. It [the crisis] is strangling us. I am no longer useful as mother, careerwoman, friend, or individual and I don't see what role I can now play in anybody's future ... I haven't even had a visitor stay over in five years since I am disgusted with what I have become'.

Mairi's spiral into her own nothingness is captured by her regular ref-erences to the emptiness of her being and escalating detachment from the people around her. She is absent from herself, residing in 'lost time' (Batta-glia 2005: 21), estranged from the order of her old world, no longer hosting guests or her beloved card-playing evenings and rarely leaving the house, let alone taking business trips to Italy or the United Kingdom. Even her phone calls to my grandfather have dried up; he tells me that 'she called at Christ-mas last year, but we didn't speak long. She was trying to sound cheerful, but it wasn't the Mairi I know'. Everything, every object, every person is superfluous to her life. The alienation of subjects and objects casts doubt in Mairi about her own validity, the point of her continued toil in the world of cascading crises, her person held in a state of empty suspension. She now has flashes of nausea that emanate from mundane objects. These episodes appear seemingly randomly, from the occasion of lifting the telephone to call a friend in Komotini to picking fruit from a garden tree. The feeling she per-ceives is pure disgust for society, a contempt so refined that it has shattered her. The nausea has become more frequent in recent years since the death and divorce of her offspring. Nausea, as for Roquentin, is associated with the difference of being something and nothing. Her existence used to mean something. Now she is nothing. She does not recognize herself in her own image. There is an unknowingness of the Self that causes vertigo.

The literary critic William V. Spanos (1978) has used Sartre's novel *Nausea* as an example of 'negative capability', a presentation of the uncertainty and dread of human existence so strong that the imagination cannot comprehend it.[2] For him, Roquentin exhibits a disgust at the meaninglessness of existence that I believe is comparable to the despair experienced by Mairi. The struc-tural precariousness of life leaves her fearing the next violence, an episode that will likely cast her further from her pre-crisis Self. Metaphorically, she is the astronaut who, caught in a catastrophic explosion, has been blasted away from her ship while on a spacewalk. She tentatively dangles at the end of her tethering, no thrusters to take her closer to home. With debris hurtling towards her, pinging off her visor and puncturing her suit, each episode of crisis pushes her further adrift from the mothership. She is left contemplating the eternal blackness of the infinite abyss, the *ilinx* of life unknown. It is only a matter of time before a piece of shrapnel ricochets to sever the cord and she is forever lost to the darkness of vacuous spacetime. Mairi is now a recluse in her home, housebound, in captivity. Her nausea, like that of Roquentin, arises from her near-complete detachment from the world, her former life, her job and her family. She has been violently torn from her timeline and the alienation from her previous life has produced a form of unknowingness of the Self, which in turn provokes the unshakable nausea.

Here is perhaps where Mairi's and Roquentin's stories depart. For Sartre, Roquentin's nausea is deeply related to the discovery – the intimate knowing – of the bare bones of life that is existence. Roquentin finds it nigh-on impossible to come to terms with his determination that existence precedes essence and further that existence in and of itself is pointless, repulsive and frightening (Nelissen and Coullet 2016: 15). That said, it is this knowing of what Sartre frames as an existential truth that, despite creating nausea, does eventually provide Roquentin with a base from which to begin reconstructing his essence through art and literature. Indeed, in sharing his discovery of existence with his former partner Anny (who has also realized the same thing, but remains in denial), we are invited to participate in what feels like a secret circle or private members' club with other people who are privileged to see beyond the usually convincing façade of essence. In short, Roquentin *knows* something and it is this knowing that makes him feel detached, unable to recognize himself, and induces nausea. For Mairi, the nausea is based on the *unknowingness* of the Self, the unrecognizable figure staring back from the bedroom mirror. Yes, both Roquentin and Mairi feel alienated from their reflection and from their former selves, but Mairi does not experience a sense of discovery or find the apparatus to reconstruct her identity. As she teeters on the edge, overcome by vertigo, she cannot find creativity in her destruction (Runia 2010); in Kierkegaard's (1980) terms, she has not been able to educate herself to find freedom in the vertiginous, or the 'audacity', as Serres (2014) would have it, to reinvent a new person for a new world. Her indifference does not have a positive affect (cf. Herzfeld 1992). Unknowingness intensifies her disorientation – layer upon layer of nauseating vertigo.

UNKNOWINGNESS

In his landmark philosophical reading of Alfred Hitchcock's 1958 psychological thriller *Vertigo*, Robert Pippin takes the reader on a grand tour of the anxieties of unknowingness. While acknowledging that the term is 'rather clumsy', Pippin argues that it captures a condition where 'we don't know enough to be globally skeptical' of all possibilities of a character's persona (2017: 16). Vertigo is created in the disparity between the moments when characters (and audience) recognize that they are right – when the evidence has led them to correct conclusions – and the instances when they end up in dead-ends, are misled or arrive at unrecognizable situations. Simultaneously understanding something and nothing about life scenarios is vertigo-inducing in a pulsating zooming-in and out between knowing and unknowing. For Pippin, 'there is no "solution" to such anxiety about our not knowing ... and in exploring the lived-out implications of such a condition' (2017: 16). The persistent searching for something recognizable elongates the periods of suspension where characters live in 'shadows of doubt'.

Unknowingness is thus neither straightforward ignorance nor purely scepticism, nor 'knowing when not to know' (Geissler 2013; on ignorance, see High et al. 2012). Ignorance as a virtue differs in many respects from our concept of unknowingness, as does deliberately averting one's attention from the undesirable, wishful thinking and self-deception (Smith 2016: 276). In a state of unknowingness, the suspension between the polemics of (un) recognition is what cultivates a sense of vertigo. Further, once self-doubt sets in, on the occasions that a character recognizes a reflection of Self based on congruent evidence that seems all too convenient to be true, the vertigo of unknowingness means that they might 'hide' from themselves in a form of self-deception based on uncertainty. Pippin explains:

> Being deceived, being self-deceived, being uncertain, but partly right, living over an extended period of time in a kind of suspension, having to make decisions about trust or disapproval, while uncertain of the relevant act descriptions or ascriptions of responsibility on which they are based, but not devoid of some markers of what would be an appropriate response, all amount to a swirl of uncertainty and partial confidence that, it seemed to me, required some capacious if unusual term. (2017: 17)

Similar to Runia's multiplier effect that details the concentric circles of recognition of fear and desire when stood at the cliff-edge, peering into the *ilinx*, suspension in an extended period of uncertainty leads, Pippin suggests, to characters in *Vertigo* second-guessing what they know about themselves, other people and the world around them, contributing to existence in the realm of the vertiginous. This definition quite clearly relates to life in endemic crisis and to the case of Mairi in particular: her vertigo is a product of her suspension between the certainty of her former Self and the life of someone stripped bare by sequential crises, perpetually existing between knowing and unknowing. Her searching for recognizable elements of her past while appreciating that she can never return to her former life elongates her period of suspension, the transformative gap between past and future orders. But further, Pippin suggests that, via Jean-Jacques Rousseau, self-doubt leading to a deeply ingrained unknowingness of Self is part of 'the formation and structure of modern industrialized, bureaucratically managed societies that leads to an increasing likelihood of and anxiety about theatrical public personae' (2017: 18). Also placing unknowingness at the heart of debate about the nature of modernity, Friedrich Nietzsche (1974: 23) warns against an overcommitment to knowledge, a culture characterized by what may be termed knowingness, which arises in the industrial age. Without the abstract nature of unknowingness, for Nietzsche captured expertly in the power of myth, all modern society is doomed to creative decline. Unknowingness can be a delight that 'flares up again and again like a bright blaze over all the distress of what is problematic, over all the danger of uncertainty' (Nietzsche 1974: 3), although perhaps not so in Mairi's case.

In Chapter 4, I will argue that emptiness is a characteristic of being suspended between two timespaces of crisis and of being trapped between collapsing and emerging social orders. This, I suggest, is a marker of European late-neoliberal modernity, in much the same way as Rousseau and Nietzsche both see unknowingness as an anxiety inherent in the structure of modern industrialized societies. In creating the modern, there is a destruction of past worlds, both individual and collective, and, as we already know from Kierkegaard, anxiety over the creation of the new is manifested as vertiginous 'dizziness' (1980) or 'trembling' (2012) when suspended above the swirling unfamiliarity of the existential abyss. In a Time of Crisis, Mairi is held in suspension on the tightrope precariously bridging the promises of futures past to which she is still agonisingly clutching, and violent new orders that decry the glories of the previous empire.

Considering Rousseau, we could then assume that Mairi's unknowingness is accentuated by the pressures of her public persona and what it is to be – or what is perceived to constitute – an upper-class businesswoman in twenty-first-century Greece. Mairi's existential crisis, then, following Pippin, is a product of what happens when something like an economic crisis catastrophically and irreversibly ruptures the assumed trajectory of modern, bureaucratized, industrialized society. Mairi can no longer fulfil the expectations of her own publicly formed persona financially, professionally or in her matriarchal role, as demonstrated in her expressing how she has failed in her parental responsibilities towards her children. Although these expectations may be a thing of the past since Mairi has been overtaken by the world around her, she cannot shake the fear to conform. She experiences the continued need to fulfil her former glories, creating a breathtaking, energy-sapping anguish of losing her presence (in de Martino's sense) in a recognizable timeline. The growing fear of untrustworthy public personae filters into the mistrust of one's own public persona, blurring the boundaries between sincerity and theatricality. For Pippin, unknowingness is a social pathology with its roots in Rousseau's and Hegel's political thought that goes beyond the violation of rights and unequal material welfare of post-Enlightenment Western society and, I would add, transcends being merely a condition of crisis (although arguably neoliberal financial crisis perpetuates unknowingness more widely).

It is this scaling-up from personal and intersubjective narratives to the societal level that begins to shed light on structures, vernaculars and affects of vertigo that allows us to apply the concept beyond the character of Mairi, the context of Greece and purely societies in a Time of Crisis. There are often minor but extremely important distinctions in all social relationships between 'who I take myself to be', 'who I am' and 'the person you take me to be', Pippin would have us believe, particularly in relations where there is much affective investment (2017: 24). Giorgio Agamben advocates the importance of a state of unknowing in the construction of a complete social identity, noting that 'the ways in which we do not know things are just as important (and perhaps even more important) as the ways in which we know them' (2011: 113). Forms of unknowingness are 'precisely what defines the rank of what we are able to know and that the articulation of a zone of nonknowledge is the condition – and at the same time the touchstone – of all our knowledge'. For Agamben, unknowing is an essential part of the art of living. Richard Smith (2016) takes this forward in his work on the transformative capacities of unknowing by connecting Agamben's insights with recent debates in the philosophy of ethics that asks us to reorient ourselves to other people as unknowable. Our ethical encounter with the Other is not to be thought of as based on knowledge about them, but rather approached from the stance of unknowingness (see also Rapport (2012, 2018) on Otherness and cosmopolitan politesse). It is from this starting point that vertigo as unknowingness as a method to understand personal, interpersonal and societal relations can begin to break free from the context of endemic crisis as we assess it here.

For instance, in the burgeoning literature on honour and social status in the Mediterranean, one may find abundant examples of performance and theatricality that fulfil public demands by way of spectacle, while concealing the 'shadows of doubt' about individual personhood and collective reputation in the private domain (see e.g. Argyrou 1996; Campbell 1964; Kirtsoglou 2004; Pipyrou 2014a). Without wanting to get sidetracked, I wish to consider just one case, since the author so clearly pins the demands of class status and public recognition to the age of modernity in the Mediterranean during the pre-crisis years.

In his 1996 work *Tradition and Modernity in the Mediterranean,* Vassos Argyrou tracks changes in wedding celebrations in Cyprus, detailing the necessity of elaborate performance in both maintaining status in the public eye and preserving a sense of self-worth. Argyrou (1996: 21) presents the *fouartas* (big spender) who theatrically shows no respect for money regardless of the economic context. The slightest allusion that a man might be stingy – such as not buying a round of drinks in a cafeteria – is a cause of great embarrassment and may bring shame upon the person and the family in the classic sense long debated in Mediterranean ethnography (see e.g. Campbell 1964; Dubisch 1995; Gilmore 1987; Herzfeld 1980, 1985; Peristiany 1965). For the *fouartas,* the pinnacle of public display comes at a daughter's wedding where extravagant, extremely expensive spectacles are staged, often requiring bank loans and the calling-in of family and political favours. However, in the mid-1990s, the rising cost of living challenged the *fouartas,* who was gradually becoming unable to live his public persona, particularly when it came to wedding ceremonies, leading to public scrutiny and self-reflection on categories of associated character attributes, including possessing a 'good heart' and being 'respectful' of neighbours and friends (Argyrou 1996: 74). The *fouartas* was being torn from the categories of his public persona and sent into a spiralling internal questioning of self-worth, character moralities and long-standing cultural attributes associated with masculinity, family care and political prowess.

In some cases, the inability to fulfil the performative expectations of the *fouartas* led to a sense of unknowingness of Self as described by Pippin above, where the man (for it is always a man in Argyrou's ethnography) was knocked around between the character definitions of 'who I take myself to be', 'who I am' and 'the person you take me to be'. Perhaps the quote from the timeless work of Carmelo Lisón-Tolosana sums up the loss of self-worth, the vertiginous questioning of one's place in the world: 'When I had money they called me *Don* Tomas; now I have none they just call me Tomas' (1966: 81). Or, to flip our situation on its head, we might consider Dimitris Psathas' (1944) account of the elevated status of the greengrocer who distributes rations during the Second World War and who might be open to a little black-market bargaining. The greengrocer's public persona is temporarily exalted, people addressing him as 'Kyrios' (Mister), which was not the case before the war (Knight 2012a; see also Hart 1992: 74–75; Just 1991: 129).

Revisiting the ethnographic detail of Argyrou's or Lisón-Tolosana's accounts allows us to consider unknowingness in situations beyond crisis. For both authors, their research participants are experiencing the pressures of modernity, industrialization and the financialization of everyday activities that are what Pippin would have us believe to be the foundations for increasing situations of unknowingness. Those who can no longer fulfil the traits of their long-established public persona become slowly stripped of their essence, their identity and their self-worth, no doubt provoking anxiety, a crisis of presence and, I would argue, a sense of vertigo. The world becomes strange to them, an uncanny new timespace of unfamiliar values, their existence rocked by an inability to perform as both self- and public expectation might dictate.

In earlier pre-crisis work in the central Greek town of Trikala, I too encountered someone who was experiencing a sense of vertigo after going bankrupt (Knight 2015: 149–51). After losing his business and house and being threatened with time in jail, Andreas, in his sixties and from a working-class family of builders, described feeling 'lost', 'dizzy' and 'physically sick' as he scrambled around attempting to borrow money from networks of friends and acquaintances while trying to hide the reality of his dire situation from his close family: 'I feared every knock at the door and every time I went to pick up the mail. When I went into the cafeteria [to collect the mail] my eyes would blur as my blood pressure started rising and then my head would start spinning. A high-pitched screeching would pierce my ears. My tongue felt fat and sometimes I could hardly speak to the landlady. It was life lived in constant panic, suspicion. Paranoia.' After a brief period of what he termed 'relaxing' after being declared bankrupt in 2006, on revisiting him in 2012, I found his life in a tailspin, Andreas declaring: 'The crisis has taken away my peace of mind, I am anxious again.' His children were in their thirties and unemployed, living at home. They still demanded stylish clothes and dined at fashionable restaurants. Andreas had started borrowing money from family members again to the tune of €8,000 and rising: 'Once again, I am caught between who I want to be, my capacity to be that person, and the demands of my family and friends. I am being torn in competing directions and I am trying to be too many people at once. I am in tatters.'

Of course, unlike in Argyrou's, Lisón-Tolosana's or my own encounters mentioned above, Mairi's state of unknowingness was not primarily linked to her newfound inability to perform elaborate displays of wealth in the public domain, but could be construed as similar in that she was experiencing a loss of self-worth and was unable to live up to her public persona. Everything she had built over the course of half a century that had come to represent 'Mairi' both to the onlooking world and in her own reflection staring back from the bedroom mirror had been dismantled by an outside force beyond her control – the economic crisis and subsequent related episodes of personal misfortune. In Sebald's *Vertigo*, it is suggested that the conscious identity of an individual is his personal memories and the integrity of his body inside his skin (Moss 2000). Mairi questions her memories and her integrity in the current moment, expressing helplessness as she ricochets between her past certainties, her current suspension and her defeated futures manifested as intolerable unknowingness. The associated nausea of unknowingness was triggered by such mundane activities as making a telephone call or glancing up to the hillside where her now-repossessed villa stood. Even picking fruit induced the nausea of unknowingness, a feeling of detachment from the Self, a realization of the futility of existence. Referring to the fruit-picking, Mairi exclaims: 'That one is extra-strange. I just don't understand it. And it is regular. I was never a village-person, always living in Athens. It is not like my mother had fruit trees or a vegetable patch or that I ever used the fruit in cooking ... I have no memories but picking a pear or plum can make me retch.' She concludes that she is being transported to a place she has never visited that is both eerily familiar and absolutely unknown.

My friend in central Greece has been experiencing something similar when tending to her vegetable patch. For Popi, her garden was her pride and joy. A visitor to her home in a small village on the agricultural Plain of Thessaly would receive a full guided tour of well-kept flowerbeds bursting with colour, held in place by carefully selected local stone. On a trip to the hospital in Thessaloniki in 2006, I remember Popi loading up the back of her Nissan Micra with scented flowers, luscious ferns and exotic imported orchids. The boot would not shut, so we lay plastic carrier bags on the rear passenger seats and continued shopping. She would drive a significant distance to uproot a wild flower reported to her by a friend or relative, delicately extracting the specimen to be replanted in her garden. Lazy afternoons would be spent cruising the banks of a river or the foot of a mountain in search of an enticing addition to her botanic bonanza.

After the crisis struck, Popi became obsessively anxious about food provision, hoarding supplies and chastising those who wasted food at mealtimes (see Knight 2012a, 2015). One of her first acts was to dismantle the flower garden and replace it with a makeshift greenhouse and substantial vegetable plot. In doing so, she lost a major aspect of her identity. Onlookers comment to this day on how the crisis took away 'Popi' in that single act of landscape remodelling. Popi is almost incapable of reminiscing about how her garden once looked, choosing to ignore opportunities to engage in conversation and preferring to redirect proceedings towards alternative topics. It seems like another world, another life, another Popi.

Like Mairi, a series of crises emanating from the original economic turmoil have left Popi housebound, a nervous wreck who rarely ventures further than her own front gate. Reclusive, her hands shake, and she is a bundle of anxiety. Since the onset of the economic crisis, her husband has passed away, her son has lost his business and her pension has been cut. She has unpaid bills. Debts. The taxman. New obsessions, new anxieties, a shadow of her former Self stalking a world of anguish and self-deprecation. On the rare occasions when she does comment on her past exploits in the garden, her narrative is always preceded by a hearty sigh. She physically cannot bear to engage. 'That was a different me in different times. A long time ago. Too much has happened to recognize it', she comments. When she goes to pick her vegetables to use in her home cooking, she 'prefers not to look' at the garden (a phrase that reminds us of Mairi turning her eyes away from the hilltop where she once owned a villa), 'remaining focused on the job'. 'I go crazy if I allow myself to think too much. Please, don't pressure me [to talk about my garden]', she politely requests.

Popi is deeply saddened by the long unsightly grass pressing up against the side of her greenhouse and the muddy mess bordering her cucumber patch, but her anguish about providing food that, her family and friends note, has toppled over into obsessive compulsive behaviour takes over. She does not wander into the village or drive more than a few miles from the home because, her daughter believes, she is 'held captive' by her garden: 'Her anxieties are all related to the vegetables and what might happen if she leaves them alone. She is afraid that she will not be able to feed the family and the crisis will take their lives.' Although logically this is very unlikely, 'the crisis instilled in her the sense that she must be the provider in any way she could. All her worry was targeted and manifested in the garden', her daughter comments. 'When we lost the flowers, we lost our mother. She has never been the same. She lost a huge part of who she is. She is unrecognizable to us and, I believe, to herself.' Poignantly, her daughter believes that Popi 'now depends on her anxieties. The crisis has eaten away at her mind and her body. Nervousness is her life now. She is dependent on her anxiety'.

For Mairi and Popi, unknowingness has become a condition of dependence, as Pippin has propagated, a form of captivity between the person, their social relations and the wider world (on captivity, see Chapter 5). Trapped in a post-rupture timespace of emptiness and suspension, the search for the familiarity of the past in a world now operating on different social and material terms of engagement has left Mairi and Popi in a spin. They are the Wile E. Coyote to the crisis' Road Runner, holding out a 'Stop' sign, but being left behind pivoting on their big toe, spinning in a cloud of dust as the world speeds by.

The shuffling back and forth between old versions of the Self and a persona undergoing schismatic externally enforced change is a neverending process that has no final solution – the vertiginous suspension seems permanent and the dependence is rarely broken (on permanence as futural orientation, see Knight (2019a)).[3] The reliance on unknowingness creates vertigo by suspending the person between desire and fear, past and future, knowing and unknowing, trying to recognize the unrecognizable. Mairi and Popi have been dispossessed of the mundane aspects of life that held together their sense of Self. They have been sent spiralling away from what they once held dear, existing in suspension with nausea and anxiety, being held captive in the timespace of chronic crisis.

RICOCHETS

Vertigo can be generated by a deep-rooted unknowingness that is experienced as nausea, anxiety and obsession. For Mairi, vertigo is being suspended between an attachment to and a melancholy detachment from her own life. She is caught in the ceaseless ricochets between the loss of past plans and desires, her limbo in a permanent present filled with fear and dispossession, and defeated futures. There is a struggle to recognize herself and her situation that is manifested as intolerable nausea-inducing unknowingness. For most of her life, Mairi believed that she was in control of her own destiny, setting and achieving goals, creating her future, and fulfilling the demands of her personal and public personas. The economic crisis reshaped what she saw as her destiny, obliterating her anticipated futures. Now, like Sartre's character Roquentin, Mairi exists in disorientation, unable to come to terms with the strangeness of crisis, feeling overwhelmingly powerless and convinced of her own uselessness. 'Mairi' is unrecognizable to Mairi, provoking an unknowingness of Self that is the cause of persistent nausea.

Questions of power and freedom are, according to Sartre, fundamentally threatening and always fraught with unresolvable anxiety associated with mundane tasks and objects. For Kierkegaard, the anxiety of freedom is dizzying, a threat that is overcome through educating the Self towards embracing the creative potentialities of new social forms. For Mairi, the division of her home was the ultimate step in stealing away her person, while for Popi, the transformation of her flower garden was the essential loss of freedom. When Mairi reconfigured her home to accommodate her returning adult children, she ceased being able to host houseguests and hold card-playing evenings. One may dismiss such changes as superficial or surmountable, yet the impact went so deep as to sever an aspect of Mairi's person. Both Mairi and Popi describe a blankness, a numbness to the world and a questioning of the purpose of existence when carrying out mundane activities. They doubt their own validity in a world of uncontrollable cascading crisis and problematize the point of a life without freedom or direction.

Adding to vertigo as unknowingness is the aspect of the multiple velocities of crisis. By this I mean that for Mairi, the numerous crises within a Time of Crisis have been manifested as both sudden rupture and the slow-motion violent erosion of everyday life. On the one hand, the death of her child was an unexpected lightning strike to the heart of an already vertiginous life, emphatically intensifying Mairi's questioning of the meaning of life and her own inabilities to control her future. As I am sure my own mother and father would confirm, the death of a child is enough to knock anyone into a vertiginous spin and constitutes a sudden and unimaginable rupture, a state of suspension from which one may never emerge. On the other hand, Mairi mentions that tedious tasks such as cooking for her grown-up children and the orientation of her living room sofa are nagging nausea-inducing instances that represent the slowly corrosive drip-dripping of crisis. Together, these multiple velocities amount to Steve McQueen crashing his racing car – which Charles Stewart refers to and that I mention in the Introduction – in a mixture of slow motion and regular speed, with flashbacks and flashforwards, zooming in and zooming out, leaving one feeling dazed, confused and seasick (Knight and Stewart 2016: 3).

Sequential crises within the wider framework of a Time of Crisis have left Mairi perpetually existing between knowing and unknowing where her being once meant something, but now, through layers of detachment and tragedy, she is absent from herself. She is skittish, anticipating the next violent event. She does not recognize herself in her own reflection and it is this unknowingness of the Self that creates the nausea. The division of her home is the prime example of how unknowingness is an overarching condition that spans multiple scales of self-definition. The categories of 'who I take myself to be', 'who I am' and 'the person you (the public) take me to be' are infiltrated by parasitic unknowingness. Alongside abrupt rupture, the slow-motion violence of everyday life leads to self-doubt manifested in the performance of mundane activities. This anguish extends to a second-guessing of how she is perceived in public by friends and neighbours. The division of her home has an immediate spatial impact for Mairi, who is now sleeping in the former cellar, but also a conceptual bearing on her ability to perform social roles that are imperative to the reproduction of her public-facing personhood. A proportion of Mairi now resides in emptiness, a vacuous timespace of transition and transformation stuck between the destruction of old world orders and the gradual emergence of the alien new, which she ostensibly rejects.

Unknowingness expressed as existential emptiness and temporal suspension is a marker of late modernity exacerbated at a Time of Crisis where the world is moving at a different speed, accelerated, as suggested in Thomas Hylland Eriksen's (2016a, 2016b) recent interventions. As some clamber to catch up, to adapt, to leap into the vortex of creative history-making or embrace the dizziness of the new world, others are left behind, scrambling towards the past, the unattainable familiar. Locked into a crisis of presence, in a hyperconscious state of self-reflection or numbness, Mairi and Popi exist in relative stasis. The rupture of critical events and the slow-motion violence of microfissures accumulate and aggravate the sense of shock and anguish.

Unknowingness has become a condition of cyclical dependence, a form of captivity emerging between the person, their social relations and a world in crisis. In Chapter 2, we move from vertigo caused by unknowingness and detachment to overconnection and affinity. Although futures may not have unfolded as once expected, returnees to an abandoned village have a more optimistic story to tell of their vertiginous lives.

NOTES

1. Michel Serres notes how looking at objects oozing in historical significance makes him feel sick to the core, transporting him to timespaces in which he would rather not be. Serres recounts how he cannot look at Pablo Picasso's *Guernica*, for instance, due to its association with the Spanish Civil War (Serres and Latour 1995: 2–3). When he looks at such pictures, he physically feels history seeping from them, as witnesses to terrible events. Such things are 'symptoms of evil', not merely reactions or analysis.

2. Interestingly for our study of temporality, Roquentin believes that history is pointless, for it concerns what *was* rather than what *is*; thus, only observing the present has any form of meaning. Although scholars as diverse as Bergson and Croce, Koselleck and Deleuze would have surely contested this stance, for Roquentin, history is about what has existed before.

3. One might think here of the literature on trauma and the therapeutic techniques of reintegrating detached versions of the Self (see e.g. Argenti and Schramm 2010; Caruth 1991; Fassin and Rechtman 2007; Kenny 1996). This approach also resonates with de Martino's remarks on rehistoricizing people suffering a crisis of presence.

CHAPTER 2

DIMITRIS
Rebuilding from Rubble

❧❧❧

The distant purr of a chainsaw echoes around a mountainside slowly waking from the slumber of another unforgiving winter. The creaking of a falling tree. The faint yet unmistakable scent of smouldering firewood on the breeze. It is March 2015 and a ghost village is coming to life. I follow my senses to a small clearing on a hilltop facing the village of Petrochori in Greek Macedonia, where my gaze fixes on the imposing figure of Dimitris mopping beads of sweat from his brow, glancing up towards the pristine sky. I salute the unshaven, weather-beaten 39-year-old as he takes stock of his morning's work. A former clerk at a tax office in Thessaloniki, Dimitris resigned in 2012, permanently moving with his family to Petrochori later that year. I remember him telling me then that he and his wife 'had been talking for a while' about how best to live through the 'difficult years'. Since the start of the crisis in 2009, they had been 'hearing stories about people getting back to basics, returning to their villages in the country to work the land or just cut down on expenditure'. Born and raised in a small apartment in the suburbs of Thessaloniki, Dimitris' grandparents owned a home in Petrochori, some 1,100 metres high in the Pindos Mountains, that was abandoned during the 1946–49 Civil War. Picking up the conversation this glorious spring morning, Dimitris swigs from his water bottle as I ask him how life is progressing among the rubble of a deserted village: 'OK! The house was crumbling, and we didn't know what we would do to make money, but to be honest we had nothing to lose. Everyone was asking the same question at that time "should I go back to my village?" We were strong enough to make the decision.'

Throughout the early crisis years, the idea of 'returning to village life' swept through conversations across the nation. I first encountered the desire to return while caught in infuriating traffic on a taxi journey across central Athens in 2011. Ninety minutes for all of five miles. The driver, most probably in his early forties, expressed his intention to 'just leave this place and get back to [my] village'. He and his wife had both inherited property in the same Peloponnesian village where they could set up home, 'work the land', 'get away' from paying so much tax, reduce their living expenses by growing their own fruit and vegetables, and generally 'escape' and 'calm down' away from the chaos of the crisis. The vision of village life was, the driver suggested, 'idyllic' and 'perfect', although 'pre-modern'. There were, he identified, a few small catches. First, he owned only undeveloped land, while his wife had inherited a sizeable house. But the house was in disrepair, having not been occupied since the 1960s. Daylight beamed through a gaping hole in the roof and much of the perimeter wall had fallen into a drainage ravine and was slowly being dragged further down the mountainside by heavy winter storms. 'We go for summer breaks, maybe two weeks in August for the *Paniyiri* [religious celebration] and take the kids to see where their family comes from. But the house has no electricity, and the roof is falling in.' Admitting that renovating the house would amount to a substantial – and expensive – project, the driver moved on to problem number two: 'What do I know about working the land?!'

Born and raised in central Athens, living in a sixth-storey two-bedroom flat, he had never even had a courtyard garden let alone an orchard or vegetable patch. Indeed, it is common banter that when someone replies to your enquiry 'Where are you from?' with the answer 'Athens', the inquisitor must repeat the question, 'yes, but *where* are you from' (implying that nobody is *really* from Athens, but everyone descends from a village in another part of Greece, even if they rarely frequent it). The driver continued: 'Making a life from the land seems like hard work. To retrain I mean. To learn. I guess the old people who still live [in the village] could teach me, but ... I suppose it's possible.' Finally, point three: 'Would my fifteen-year-old and twelve-year-old really want to live in a remote village? No internet, no movies, away from their friends?' The question was, of course, rhetorical. Nevertheless, the driver seemed to be truly contemplating the advantages of 'going back to the village', despite the fact that neither he nor his wife had ever resided there for more than a fortnight in the summer.

In 2012, Dimitris, his wife Voula and their teenage son Michalis relocated to Petrochori, retaining their apartment in Thessaloniki, which had been an *inter vivos* gift from Dimitris' widowed mother. 'We didn't have anything to lose', he jests, carefully picking splintered wood from the teeth of his chainsaw. 'The debts were piling up, all those new taxes, the cost of living in the city ... and just the stress ... it was killing us.' Expressing similar doubts to the aforementioned taxi driver, at first it was unclear to Dimitiris how he might make a living or simply adapt to a life towards which he had little affinity and virtually no experience: 'I had this small house in Petrochori that was beyond saving really. It looked like if you were to lean on it or flick a cigarette butt in its direction, it would just collapse in a heap of dust and stone ... I remember playing in it in the 1980s when I was still at school. My siblings and I would spend a few weeks up here with my grandparents during the summer holidays.' The house was finally abandoned in 1989 when his grandparents went to live out their final years with his parents in the city. When Dimitris and Voula first visited with the intention to relocate, dense foliage had reclaimed the house. They found the roof half-collapsed, severe damp problems, and infestations of mice and scorpions. There was no mains electricity, meaning no heating supply apart from an old wood-burning stove. The first job, Dimitiris explains, was to make one-half of the building watertight: 'I got together with a couple of friends from Thessaloniki, promised them beers and told them of the beauty of the place. We spent three weeks in the summer patching up the roof and generally clearing away the forest. And then we [his family] had to just get on with it, close our eyes and make the move.'

Dimitiris and Voula eventually established a small coffee shop in the village to catch trade passing through towards the UNESCO-protected Zagorochoria in the summer and cater for winter hunting groups. The village coffee shop had been closed for years and Voula remembered the surname of the owners. Dimitiris explains: 'The children of the last people to run it now live in Ioannina [in Epirus, a region to the west] so we tracked them down. They offered us a ten-year lease whereby we give them a small percentage of our earnings.' The coffee shop building was in relatively good condition and, located in the central square, was prime real estate pressed up against the only road in and out of the village. Their son Michalis now manages the coffee shop, deals with wholesalers and runs the website. Voula cooks local delicacies, primarily sourced from the surrounding environment, while Dimitris organizes the financial side of the business and is something of a local handyman, cutting firewood, maintaining common land neglected by the cash-strapped council and running elderly villagers into town for hospital appointments.

Over the course of eight years, Dimitris, Voula and Michalis have quite literally rebuilt their futures among the rubble of the past. And others have joined them. Petros, university-trained as a biology teacher who cannot find work because, he insists, he does not take 'political sides' (he has not found patronage from local politicians), resides in Petrochori to tend to his bees and sell firewood in Grevena, scratching out enough money to pay for his children's private English and mathematics tuition. His wife and children live in Larisa, some 110 miles away. Kostas, a young shepherd, declined university education with its supposed dead-end prospects to re-establish his grandfather's flock. Fotini, an architect in her early thirties, finds that she can cope with her sporadic workload from her base in the village while keeping her living costs down, travelling to urban centres as and when the job demands. All have found a bolthole in Petrochori since the onset of crisis, renovating ancestral homes and communal areas. Other properties have been purchased by diasporic Greeks with kinship ties to the village – a businessman now based in Hong Kong has begun renovating a three-storey stone house bought from a distant relative for €20,000 and a dentist from Boston whose family last lived in Petrochori in the 1930s is rebuilding a house from the foundations up, a project that has already taken over five years owing to strict conservation laws.

The crisis has been regenerative for Petrochori as return has meant restoration, a village rising from the ashes. With the rejuvenation of village life has come a dual-aspect disorientation openly expressed by the returnees. First, the unforeseen move from urban to rural setting has inverted commonly held perceptions of linear progress on the timeline of late modernity. This vertigo is associated with the elsewhere of life in crisis, the geographical uprooting of families from urban to rural environments, triggering 'mobility anxiety', a leap in imagination leading to paranoia owing to the dramatic rearrangement of social relations involved in losing place (Battaglia 2005: 14, 21). Relocation to the village has undone movements that commenced in the 1960s, when, Ernestine Friedl was among the first to note in the Greek context, the desire for urban living was first linked to notions of class mobility, cleanliness and prestigious employment (Friedl 1976: 365; see also Argyrou 1996: 35; Hart 1992: 77). In the pre-crisis years, a return to the rubble (physical and metaphorical) of rural life was unthinkable, fostering connotations of peasantry, backwardness and pre-modernity. Trajectories towards the material and conceptual comforts of urban living have been generally considered birthrights for people born into post-dictatorship Greece (Knight 2017a; on future as birthright, see Rapport (2019)), with mainstream expectations post-1974 being material accumulation, advancements in home utilities and the unquestioned investment in ubiquitous political promises of 'plenty' associated with Greece's belonging to the West (Herzfeld 1987). For people like the Athenian taxi driver – and indeed Dimitris before he relocated – moving back to ancestral villages is discussed as returning to a place of pre-modernity, somewhere belonging to a timespace before Europeanization. Second, the material landscape of abandoned villages generates a whirlwind historical consciousness. People cite how the rubble of ancestral homes is infused with past events, relations and emotions that have a physical and extraordinarily affective presence (Gordillo 2014; Navaro-Yashin 2012; Stewart 2012; Stoler 2013). The tangibility of the past extends to the natural environment, ingrained with centuries of bloodshed, conquest, toil and narrative. Together, inverted expectations of *where* twenty-first-century life is situated and the overpowering physicality of the past embedded in the materiality of the village is enough, to paraphrase Dimitris, 'to take the breath away', transporting people on a topological journey, stretching, twisting, braiding and crumpling, but in this case, it will become clear, not tearing the fabric of time.

This chapter explores how these 'geographies of loss' (Bryant 2010: 79) – physical relocation and temporal reorientation – combine to cultivate vertigo among returnees to Petrochori, with special attention to the vertiginous elsewhere. The vertigo of the elsewhere is situated in the material environment of the village and the inverted trajectories of expectation associated with life in twenty-first-century Greece. Of course, the vertigo discussed here also encourages contemplation of the elsewhen, the temporal confusion caused by living in different times – which is the theme of Chapter 3. But for now, it is beneficial to dwell on the more mundane aspect of vertigo, the everyday consequences of relocation to an abandoned place of debris. As returnees begin to fashion their futures from the rubble of the past, it becomes apparent that in Petrochori, vertigo centres on an overconnection to the affective qualities of time and place. This is quite a different manifestation from Mairi's vertigo in Chapter 1, which is situated in unknowingness and detachment where she is unable to find a positive basis to rebuild her life in crisis. Vertiginous lives in Petrochori belong to people who have pushed the reset button during the crisis years, taking the leap off the cliff-edge into the unknown to create new livelihoods. Rather than defining themselves as pioneers or the courageous few forging new frontiers, as Runia or Kierkegaard might read the creativity of action at a critical horizon of history, people like Dimitris see a return to Petrochori as escapism and a search for familiarity in the *ilinx* of crisis. Instead of critiquing philosophies of the positive creative properties of the vertiginous, here I choose to focus on the everyday optimism found in the material and spatial rupture of relocation. Although lives may not have unfolded as once expected or hoped, villagers find much to celebrate in their rebuilding of Self and family among rubble.

RUBBLE

Aiming to further an understanding of how the tangible qualities of rubble and debris are embedded in the continuous transformative negotiation of subjectivity, this chapter charts the uneven temporal sedimentations among the ruins of Petrochori that 'contour and carve through the psychic and material space in which people live and what compounded layers of ... debris do to them' (Stoler 2013: 2). Villagers such as Dimitris have an affective connection to the rubble in which they live, including experiences of reliving times past and the comfort, familiarity and embodied disquiet found in debris (cf. Trouillot 1995). For Dimitris, the material environment unites 'apparently disparate moments, places, and objects' (Stoler 2013: 7) where the past weighs heavily, although not necessarily negatively, on the present and future, evoking what he terms a 'whirlwind' experience of time and place.

One of the leading proponents of the study of what is referred to variously as ruins, rubble, debris and detritus, Ann Stoler paces Walter Benjamin in arguing that ruins have the potential to make material and affective connections between incongruent timespaces, affectively burdening material and social microecologies in multiple ways. She asks:

> Under what conditions are those sites left to decompose, remanded, reconsigned, or disregarded? Some remains are ignored as innocuous leftovers, others petrify, some hold and spread their toxicities and become poisonous debris. Others are stubbornly inhabited by those displaced to make a political point, or requisitioned for a newly refurbished commodity-life for tourist consumption, or occupied by those left with nowhere else to turn. (Stoler 2013: 13)

More than solely encapsulating 'petrified life' in the classic terms of Benjamin (Buck-Morss 1991: 159, Frederiksen 2013: 15), rubble is at once a product of the past that permeates the present and shapes both the conditional subjunctive and the uncertain future (Stoler 2013: 10). In the early crisis years, Petrochori was a last-resort hideaway for people 'left with nowhere else to turn' in the wake of crisis. But despite the desperation with which people first sought to return, and the complex temporal indices involved in reforming materiality and psyche, living among rubble has cultivated novel social outlooks and political subjectivities. The initial abandonment of Petrochori was the result of targeted governmental projects over the course of sixty years, the village slowly receding into a site of remembrance, a carefully controlled representation of the past with little impact on the present and future. The re-activation of Petrochori as a place of permanent residence more than six decades later has had visceral and visual repercussions, the rubble 'actively morphing, changing, and being recycled in the local imaginaries around displacement, suffering, and life-making' (Rao 2013: 316). Since the onset of crisis, the petrified life of Petrochori has become enlivened in novel ways.

The term 'ruin', Gaston Gordillo (2014: 4–5) advocates, is infused with 'abstracted veneration' that detaches the material form from the present, prioritizing 'culturally specific habits' that have an overtly Western genealogy. Classifying objects as ruins emphasizes their pastness, Gordillo continues, and thus underscores the modernity of the present and the Western obsession with preservation and heritage (2014: 9). Conversely, in common parlance, 'rubble' usually refers to shapeless and worthless debris rather than something to be protected and revered. In line with Gordillo, I would suggest that this polemic is unhelpful and advocate the textured, affectively nuanced and temporally charged qualities of materiality, regardless of label. For the present purposes, the material landscape of Petrochori is referred to primarily as rubble, stripping it of any potential overtones of protected grandeur, reflecting the grassroots reality of neglected buildings, crumbling walls, pathways slipping into the rapids of raging rivers, and wilderness encroaching on all material traces of past inhabitancy. However, the area does fall under European Union (EU) and Greek state conservation law, something that has added extra challenges to the literal rebuilding of the village since it has been granted a form of de facto 'ruin' status.

No matter terminology, the social afterlife of structures, sensibilities, and things produce the microecologies of matter and mind in an ongoing process through which one can locate a 'trail of the psyche' (Stoler 2013: 9). The afterlife disturbs everyday life, Yael Navaro-Yashin (2012: 20) suggests, with its 'irritability' – the uncanny qualities in which material objects discharge affect. In Petrochori, the vertiginous affects of rebuilding from rubble, both metaphorically and practically, do not consist of implacable resentment, domination and ongoing structural violence, as Stoler has suggested for the postcolonial context. Instead, relocations to life among rubble have been overwhelmingly optimistic. Taking Gordillo's (2013: 246) statement that no ruin escapes the tension between 'positive and negative elements' with social actors, depending on perspective, tending to 'gravitate toward highlighting one over the other', in Petrochori villagers certainly highlight the positivity of rubble, despite the violence ingrained in the material and natural landscape. Rubble has provided an avenue out of crisis, or at least an alternative to the suffocating stresses of the city, and people report feeling an intimacy with past generations who once made the now-ruined village a lively hub of sociality and commerce. The lifeblood of long-departed ancestors invigorates the new occupants of Petrochori. An abandoned landscape that was once detached from future-making and considered beyond the desired trajectory of late capitalist modernity is now the centre of reconceptualized futures for a community enlivened. The crisis years have still been extremely challenging, but residents of Petrochori cite the physical qualities of the material landscape, imbued with the stories of ancestors and events of the past, as being seminal to their own endurance. The vertigo experienced upon relocation to the ruined village, although disorienting in multifaceted ways, is based in an overpowering connection to this material elsewhere. Debris works on matter and mind to engender political actors with resilience and a renewed sense of belonging, sometimes verging on the obsessive (think Scottie's obsession with Madeleine in *Vertigo*). The villagers of Petrochori embrace the vertigo to forge unanticipated, entangled and courageous lives among rubble.

I wish to argue for the optimism of rubble that transcends both the modernist world and the need for distinctions such as enchanted/irritable. In his thesis on Parisian arcades, Walter Benjamin famously said that positive spatial forms were a feature of the bourgeois modernist world, a consequence being that rubble is left to reference uncoded negativity, distinguishing what Georg Simmel called the 'work of man' with recognizable form from a mere 'heap of stones' (Gordillo 2014: 9). Experiences of life among the rubble of Petrochori inverts this observation, since my interlocutors find positivity and familiarity in rubble that to outsiders – and from the perspective of the pre-crisis years – may index pre-modernity and archaic pasts. Instilled with turbulent, at times bewildering affect, the crumbling walls and collapsing buildings perspectivize and guide life choices in a polytemporal smoothie of disturbing pasts, critical presents and potential futures. Rubble, then, is not a feature of negativity, but 'exerts positive pressure on human practice' (2014: 11) often experienced as a gravitational pull holding captive those within its sphere of influence.

The disorienting rubble of Petrochori speaks from multiple overlapping timespaces, becoming a fraught and destabilizing punctuation of the present. However, this does not imply that the disturbance is undesirable, but rather that rubble can cause pause for reflection, reassessment and, in Martin Heidegger's (1993) terms, gather people, memories and affects around it, revealing modes of ordering and ways of bringing forth manners of Being. To invoke Heidegger further, in Petrochori rubble is a kaleidoscope of spatiotemporal coordinates that may at first make one go cross-eyed before a beautiful picture emerges.

PETROCHORI

Situated in a tranquil corner of Greek Macedonia, the village of Petrochori perches on a mountainside deep in the Pindos Mountains. With winter temperatures sometimes exceeding -20°C and snow often covering the 20 miles of road from the town of Grevena, in the decade preceding the crisis, the village summer population of approximately 170 souls dropped to between four and ten from November to February. Petrochori had become a 'summer community', representing a past that was cordoned off from the flow of time and whose effects on the present and future were carefully restricted to controlled visits in the mid-summer months. Similar to many villages of Greek

Macedonia, life in Petrochori was drastically transformed by the events of the 1940s. During the 1946–49 Civil War, kidnappings and murders by both communist and nationalist groups were commonplace in the mountains north of Grevena. The civil war crippled the economy of Petrochori, where stone-masonry had been thriving for centuries. From at least the mid-Ottoman period until the Second World War, teams of builders from Petrochori would travel as far as Albania, Bulgaria, Thrace and even Istanbul to fulfil lucrative building contracts. Petrochori became synonymous with high-quality masonry, and the village enjoyed a sustained period of relative wealth and prestige. Owing to expertise in building with stone, today the village still holds masterful, if dilapidated, examples of the local craft, with most houses dating to the early 1900s and constructed in the traditional way.

The Axis occupation of 1941–44 and the subsequent civil war disrupted the movement of stonemasons, who could not find enough local work to maintain a livelihood. The dangers of travelling in the mountains owing to violence by both sides meant that those without political or economic interests in the conflicts had little choice but to abandon their village. The government created 'safe zones' (sometimes inverted and called 'dead zones' in reference to the abandonment of masses of mountain communities) for people wanting to relocate from the mountains to urban centres on the plains. Government enticements towards urban life on the plains were part of a wider programme of wartime population control aimed at breaking the communist supply chain running from Yugoslavia through the heart of the Pindos Mountains. The safe zone project constituted a deliberate governmental initiative towards ruination that, in a postcolonial context, would fit neatly into Stoler's and Gordillo's argument on 'the ongoing nature of imperial process' (Stoler 2013: ix) that creates 'spaces constituted by absences' (Gordillo 2013: 228; see also Rao 2013: 309).[1] There were rumours about copious employment opportunities for construction workers in towns such as Kozani (50 miles from Petrochori), Trikala (80 miles), Larisa (110 miles) and Thessaloniki (125 miles), urban environments that required substantial renovation after a decade of war. When combined with the movement of those who enlisted with either the communist or nationalist militias, alongside the well-documented forced relocation of children from the area (Danforth and van Boeschoten 2012; cf. Pipyrou 2020), there was a mass exodus of villagers from 1946 to 1949. Some returned in the 1960s to rebuild homes and hack away the encroaching undergrowth, but, with no mains water, electricity or telephone service, by the 1980s Petrochori was empty once again. Many extended families are nowadays split between various urban settlements, although most retain at least one house in the village, often in a state of disrepair.

The abandonment of Petrochori was partially a large-scale process of 'ruin-making' that Stoler (2013: 21) pins to government resources and planning that enforce the creation of new zones, uninhabitable space and strategic politically charged nation-building. In addition to the 1940s 'safe zone' project, more recent programmes to reform local government under the rubrics of *Ioannis Kapodistrias* in 1997 and *Kallikratis* in 2010 dealt a further blow to the depopulation of the Greek periphery. The amendments accentuated and accelerated the depopulation of Petrochori, which became almost exclusively a summer community with only a few elderly villagers choosing to stay outside of the months of July and August, arriving at the end of March and leaving before the first snow in October. In the pre-crisis years of my visits, which commenced in 2003, between November and February Petrochori was usually permanently inhabited by only one family: Giorgos the shepherd and his wife Soula, both in their seventies, and their two children, who sold their dairy products at market in Grevena. In the summer months, the village would come alive as families returned for vacations and to participate in public and religious celebrations (*Paniyiria*) held in July and August. People in their forties and fifties who remembered their childhood summers holidaying with grandparents in the village would open up the ancestral home, bringing their own children and elderly parents. Before the crisis, life in the village swelled for six weeks in July and August, only to return dramatically to its seasonal empty slumber. As such, the material and social past embedded in the village environment was carefully and selectively controlled. Petrochori became a site of nostalgic remembrance that was detached from real-world future-making. Structural nostalgia facilitated the selective remembrance of the past laden with qualities that no longer had a purpose in the present where the material, spatial and temporal landscape had been reshaped (Herzfeld 2004). Village life was kept at arm's length in a form of comfortable and controlled detachment.

The rubble of the decaying village was in the pre-crisis years symbolic of decades of neglect in favour of modern urban living, as well as being valorized from a distance as a site of incessant remembrance – summer holidays, grandparents and simpler times. Yet now things are different. The village still witnesses a seasonal soar of residents, but the winter numbers have taken a remarkable upturn. The permanent residents of Petrochori numbered twenty-five in 2019. This may not seem too impressive, but represents a 525 per cent increase on the single family of four from 2003. When factoring in people, usually retirees, who arrive in March/April and leave in September/October, the number rises to approximately fifty residents. The stories behind the new arrivals are very similar: inherited houses left uninhabited for decades, and desires to escape the pressures of crisis Greece and return to

what is perceived to be a simpler way of life. Their reports on their experiences of village life are extraordinarily comparable, regularly referring to
'returning to the rubble' of the past to rebuild their lives. The tangibility of
the past permeates the narratives; rather than talking of abstract elsewhens
or fluid concepts of temporal displacement (discussed in Chapter 3), the
buildings and the landscape provide grounded experiences of living in an
elsewhere once associated with a long-vacated past. Vertigo here is palpable
through the physical environment; the re-insertion of historically rich place
into timelines where it was supposed to be long redundant.

Dimitiris describes his experiences during the first days of relocation to
Petrochori as 'breathtaking' in the literal sense: 'Everything I touched, everywhere I walked, I felt history gushing through my veins.' On one occasion
after an arduous trek to the nearest freshwater spring (mains water was not
restored to his home until two months after his return), he stopped for a cigarette outside what used to be the village school that closed in 1985. Leaning
against the stone wall, Dimitris' heart suddenly started beating faster, 'like
it was going to blow up'. He gestures with his fist pumping back and forth
close to his chest, 'bam bam, bam bam, bam bam ... Honestly, I could feel
the energy running through my body, I was having palpations, I thought that
I was going to explode'. What he describes as 'the most intense experience'
that 'transported' his body to another place was caused by 'the generations
of children who have passed through that place, kids I used to know, the
old people who were once young too, everything they have witnessed. The
builders who constructed that marvellous structure [the school] ... everything was surging through me'. Dimitris insists that it is 'not just some memory', but an all-encompassing feeling: 'I was there, living those decades, all
those lifetimes together, swirling ... the people and the history whooshing
through me. I was still in Petrochori, but in a different place, another epoch ...
it was all such an intense blur.' The school walls had captured in them the
petrified life of a vanished world – visual images, relationships and events
(Buck-Morss 1991; Frederiksen 2013).

The topological experience of time and place Dimitris relayed is intimately linked to the physical environment, leaving him feeling as though
he was being sucked through a vortex. In very much a Proustian sense, he
became giddy as the years of history stacked higher and higher, released
into his fingertips through powerful waves upon contact with the stone. The
depth of history, tangled and energized, had a bodily affect. Other villagers
report the stone being 'alive', one person insisting that 'the stone is a living
being, a witness, and a friend', another insisting that it is 'haunted' by the
beings of ancestors long departed. For Dimitris, the stone walls of the school
collapsed space-time, producing a feeling that everything was happening at
once. He now knows what to expect, he says, when touching the stone that

is always warm but ever cold, in the here and now but existing throughout history: 'I now take great pleasure in placing my hand on the stone walls and buildings ... I anticipate what I am going to receive. It is a bit different on each occasion, but you always feel the life of hundreds of people from hundreds of times rushing through you.' Feeling the past pulsating is a vertiginous experience that can be located beyond a generalized aura of feeling lost or dizzy. Touching the stone, Dimitris confides, not only reminds him how things used to be, but also provides him with insights to his own futures. At first, the vertigo made him feel vulnerable, not knowing when or where he was going to travel upon interacting with the material environment, but now he reports that the 'whirlwind' of history provides him with courage that he will 'make it, no matter the cost'. In a sense, Dimitris has educated himself to embrace the creativity of vertigo in the manner suggested by Kierkegaard. Through schooling the Self to safely navigate the *ilinx*, Dimitris' vertigo is pedagogical, something he actively seeks out. He anticipates the cliff-edge and braces himself for the onrushing force each time he interacts with the material environment. The stone 'guides him', he says, and he has learned to harness the vertigo for positive futural orientations.

The pulsating past is not restricted to humanmade structures such as the school, but extends to the natural environment. On walking through the mountains each cave, bend in the river, every cultivation terrace and overgrown track is seeping with the past – 'everywhere, every detail in the landscape has seen war, bloodshed, family tears and laughter', Dimitris explains in what for Benjamin constituted the arrested 'marks and wounds of human violence' (Buck-Morss 1991: 163). Dimitiris is deeply affected by his interaction with 'forgotten times' that he had assumed were 'dead'; 'There is so much history to this village, we have all heard the stories of our grandparents who lived up here and [we thought] that these years were in the past, that the stone houses and wells were just relics ... they are still very much alive!' In this statement, Dimitris references how returning to life among the rubble of the past he had assumed 'dead' has re-ignited what Stoler (2013: 11) calls the 'consequential histories of different futures'. In his evocations, the past has 'returned' or been 'activated' in the continuous formation of present subjectivity holding consequence over the construction of alternate futures that were once unimaginable. The proximity of the rubble, associated with the abject poverty of a former (collective) life, and the new sense of the future embodied by the current residents, collide in what Vyjayanthi Rao (2013: 291) has termed 'schizophrenic' relational history. Movement among the rubble of the long-abandoned village creates a new way of relating materially and mnemonically to the past as well as to the future (Rao 2013: 294).

It is one thing, Dimitris tells me, to know that you are making a decision to return to an ancestral village, to go back to a way of life and a place last occupied by your grandparents, but quite another to relive history in such a tangible way. These are two interconnected aspects to his vertigo that are associated with reliving what to him were dormant histories. First, there is the conscious decision to 'go back to basics', 'peasant' and 'village' life, hence rupturing the otherwise commonly perceived trajectories of late capitalist modernity. Dimitris describes his relocation to another place as enforced by outside actors, foreign agents (especially the Troika and 'Germany') and abstract entities (markets, finance and taxes). This undoing of the rural to urban migration of the 1940s and 1960s that led to the village's dereliction might seem like the more obvious form of displacement and is the common narrative when people express desires – fulfilled or not – to return to their villages in the crisis years. The original depopulation of Petrochori was part of an administrative plan to reshape the material environment, creating a space void of human habitation for political reasons. The geographical and material reconfiguration witnessed since 2009 as people return to abandoned villages has also been heavily influenced by outside policy and bureaucratic decisions.

The second feature of Dimitris' vertigo is being sucked into the vortices of swirling lifetimes past by the physical environment of Petrochori. Upon moving to the village, affective histories came to life topologically and topographically (Knight 2017b; Stewart 2017); pasts enlivened by the physical landscape are mixed in a manner that Dimitris says has left his life 'spinning'. Subjective feeling, Navaro-Yashin (2012: 161) has argued, is intertwined with environmentally produced affect and this seems to be central to Dimitris' sense of vertigo. The landscape, he proposes, has not changed, but has been waiting for people to return to re-experience the events it has witnessed – the voices of children, screams of civil war ancestors executed in the village square, and the tap-tap of stonemasons' chisels. Such stories tie history to the sublime aesthetic experience of landscapes representative of the past (Rao 2013: 301). The 'ecologies of remains [with their] wider social topographies' (Stoler 2013: 22) intensify and complicate the vertigo experienced by Dimitris' crisis-enforced relocation from Thessaloniki.

Even everyday items carry Dimitris on a vertiginous ride. Picking through the rubble of his deserted home back in 2012, he found newspapers dating to the 1980s, one bunch deliberately fastened together incorporating pictures of the Greek national basketball team so revered in the 1980s. 'These seemed to be deliberately bound together', a keepsake or time capsule, he reflects, from a bygone era. When we return home for an afternoon *tsipouro*, he disappears without speaking. Waiting patiently in the living room, I have half an eye on the television when he appears with two beaten, rusting metal boxes in hand. 'Look at these. These were tossed on the floor by the staircase when we opened up the house with Voula.' I delicately turned the first rectangular case over in my hands, my eyes piecing together partially corroded lettering on the lid and one of the sides. The faded white wording on the battered green box was in English and the date '1944' could be deciphered alongside an insignia – it was a wartime British ammunition tin, a collectable of war (Bryant 2010: 145, Navaro-Yashin 2012: 202). 'Just lying there on the floor of my hallway!' remarked Dimitris, scoffing at the perceived absurdity of his find. The other was a biscuit tin, elaborately decorated, again with English writing. While mushroom hunting, another villager had found an identical tin a couple of valleys away, part-buried in the mud among thick confer trees. Dimitris supposes that these tins are also remnants of the British-led wartime effort in northern Greece. 'How not to feel jarred, knocked off your stride, or left shocked?', he rhetorically poses, 'War!? In my home!' The tins highlight the tangibility and visibility of disturbing objects that displace temporal experience.

For Dimitris, the relocation to the village and life among rubble brought new relations into the world. His new geography, itself an inversion of all his futural expectations, brought with it the proximity of the past in its material forms, drawing the place into multiple lived times and spaces. He developed deep affinity with his dual-aspect vertigo, the forced relocation from modern city to traditional village and the dizzying pasts ingrained in the debris of the material landscape. In 2012, Dimitris embraced the task of rebuilding a future from metaphorical and physical rubble.

SUCCESS

The cafeteria business has been a modest success, Dimitris and Voula operating at a small profit each year. They have gained a reputation as the only place in the immediate area to offer year-round food and drink, and have a steady stream of regular custom from neighbouring villages. In the summer, their small courtyard is packed with fellow villagers vacationing in their ancestral homes, day-trippers from Grevena and Ioannina, and the occasional group of foreign tourists. Voula is kept busy in the kitchen preparing stuffed peppers and tomatoes, mushroom and onion pies, and a range of scrumptious sweets. Forever smiling, son Michalis is run off his feet as the sole manager, waiter and public face of the enterprise, while Dimitris spends much of his time engaged in maintenance chores in the village – from chopping, delivering and stacking firewood for the winter months to patching up leaky roofs or painting railings in one of the village's three churches. The winter is much quieter, but the family get by on their summer earnings, topped up by regular custom from hunting groups passing through the region. Christmas also sees a spike in profits as a smattering of people visit the village for a short break over the festive season. The consensus among the family is that they would not want to be elsewhere.

'It's not all perfect', Dimitris insists. 'But look at what you have around you. Clean air, the scenery, and not so many assholes telling you what to do every day. The pace is slower and the quality of life much better.' Early one summer's morning, I find the opportunity to sit with the often-elusive Michalis, managing to secure his attention before the start of another hectic day. Sat in the shade in the corner of the courtyard with a cold coffee in hand and a gentle breeze flowing through an ever-receding hairline, I enquire whether he misses his life in Thessaloniki. It must be difficult, I propose, for a twenty-five-year-old to be away from the social scene of an urban centre, residing in a place where permanent inhabitants number around only twenty, of which he is one of only two people under the age of thirty. A quiet, reflexive, calm yet charismatic character, Michalis is adamant that he is more than happy with living in Petrochori and emphasizes that it is his decision: 'Mum and Dad have never forced me to stay here. This is my life. Sometimes I go back to Thessaloniki. Perhaps once every two months for a few days and honestly I cannot wait to leave [the city].' The visits to the city are usually to run errands such as paying taxes on the urban flat, servicing the car or taking care of medical issues. On occasion he might attend a soccer match featuring his beloved club, Aris. Michalis says that he cannot believe how some of his own friends 'waste life' sitting on the seafront drinking coffee and playing backgammon: 'There is not much of a future for them. The city doesn't offer them anything. The crisis is deep-rooted wherever you live. You have to be proactive.' He maintains that he does not miss anything about urban dwelling and explains how he is better off psychologically, socially and financially in the elsewhere of Petrochori: '[In Petrochori] I have a life, a job, my family. I don't want to be like them [in Thessaloniki] – here I am my own boss and making a living among the rubble of the homes of my grandparents and great-grandparents.' It is essential for Michalis to have 'peace of mind, no loans, clean air to breathe, and a close, although you might say eccentric, community of people around'. In Thessaloniki, he concludes, he would either die of anxiety or boredom (on boredom, see Frederiksen (2013)).

He realizes that as someone in their mid-twenties, his lifestyle choice might be perceived as unusual by outsiders, particularly young adults, and former friends from urban Greece. 'It doesn't bother me', he says in a confident and reassured manner. It is obvious that he is used to addressing this line of enquiry: 'You could say that I am a person out of place. That I do not belong in a crumbling village. A twenty-five-year-old guy, into soccer, music, the usual stuff, living with his parents 1,000 metres up in the mountains with the bears and the goats. It is my choice, and it does not seem strange to me.' Unlike Dimitris, who experiences a form of temporal displacement by moving away from a trajectory of urban modernity to live among the rubble of his ancestors, Michalis displays comfort with his surroundings. Perhaps this is because he has lived all his adult life in the village, moving to Petrochori at the age of seventeen. He does not describe the same sense of pulsating vertigo as Dimitris – rather, a quiet contentment that he has made something of his life while others of his cohort are withering at the hands of endemic crisis. Put bluntly, crisis is all that Michalis has known (he was fourteen when former Prime Minister Giorgos Papandreou 'discovered' that Greece had no money) – the village is the only place he has experienced, whereas Dimitris has been torn from a respectable city job, expectations of material accumulation and the belief in a global system where Greece firmly belonged to the time of Western late modernity.

Michalis is keen to note that he too feels the weight of the past rushing through the stones and the mountainsides. He spends much of his spare time walking the forested mountains in search of wild mushrooms, 'but I am never alone ... the mountains are alive with the people of the past, everything that has happened here'. He also expresses a deep love for the built environment, the tangibility and what he terms the 'personality' of the stone: 'Every structure was built by a relative, someone you have heard stories about or can vaguely recall the face of, like in a far-off half-dream world. You can't quite remember if you have met, say, Pappou Ilia or Barba Gianni, or whether they were alive only in your childhood imagination.' He reserves special affection for the school and a mountain shrine – built in stone, with a freshwater spring – situated a few miles' walk west. He talks of the material landscape with intimacy and comfort rather than a sense of displacement or disorientation. The extraordinary is embedded in the traditional materiality of the mundane (cf. Avieli and Sermoneta 2020) – the stone buildings and the natural environment. Despite feeling the past present in every stone and valley, this does not induce the vertiginous palpitations experienced by his father. In his narrative, Michalis describes being 'a person out of place', a twenty-five-year-old man born in an urban centre with expectations of a modern European lifestyle to be shared with his friends and neighbours in the city. This is the elsewhere of Michalis' existence, being out of place in the eyes of his peers and external observers. He is a unique figure in his new environment, residing among the rubble of an abandoned village, visually standing out as one of only a handful of youngsters making life deep in the Pindos Mountains. His life has not been reduced to rubble by the crisis, but rather he is building a future, as he aptly quips, 'among the rubble of the past'.

Another member of the 'crisis generation' is Kostas, the grandson of the only permanent pre-crisis residents of Petrochori, shepherd Giorgos and his wife Soula. Kostas was born in Petrochori to their second son, Dionisis.

Obtaining an overall grade of nineteen out of twenty in his high school exams in 2011, Kostas had intended to study architecture in Athens until the onset of the crisis. After a year out to contemplate his future, Kostas came to an agreement with his grandfather that he would take over the herd of goats full-time from 2014. Learning the occupation intimately over the period of two years, Kostas, now in his late twenties, has married a woman from the neighbouring village and has settled in Petrochori. It was a job he was familiar with from his childhood when he accompanied his grandfather, striding the mountains from dawn to dusk. He explains how university has become 'just another dead-end now', offering no future for young people. The marketplace is flooded with qualified university graduates, but endemic austerity has meant that there simply are no jobs to meet the demand (see Chapter 4).

Sitting on the stone steps outside the school late one summer afternoon where he is waiting to catch a snake that has disappeared beneath a rock by the dilapidated children's swings, Kostas muses on his childhood affection for the village and his expectations for a life elsewhere. He highlights how the school in particular is a special place, even with the roof caved in and the back walls falling away down the mountainside one stone at a time. He reflects on how some of the most important and intimate moments of his life have been witnessed by 'these stones' of the school: 'The smell of meat on the barbeque during the *Paniyiri*, childhood friends and the taste of sweat on the lips as we tear around in the midday sun. My first love, my first kiss ... Yes, here with a girl from the next village. Black and white photographs of my grandparents and other villagers posing expressionless on these very steps. This is Petrochori.' He pauses, seemingly lost in thought, staring into the middle distance, exploring his innermost memories, nostalgias of childhood, until he continues: 'the scent of thyme as your boots rustle through the undergrowth in the mountains, the itchy warmth of my grandmother's goat-hair blanket. This is ... This is Petrochori to me.' However, during his childhood, Kostas imagined his future lying away from the village; he dreamed of Athens, an office job, a 'career in the city'. He believed that these memories, senses and the nostalgia for Petrochori would be confined to a past life, not part of his present and future in the village: 'I always thought I would leave these stones behind. But they remain part of me. The crisis meant that my future was to be made here, not where my childhood self would have expected. Perhaps you could call it fate, but my life was certainly changed by the crisis. I am a different person to the one I might have been.'

Kostas lives in his great-aunt's house, which was in a ruinous condition after she and her family migrated to New York in the 1930s. The house had not been inhabited again until Kostas got the keys in 2015. He rebuilt the boundary walls in the old drystone method he had been told about in stories of times past and, with the assistance of a builder from a nearby village, set about patching up the roof and repointing the walls of the house. The garden is still strewn with sizeable chiselled stones, remnants of former walls, terraces and outbuildings. Kostas resides primarily on the ground floor of the imposing three-storey building, knowing that he requires planning consent to renovate the house any further. The structure remains in a precarious state, but is substantially more secure than the surrounding dwellings, many of which have been reduced to piles of stone and roofing tiles.

As Kostas rightly anticipates, one source of great frustration has been in planning consent for renovating buildings in Petrochori. Voula, the cafeteria owner, describes the friction as 'a clash of civilizations', referring to the needs of villagers conflicting with the 'foreign bureaucracy' of the regional planning office. Voula endured years of struggle before eventually being able to legally refurbish the coffee shop and the ancestral home. She laments that 'after forty years of Petrochori being in a conservation area they [the regional council] suddenly remembered to apply the law, or more like their misinterpretation of it'. Her exasperation is based in her belief that councils and governmental systems more generally should support the rejuvenation of abandoned communities.[2] She also thinks that conservation law is now implemented because of the influence of foreign auditors appointed to report to the Troika or international observer boards in Brussels and Berlin. At first glance, she seems to have good reason to lambast the bureaucrats who 'suddenly remembered' that Petrochori was in a conservation area, for the village is dotted with nontraditional construction erected over the past forty years. EU conservation law is at odds, she says, with both the 'Greek way' of building and with 'the need' for people to return to their villages and renovate their homes to ride out the crisis years. Her words echo what I had heard from Kostas when he was guiding me around his rapidly deteriorating home, which he is doing his best to save before it 'completely collapses'. Every time he shores up one wall, another piece starts bowing or slips into the passing road: 'What they [the committees] have written on their guidelines is just not practical, it doesn't fit the reality.' With exasperation, almost desperation, in his voice, he says: 'The styles of buildings they insist upon are *not* traditional anyhow, but some foreign interpretation of what a traditional village should look like.'

It took Voula and Dimitris five years to have their cafeteria signed off by building control: 'People suggested bribing the committee, but we didn't want to do that. I wouldn't lower myself to that. But anyway, it doesn't work now because they have to report to the Troika auditors.' Voula has heard that people from other villages have attempted to bribe the committee, but to no avail, 'and they just will not listen. There is no negotiation. They tell you what colour to paint the building, what trees to plant, where to quarry the stone ... It's so expensive and completely inhibits people who need to return to their village [during the crisis]'.

This clash of what both Dimitris and Voula term 'European' with 'traditional' frameworks represents a disorienting discrepancy. European conservation law does not translate to the needs and pressures of people living in crisis who have chosen or been forced to relocate to homes that have been abandoned for decades. What is more, the interpretation of the law is in the hands of Greek bureaucrats based in the city, who 'are completely out of touch with village life. They have never been to Petrochori and don't know the first thing about either the traditions of the place or the needs of the current inhabitants', bemoans Voula. (on Greek bureaucracy, see Herzfeld (1992)). She feels that such a complicated and restricting system that 'does not match' the critical context in which many Greeks find themselves actually leads to more illegal construction than it prevents: 'Why would people bother engaging with the planning committees? They reject your application because you want a small window at the back facing the mountain, or you want to put in aluminium instead of wooden window frames to save €1,000, or you refuse to paint your balcony lilac!' These things, she rightly suggests, get done anyway, but through illegal means, since 'the city boys sitting on the committee will never visit anyway. How will they know? They threaten you with their "satellites" that can see your home from space and "Google Maps" that can tell them if you have followed their instructions, but then you reflect and say "Wait a minute, are you serious? We are in Greece, no public sector worker will bother checking that, it's a dream of some European bureaucrats!"' Again, one can identify a grinding disparity where the bureaucratic guidelines of external Others are believed to be inappropriate or unworkable for the time and place of crisis Greece. European conservation law does not accommodate the needs of people returning to ancestral homes, nor does it connect at a practical level with 'the Greek way' of doing bureaucracy (Herzfeld 1992).

For some returnees, the process of home renovation in Petrochori was complicated further by the discovery that several buildings had been seized by the Greek state owing to their 'uninhabited' status. When investigating the potential to return to his grandparents' home permanently, Petros inadvertently discovered that the house no longer belonged to him. The year was 2014 and he had relocated from Larisa, living away from his wife and two children for a trial period of two months in the autumn with the idea to set up a beekeeping and logging enterprise to provide enough income to pay for his children's extra pre-university tuition. It was a sacrifice of the present for the future of his family, he recites. He had the deeds to the house, abandoned by his grandparents in the 1940s, but passed down through inheritance via his mother: 'It was only when I went to Grevena to file the papers for the house to be connected to the mains water and electricity, as well as putting the tax papers in order, that I discovered that according to the state – or some parts of the state – the house wasn't mine!' Petros was informed by the local tax office that despite the fact that his family had been paying tax on the property via the Larisa office, in Grevena they had documents showing that the building was repossessed in the 1960s and, further, that the property had been leased to the local shepherd (a family friend) since the 1980s: 'They gave me a stack of forms that supposedly showed I had been informed of the repossession. They said that I would have received numerous letters about this, all addressed to the abandoned property in Petrochori.' The abrasive clerk ironically smirked that surely on arrival Petros had 'noticed the goats grazing in [his] flowerpots and shitting in [his] living room'. A university-educated biology teacher, Petros could not understand the logic or wording of the notifications and commenced an eventually successful three-year legal fight to prove the building still belonged to his family. He says that he 'can easily believe' that parts of the state apparatus do not speak to each other – he was the legal owner according to the Larisa office, yet the corresponding office in Grevena disagreed – but he was astonished that the shepherd whose family were distant relatives had 'pretended not to know' that he owned the property: 'He took advantage of our absence and used it for his goats! He can't claim that he thought we were all dead because his sister, niece, and nephew live in our neighbourhood in Larisa.'

On returning to his village, Petros was made acutely aware of what was missing, not only in the material but also in the social landscape. His presuppositions about unchanged sociality were rapidly deconstructed. Living in a zone of abandonment reached beyond his crumbling ancestral house to envelop the societal. His expectations for future-building among rubble – his desire to forge a living to pay for his children's tuition – were incomplete and precarious, since he was dispossessed by both state and society (cf. Azoulay 2013: 205, Rao 2013: 304). To live in rubble, Martin Frederiksen (2013: 16) reminds us, is 'to live in a world of lingering remains and residues that are both material and social' in the fragments of social and material afterlives (see also Stoler 2008). It was the social detritus as much as the physical debris that confounded Petros, leaving him in a precarious condition, not able to re-activate his ancestral pasts in ways that he might have expected or hoped.

GRAVITY

A focus on rubble provides a deeper historicization and politicization of vertiginous life, placing the materiality of space centre stage. The physical and affective configurations of rubble, to paraphrase Gordillo (2014: 264), are defined by continuities and ruptures that connect people to disparate timespaces once considered dead or abandoned. Portals to these time-spaces lay dormant for decades and most certainly did not play a part in the construction of modernist futures in the pre-crisis years – at most, the rubble of Petrochori was carefully managed, fetishized and energized for a few weeks each summer. During the crisis, with the permanent repopula-tion of the village, debris works on matter and mind, shaping new histori-cal and political actors who are forging unanticipated, entangled and newly empowered futures. Rather than rubble being 'the enemy of human beings' due to its inherent qualities of destruction and failure (Gordillo 2013: 247), it is an integral positive part of creative future-making from the position of precariousness in crisis Greece, prompting unexpected mutant political subjectivities.

The temporal disorientation of rubble is twofold. First, there is the forced relocation from urban life associated with modernist progress, accumu-lation, and belonging to the West to village life that was once thought (or not thought of at all) as a timespace of the past, perceived as pre-modern, archaic and 'dead'. Urban to rural migration undid, or inverted, the trajec-tories of previous generations, as documented in numerous works of Med-iterranean ethnography, and went against all expectations of urbanites in pre-crisis Greece. This disjuncture created a form of vertigo associated with the elsewhere that was caused by the practical necessity to relocate, upping roots from the city to fashion new lives in the village. From a position of economic precarity, people made the jump, consciously or not, into the de-structive *ilinx* of time and history, creating futures among the rubble of the past that they eventually classed as optimistic when compared to alternate paths in the city. They acknowledge that the decision to relocate has been transformative. In recognition of virtual split personas across timespaces, Kostas explicitly notes that he is not the same person he would have been if he had chosen to go to university and reside in Athens. Second, the material environment into which returnees have been parachuted provokes a pro-foundly affective 'whirlwind' vertigo where rubble has a gravitational pull that twists and braids temporal experience (Bryant 2014). Interaction with rubble, particularly stone structures such as the village school and ancestral homes, as well as topographical features, transports villagers in a confused aura-like state to overlapping timespaces densely packed with personal re-lations and critical events that disorient familiar trajectories and bounded categories of past, present and future. The vertigo induced by the material environment may cause palpitations or a shortness of breath, and may col-lapse time so that all history happens at once.

Rubble helps people understand through the body 'the ruptured multiplicity that is constitutive of all geographies as they are produced, destroyed, and remade' (Gordillo 2014: 2). It is disorienting since it is multilayered, polytemporal and points in copious directions. There are melted timespaces coexisting together. This is the jarring, disturbing feeling that Dimitris experienced the first time he lent against the outside wall of the derelict school to light his cigarette. Here, the stone wall may be viewed as one of Gordillo's (following Levi Bryant's) 'bright objects', or what Navaro-Yashin (2012: 20) terms 'enchanted' or 'irritable' sites; material that attracts, a key node in the local landscape that orients, exercises gravity and influences village life. The gravitational pull of the school wall sent Dimitris into a spin until he learnt how to navigate and eventually embrace his vertigo. Now, he and many others are held captive by the gravity of place.

Despite frustration with planning law and the giddying affect of the material landscape, it is striking how the relocation to elsewhere has generally been a positive experience for the people of Petrochori. Anna Tsing (2005: 74) talks of rubble containing 'the residue of success and failure', while the roots of the positivity/negativity of rubble can be traced back to Benjamin. Futures have not played out as once expected, yet uprooting to Petrochori with its disorienting material environment is perceived optimistically, partially due to the view that once-anticipated futures are now impossible – they are 'dead'. Resonating with Caillois' (2001: 141) notion of the 'narrow door' that people must jump through to gain access to progress and to a future, the death of one trajectory led to the opening of another, a porthole that was once itself considered 'dead' – a long-abandoned village, the rubble of Petrochori. In this sense, the geographies of loss are twofold; late modern trajectories towards a future of material expectation and monetary wealth have been defeated, while once-lost pasts come surging through the environment upon physical contact, producing giddiness as they stack up in entangled layers.

Yet the optimism provided by relocation must not be confused with succumbing to vertigo. The whirlwind of onrushing pasts has bodily impact and is respected by the villagers. Instead of framing their embrace of the vertiginous as a creative new chapter in history-making, it is rather more productive to focus on the cautious everyday optimism of the people themselves, who feel that to some degree, they have escaped the *ilinx* of crisis, stepping down from the vertiginous ledge rather than having to take the plunge, in a manner of speaking. The vertigo of the elsewhere is associated with geographical uprooting, the mobility anxiety of starting life anew in an unforeseen material environment. In the next chapter, attention will turn to how interaction with another form of materiality, namely energy technology, generates wormholes to the elsewhen of life in crisis.

NOTES

1. On the creation of 'sterile zones' by government forces – in this case, Israel in Gaza – see Azoulay (2013: 198).
2. Navaro-Yashin (2012) discusses at length the affect of government administration, as well as bureaucratic documents.

CHAPTER 3

ANTONIS
Technology and the Elsewhen

⌇⌇⌇

EXCURSION 1

Let me digress. It is 2 AM on a Saturday in late May and I am sitting in the foyer of the Austrian Hospice in the heart of the Muslim Quarter of Old Town Jerusalem. The balmy night air carries the sounds and scents of the Via Dolorosa as the crowds celebrate the end of Ramadan. My family asleep upstairs, a handful of my more adventurous colleagues filter in, their cheerful tones accompanied with wafts of spices and the babble of half-a-dozen languages from the street beyond. I am preparing a keynote lecture under intense time constraints, but I reflect that this is one of the most qualitative writing experiences of my life. At seven days and counting, my time spent in the Holy Land has not been by any means extensive. Yet the temporal disorientation I have encountered has left me reeling, scrambling to maintain my balance. The vertigo-inducing clash of timespaces is accentuated by the presence of technology punctuating my somewhat naïve stereotypes of a biblical landscape. What grabs me is the profusion of technology that has a decidedly futural or futuristic orientation and how this disturbs the almost timeless, ancient backdrop. This is not to dismiss historical or archaeological forms of technology that are no doubt abundant in the towering walls, intricate mechanics of concealed crypts, and irrigated historic gardens that overlook the city. Technology is inherently an ever-shifting category defined by professional discipline and scientific epoch. Nor is it to overlook how more modern technologies are themselves assemblages of inventions dating back to disparate eras, as beautifully outlined by Serres (Serres and Latour 1995: 45) in his dismantling of the late-model car, an aggregate of scientific and technical solutions dating from multiple periods. One can trace it component by component: this part was invented at the turn of the century, another ten years ago, and Carnot's cycle is almost 200 years old. Not to mention that the wheel dates back to Neolithic times. The ensemble is only contemporary, Serres proposes, by assemblage, by its design, by its finish, sometimes only by the slickness of the advertising surrounding it. Technology is polytemporal, with a plethora of datable pasts, potential orientations for present life, and timelines for future material degradation.

Here, as the cool night air kisses my sleeveless arms, taking the edge off the sweltering early summer heat, I pause to reflect on why I am so struck by what I see as the temporal paradoxes of technology. In all honesty, I conclude, my experience in Israel has been arresting in what I reflexively consider to be a quite naïve way – namely, the striking punctuation marks left by modern technology in spaces and places my Northern European Anglican Christian mind has immediately and quite innocently associated with tradition and the archivable eternal past.[1] In modern technology disrupting timespaces seeping in historical resonance, it has been stimulating to observe the visual contrasts of old and new, the past and future in the present, of futural momentum where desires and aspirations for – more often than not – material acquisition drive people's lives while existing amidst seemingly timeless devotion to faith. Technology is as much part of the Jerusalem melting pot as religion, kinship and politics, which for some reason, on this my first visit, surprises me.

On strolling around the truly awe-inspiring Old Town of Jerusalem with all its deep history of conquest, crusade and tumultuous coexistence, I am struck by what I see as Orthodox Muslims pushing through the bustling streets at the end of another day of Ramadan with mobile phones pressed against their niqabs or engrossed in checking what I can only presume are social media pages or other such internet mainstays. On leaving the Church of the Holy Sepulchre, the ancient walls and otherwise immutable soundscapes are displaced by cries from peddlers of Nespresso coffee machines, multicoloured electronic barking dogs and universal band remote television controls.

In the Hebrew University of Jerusalem, a doctoral candidate tells me of his research with people building small and medium-sized technology-based enterprises while having to navigate the conflicting timescapes of the Jewish religious calendar and US capitalist market systems. For his research participants, when competing calendars and time difference are accounted for, the problems of collaborating between Tel Aviv, the centre of the Israeli hitech industry, and the US West Coast leaves less than four full days a week open for business. Another student explains how psychoanalysts are being replaced by computer programmes with intricate, yet standardized, pathways to lead the patient through therapy. After seeing my childhood imaginations of the Little Town of Bethlehem crushed as we speed over concrete bypasses and through deeply hollowed tunnels, my colleagues remind me that Israel is a world leader in water recycling, which has led to new and unexpected health concerns – perhaps, I think, this technology has arrived slightly before its time.

On a train ride north to Haifa, we pass through arable fields nourished by Israeli drip irrigation systems, a technology developed for the Negev Desert in the 1960s that has since been successfully exported worldwide. Netafim, a leading provider of the drip irrigation system, advertises that its technology helps '[g]row higher, better yields every season ... no matter the crop, climate patterns, soil type or topography'. For some reason, the technologically enhanced agricultural farmland contrasts in my mind with a caravan of camels we have recently passed on leaving Beer Sheva. It also gets me thinking about the Israeli-produced inverters used on photovoltaic solar parks on the Plain of Thessaly in central Greece, developments that are simultaneously seen as promising a sustainable future and considered representative of the foreign domination by technological means of once-fruitful land that has a history of farming stretching back over 4,000 years. Solar also plays a role in another episode of technology confusing my ability to locate myself in time and space when I encounter photovoltaic panels lined up in the foreground of the Qumran Caves, home to the Dead Sea Scrolls. On my trip to Haifa, in the morning I am left in awe of the speed, efficiency, affordability and comfort of the Israeli railway network. Two hours, 60 shekels, air conditioning! On my return journey that evening, all trains are cancelled owing to the fires engulfing the centre of the country. In my anxious phone calls to my hosts Nir and Amalia, I am left reflecting on how reliant I have become on the institution of public transport and my inability to navigate a technology crisis with any ounce of dignity, and also caution myself against a growing tendency to now curse the backwardness of this cultural chaos unfolding before my eyes. It would not be this disorganized at King's Cross(!).

To cap my disorienting experience of deep pasts and speculative futures, I deliver my keynote at an interactive science park a stone's throw away from (the unverified location of) Abraham's Well, mentioned in the Book of Genesis and now accompanied by a visitors' centre complete with 3D documentary and moving audiovisual hallway. After a tour of the old city of Beer Sheva full of historical sites from biblical to British imperial times, that night Israeli warplanes thunder overhead on their latest raids into Syria and Lebanon as my daughter sleeps soundly in the reinforced safe room of our Ottoman-style apartment. I lie in the darkened room churning over the words of Martin Heidegger, who once posed that technology is 'a manner of the essential swaying of being', that is, of Being's own essential unfolding, wherever that may lead (1972, 61: 88).

*****

I have become attuned to the dizzying affects of technologies with contrasting temporal trajectories to multiple elsewhens through research on
renewable energy infrastructure (Argenti and Knight 2015; Knight 2017a).
Technology influences the ways that we draw the future into, or return to
pasts within, timespaces of the present in what Rao (2013: 291) has termed
'schizophrenic' temporal landscapes. In technology we see the messy mixing
of past, present and future in the overlapping of what philosopher Theodore
Schatzki calls 'activity timespaces' (Bryant and Knight 2019). Technology
helps establish orientations towards what we, collectively, expect, anticipate and hope for from our futures, or otherwise plunge us spiralling back
through the past to relive eras associated with reduced technological capacities. Either way, the material landscape provokes temporal displacement,
transporting people to overlapping, simultaneous elsewhens that take account, in a Bergsonian sense, of the weight of the past and potential futures
within the burgeoning bubble of the present.

From renewable energy infrastructure promising an ethical socioeconomic
model based on clean sustainable power to space exploration and innovations
in biotechnology that stretch the known limits of the human, our interaction with technology lengthens or foreshortens our relationships to the past
and the future. On the plane of the mundane, such objects can be taken for
granted as 'objective evidence' of existing in certain timespaces (modernity,
Europe, the space age) and can thus be reassuring of temporal and material
progress (Avieli and Sermoneta 2020). In extreme cases, the contrasting temporalities of technology can pull a person apart at the seams, tugging them
in polemic directions of the futuristic and archaic. This is where vertigo sets
in. As Debbora Battaglia aptly and poetically puts it, 'the articulation of anxiety and optimism in the social discourse of technoscience spirituality puts a
restraining order both on scenarios of technology-produced alienation and
of transcendental humanism' (2005: 26). The dense networks and connections between the Self and technology become 'time warped', allowing fluid
transportation to multiple elsewhens through temporal networks that do 'the
work of relationality'. Battaglia – referring to Sven Birkerts – suggests that
subjectivity becomes 'absorbed in technoscience' with a maelstrom of potentialities for imagining 'life as we know it' and 'life as it could be' (2005: 26).

The overtly temporal aspect of vertigo is foregrounded by many of my
research participants who have interacted with energy technology on the
Plain of Thessaly since the outbreak of the economic crisis. This chapter explores the story of Antonis, a car mechanic from Trikala who has retrained to
install photovoltaic panels on large solar farms during the summer months,
while working privately creating thermostats for home open-fire systems

in the winter. Antonis experiences the vertigo of juxtaposed technological solutions to a life in crisis, one associated with futuristic sustainability in the era of Western late modernity and the other with peasantry, village life and the pre-dictatorship years. These trajectories open categories of belonging that can be compared to other contexts of crisis, including the perpetual 'almostness' and 'not-quite' condition of living with anticipated conflict in the Middle East, and deep-rooted anxieties of colonization and inferior citizenship expressed in austerity-ravished South Italy. It is my argument here that technology facilitates, enhances or inverts our temporal orientation, harnessing affective rhythms that push or pull people between timespaces. People may experience multiple simultaneous elsewhens in the 'movement of becoming that links past, present, and future in a non-deterministic process that partakes simultaneously of change and continuity' (McLean 2017: 136). This may be because of a technology's perceived connections with a bygone era, its innate promises for something better over the futural horizon, or the comfort and stabilizing affect it can bring to maintaining the present as more of the same. To illustrate the multifarious characteristics of elsewhens, let me turn towards a literary excursion.

EXCURSION 2

The novella 'Elsewhen' (2012 [1941]) by renowned American science-fiction author Robert A. Heinlein takes the reader on a journey to multiple temporal realms where protagonists' lives have transitioned to alternate trajectories – what Heinlein interchangeably refers to as *elsewhens, somewhens* and *anywhens*. Five university students participate in an experiment conducted by their philosophy (speculative metaphysics) teacher, Dr Arthur Frost, who believes he has found a way to 'travel about in the pattern of times' while in a hypnotic state (2012 [1941]: 84). The professor explains his theory of analogous time, where time twists, cuts and branches into 'side canyons'. It is at the intersections of the topologies and topographies of time that the crucial decisions of life take place. There are turnings left or right towards different futures, as well as switchbacks, shortcuts and scrambles that connect timespaces of the past and future. In topological time, one may move backwards with the past ahead and the future behind (in the classic sense preached by Benjamin) or 'roam the hills' in directionless ponderance. Journeys in time, Dr Frost explains, are 'excursions into possibility' and 'extreme improbability' that can lead to 'anywhen' (2012 [1941]: 84–86), with the transition preceded by 'timeless limbo' (2012 [1941]: 101).

The five students – Jenkins, Fisher, Monroe, Martin and Ross – choose a path and are told by Dr Frost that their own beliefs and characters will partially influence the lifeworlds they encounter in their new timespace. In a crucial feature of the story – and of interest to our own ethnographic case – the protagonists' connection to timespaces past and future are intimately linked to their own religious devotion, grounding in logic and materiality or altruism. Their timespaces are shaped by what is meaningful to them, either in terms of individuality (a central theme in much of Heinlein's writing) or collective social responsibilities. The professor informs the students that he has built in a mechanism whereby after two hours they will return to the present on the main timeline and report their experiences, giving them opportunity to reflect on how their own beliefs – conscious or subconscious – have affected their journeys. They proceed to select their 'paths'. Monroe informs the professor that he wants to enter a 'brand new world' by way of a 'right-angle turn' away from the present timeline. Martin and Jenkins intend to 'climb up a bank to a higher road somewhere in the future', Fisher plumps for the 'remote possibilities track', while Ross is sent to a 'branch path in probability' (2012 [1941]: 85).

After two hours have passed, the students begin to reappear in the professor's office, except for Jenkins, who did not succumb to the hypnotism owing to his lack of belief in the possibilities of the experiment. His grounding in engineering and mechanics hinders his imaginative capacities for something beyond the observable dimensions. As the test subjects reappear one by one, it is immediately apparent that the subjective time elapsed is far longer than two hours, that the timetracks are real in their own rights, and what constitutes 'conventional' is relative to the worlds visited.

Some timespaces resembled present-day Earth, others are set in the deep future/past, while still more are divine and otherworldly. Influenced by her devotional religiosity, Ross returns as an angel, much to the astonishment of Jenkins. Dr Frost explains that this was always a probable *telos* for Ross considering that her personality was destined to tailor her experience of a new timespace of probability. Slanting through the axis of time has left Fisher exhausted – at one moment she passed out, although she eventually learned how to control the directionality of time. She mentions the Blue Ridge Mountains and New York City, but a planet with two suns and Neanderthals also form part of her story. She could see inside of solid objects and had taught herself medicine by studying the insides of her own body. Upon returning, Monroe talks of 'connected time rates' between his new world and the professor's, and is anxious to re-enter his new timespace, which he now perceives as home, to tend to the pressing wartime needs of his new comrades. He was and was not the same person in the two timespaces, being called Igor in the new world, stating that 'I hadn't forgotten Monroe ... I had *one* identity and *two* pasts' (2012 : 96). Fisher eventually joins him to help with the war against space invaders. Martin does not return to the original timeline to report to Dr Frost, much to the distress of her admirer Jenkins who is still trapped in the professor's present since his engineering background continues to inhibit his belief in time travel. When Dr Frost decides to transition to track down the stranded Martin, he finds her unwilling to return, vaguely remembering her previous life as a dream-like state, arguing that from her perspective the new world is real and Dr Frost is from her dreams, 'There is no return to the place of dreams!' she defiantly rouses, accusing the professor of blasphemy (2012 [1941]: 102). Dr Frost eventually convinces Martin that he and Jenkins are not merely a figment of her subconscious, but real forms from another timespace. Jenkins is ultimately persuaded to allow his body and mind to be overrun during hypnosis and joins Martin in her life as a priestess named 'Star Light'. There is no end to the permutations of *somewhens*, Dr Frost surmises, determined as they are by personal character, social priorities and the infinite topological combinations of time-flow encountered in the transition.

*****

It may be easy to concur that the concept of elsewhens dabbles in more abstract realms than the elsewhere discussed in Chapter 2. Yet more than merely a work of a majestic mind in the field of science fiction, numerous aspects of Heinlein's writing resemble ethnographic observations of vertiginous life in crisis Greece. For instance, in the novella, the elsewhens encountered by the five students are partially crafted by their own consciousness, characters and social priorities. Connections to alternate timespaces are fashioned by material environments and spirituality. Although there might be multiple messy trajectories to infinite connotations of the elsewhen, the timespaces visited are all anchored in some way to the person and/or place of the original timeline. Similarly, the descriptions of vertigo portrayed by my protagonists, particularly throughout this chapter, illustrate that pathways to elsewhens open according to resemblances, proximities and needs of people and places – no new timespace is completely detached from the original present. Dr Frost's students and my research participants alike dip in and out of elsewhens following topological experiences of interconnected alternate worlds based on technologies, beliefs and social concerns. Meaning and messages are dragged from disordered temporal points, while the technological environment triggers reflection on past resemblances, perceived proximities with other timespaces, and critical interrogation of future-oriented promises (on repetition and recurrence see Bandak and Coleman 2019). New realities mean that previous (pre-crisis) lives become dreamlike or vague, or incite feelings of embodying dual identities in multiple elsewhens. The story of Antonis and his interactions with vertigo-inducing energy technologies that are imbued with proximities to contrasting elsewhens highlights in ethnographic form existential 'realities' once confined to the pages of science fiction. It is Antonis' belief that technologies transport the individual on a messy journey through time, connecting pathways between topological pasts and futures, leaving the subject lost, dizzy and questioning previously assumed truths about belonging to timespaces of twenty-first-century Europe.

DIVERSIFICATION

The vast Plain of Thessaly in central Greece, the region's breadbasket for over four millennia, is now cloaked in a dense patchwork of solar panels. The agricultural region has been transformed since the 2011 relaunch of a renewable energy drive promoted by the European Union (EU) and the Greek state – energy export to Northern Europe was promoted as a way to repay the nation's burgeoning debt. In 45°C heat on the shadeless plain in the summer of 2013, Antonis, a forty-year-old car mechanic who set up his own automobile modification garage with an EU loan in 2002, is lying on his back, tools in hand, rewiring a solar panel. When I first met Antonis in 2003, he had recently opened his garage and business was booming. There was high demand for modified exhaust and engine systems, and Antonis had just signed a contract to provide handcrafted parts to a team competing in the national touring car championship. With his wife – like Antonis a trained electrician – as his assistant, he seemed unstoppable.

In 2013 Antonis' garage turned a monthly profit of less than €100, 'once you include the loan repayments, the electricity, and the cost of firewood to heat the workshop ... then account for all the new taxes'. Nobody had the luxury of modifying cars with austerity measures in full swing: 'People look after their families. Nobody has a penny to spend on anything beyond everyday survival and the government insists on punishing private sector employees instead of reforming the public sector ... all in all, I am screwed', Antonis remarks. To pay the bills and feed his two elementary school-age children, Antonis has had to diversify. After taking a short refresher course in electronics at the local evening school, Antonis now installs solar panels, informally working de facto for multinational corporations investing in the Greek energy industry that is being rapidly privatized as part of the austerity agreement with international creditors. He works cash-in-hand and without insurance, jobs sourced through a friend involved in solar panel wholesale: 'I get a call that says "Antonis, we need you on Friday in a village near Karditsa. The job will take three days. Your cut will be X euros". I ask no questions, turn up, and do my work.'

With unemployment peaking at 25 per cent in 2013, job diversification has for many years been both commonplace and necessary. Car mechanics, electricians and engineers are now involved in the renewable energy industry. Photovoltaic systems are perceived as relatively easy to install and require minimal extra training for people with a background in electronics and engineering. Courses offering certificates in correct installation practice are available from local colleges, but these are not necessary and are rarely completed. Antonis quips that installing solar panels is 'as easy as tapping into the neighbour's electricity supply or telephone line, like I did as a kid'. In 2015, he started collaborating with a friend from Karditsa rather than his former contact in Trikala because 'Giannis gets me bigger jobs and is more reliable with payment. Okay, he takes a bigger cut, but I know that the jobs will come regularly over the summer and I will never have to chase him for cash. He's more professional'. The renewable energy drive has provided a new line in second jobs as people supplement their – often failing – primary employment with informal work in the energy sector.

So far, we have a well-trodden story of the informal economy sustaining livelihoods in times of endemic crisis (Clough 2014; MacGaffey 1987, 1991). Concentrate, here comes the vertiginous bit. Despite the Plain of Thessaly being awash with solar panels, the energy generated rarely serves the local community. The energy produced by the German, Chinese and Israeli panels is transported through the national grid to urban centres and then over the Balkan borders towards Northern Europe. Unable to afford oil central heating and with no mains gas, local people light open fires to keep warm at night (often with unsuitable materials such as green firewood, old clothes and even household waste), creating health and environmental problems as toxic smog engulfs the villages of the plain (Knight 2017a). The EU and the national government had envisaged renewables to be part of a wider 'Time of Sustainability' (Knight 2020) based on the perception that the green economy could provide long-term financial and environmental stability (Knight 2017c). However, they did not count on the renewable energy initiative being perceived locally as neocolonialism, a foreign occupation and form of dispossession, and an extractive economy operating on similar terms to the oil industry in Western Africa (Argenti and Knight 2015; see also Franquesa 2018; Howe 2014). Multinationals rent the land on 25 to 50-year contracts from local farmers who feel they have no other choice in critical times.

One winter evening, Antonis invites me to join him on the second-storey balcony of his mother's house in a village 5 miles outside of Trikala. We sit huddled in puffer jackets – Antonis drawing on a hand-rolled cigarette, me with both hands around a warm cup of Earl Grey tea – with the vast agricultural plain stretching out in front of us towards the silhouette of the imposing

Pindos Mountains and the ski resort of Pertouli in the west. As dusk falls, a thick smog starts descending over the village as people light their open fires, completely obscuring our view of the fifty-plus photovoltaic panels on farmland owned by villagers. With no wind (the plain is hemmed in by high mountains on three sides and Trikala is a two-and-a-half-hour drive from the Aegean coast to the east), the smog forms a dense blanket until even the large platanus tree at the end of the driveway has become engulfed and disappears from sight.

Two seemingly contrasting energy sources – high-tech photovoltaic panels and open wood-burning fires – have become symbols of the livelihood changes brought about by economic crisis and representative of the contrasting directionality of life in Greece. Like the majority of people I have talked to in western Thessaly, Antonis associates photovoltaics with clean green energy, futuristic sustainability, groundbreaking technology, ultramodernity and international political energy consensus. Open fires conjure images of pre-modern unsustainability, pollution and extreme poverty. The contrasting technological orientations spark in him a sense of vertigo, not knowing where or when he belongs on an overarching timeline of pasts and futures. The expected linear progression of late capitalist modernity has been aggravated, stirring sensory confusion and temporal disorientation haunted by the potentiality of the past to resurface and the future to not play out as once anticipated. 'What are we to read into this?', he asks. 'We are being promised a future that is symbolized by photovoltaics. I mean, we are European, wealthy, moving forward in life. But then we are also being exploited, forced back in time to an era of peasantry like our grandparents ... where do we belong, when [in what time period] do I live?' The visual image observed from his mother's balcony beautifully captures the feeling of disorientation, the contrasting temporal trajectories, embedded in the schizophrenic technological landscape. And Antonis' use of the word 'when' in questioning his own temporal belonging is poignant to our exploration of multiple elsewhens amalgamating in the experience of vertigo in crisis Greece – 'when do I belong?' is a phrase I have encountered on numerous occasions in the last decade. Antonis says that the orientations or directions experienced through the material landscape have left him feeling 'lost', 'floating' and 'torn' between points on the historical timeline.

During the summer of 2012, Antonis commenced construction of an open-fire heating system in his home. The price of petrol required for central heating was dramatically increasing, and, he insists, his mechanic business was on the verge of bankruptcy, 'only bringing in €30 one month after rent and utility payments'. Over the course of two months, Antonis built the fireplace, ventilation system and flue, connected it to the hot water and installed a thermostat. He also bought a new handsaw, something he used to cut down his neighbour's crab apple tree for firewood. Since creating and installing his own open fire, Antonis has a sideline in selling and connecting motors for woodburning heating systems that he stores in his garage alongside car exhausts and turbos. He now charges clients identified through his friendship networks for his services installing open fires in their homes and private businesses, again taking cash payments. In the winter, he is an open fire expert, travelling around western Thessaly hooking up ventilation systems and thermostats. In the summer, he is a freelance photovoltaic mechanic, all while still owning and running a stuttering automobile garage, a triple undertaking that he describes with a wry smirk as 'crazy ... what else to say!'

Firewood is now imported to western Thessaly from as far away as Bulgaria and the Republic of North Macedonia, where it is purchased in bulk at low prices by opportunistic entrepreneurs to be sold at a profit south of the border. Illegally felled wood is also transported in articulated lorries from the forests around Metsovo, Epirus, just over the regional border, and sold for €180 per ton in western Thessaly. Clandestine deliveries of illegally sourced wood regularly take place in the dead of night by men in convoys of blacked-out pick-up trucks. Torrential winter downpours coupled with an increase in illegal logging have recently caused substantial flooding and landslides in Thessaly and Epirus as a result of deforestation. Wood burners are also imported across the Balkan borders to be sold in showrooms in central Greece. Antonis comments on how people are 'doing the best they can' to get through the crisis years, trying to 'put their skills to use'. On his sideline of installing open fires, he says: 'If I can do it for myself, I can do it for other people too. It is better than sitting around doing crosswords [in the garage] all day.' He is conscious of the paradoxes involved in working on technologies with very different temporal orientations, material that he sees as being invested with 'different promises' for the future of Greece: 'It is strange jumping from installing open fires, which are so much to do with poverty and peasant life, the life of our grandparents, probably great-grandparents actually, and then working on those futuristic photovoltaic panels.' Following Henri Bergson, we may say that by drawing on memories of the life of his ancestors, Antonis detaches himself from his present and places himself in a specific region of the past with an image drawn in accordance to his needs to explain his present (McLean 2017: 136). It is, he poignantly points out, 'like going from the Dark Ages to the space race ... like falling back through time while being slingshotted into the future ... How can someone believe in both, live in both times, without feeling dizzy! My head spins ... I feel lost.'

LOST

Technology provides a lens through which to approach how people experience the thinning of the temporal horizon, with technologies possessing rhythms and orientations that make futures or pasts more tangible. Two contrasting technologies take Antonis on different trajectories towards alternate elsewhens, on the one hand providing hope for a radically improved quality of life (in the post-apocalyptic, post-crisis world) and, on the other, the anticipation that long-dormant livelihoods of the past will once again rise to the fore and shape the ruins of the collective future. These multiple overlapping timespaces compete and cohabit within contemporary crisis experience, leading to questions of 'when?', opening classificatory categories of belonging such as '(pre)modern' and '(pre-)European', and adding to feelings of being 'lost' or 'suspended' in time (Battaglia 2005: 4). Technology here provides affective structures to everyday life and has provoked people like Antonis to speculate about their temporal trajectories: are they part of a prosperous European and corporately endorsed future or destined to 'go back in time' to some archaic elsewhen of pre-modernity? The topological entanglement of contrasting energy paraphernalia offering alternative versions of the temporal location of a Time of Crisis prompts people like Antonis to rethink their worldview. One research participant, Sotiris, a 46-year-old farmer from western Thessaly for whom Antonis occasionally works, says that 'the paradoxes of current energy technologies' with their intermingling allusions to a high-tech future and a low-tech past make people 'reconceptualize their place in space and time ... do we belong to a modern Europe ... are we in the same time as Germany and France?' It is the materiality of temporal displacement that seizes and contorts what Stuart McLean (2017: 239) has called 'habituated space-time' in the sense that Heinlein portrays in his novella – are the timespaces of Germany, France and Greece connected? What resemblance links these contexts? This all adds to the sense of vertigo. As such, technology warps time, or opens new portals, leading to reports of feeling 'lost', caught between nonlinear past and future elsewhens. As for Heinlein's characters, shadows of potential pasts and futures shape life trajectories in a Time of Crisis, connected yet somehow still weirdly alien, hazy and partially out of reach.

In a web of tangled trajectories, people question their belonging to timespaces of Europeanness, cosmopolitanism, the so-called 'First World', and the future as a place of material progression. This sense of disorientation as to where and when one belongs is something that I have become intimately familiar with in Greece over the past decade. The question of belonging to the era of modernity, Europe, the First World or to some archaic pre-modern non-Western timespace brings into sharp relief preconceptions of progression and trajectory inherently linked to late modern Europe. It is also an issue that I have seen raised in at least two other contexts of chronic crisis – Israel and South Italy – to which I now briefly turn to make the case for vertigo as part of an affective structure of a Time of Crisis beyond Greece.

Many scholars have discussed Israel and the wider Middle East as being in the clutches of perpetual crisis, often in relation to ever-impending violence. The academic conversation has regularly focused on how violence (past and future) seeps into the present and is manifested in everyday activities and temporal orientations. For instance, Sami Hermez (2012, 2017) has explored how the anticipation of violence permeates ordinary life in Beirut, leading to an underlying state of anxiety and uncertainty. Suggesting that the 'absent presence' of violence causes war to be a permanent existential condition even in peacetime, Hermez describes how everyday activities – such as buying a generator, stocking up on diesel or sharing anxious laughter – are affected by a grey zone of almostness and not-quite (on anticipation and a 'Time of Peace', see Bryant and Knight (2019)). Over the border in Israel, Joyce Dalsheim (2015) engages with the Bergsonian notion of duration in her article tellingly titled 'There Will Always Be a Gaza War'. The endurance of conflict beyond event time is explained through a 'consciousness of duration' – the folding in of heterogeneous pasts and multiple anticipated futures that inform the topological experience of a crisis moment. Providing the example of the 2014 abduction of three Israeli boys and the ensuing war, Dalsheim proposes that each repetition of conflict 'includes the memory of previous actions and their own imagined futures. Events of the past and present are juxtaposed, but not necessarily in discrete order like beads on a string' (2015: 11). When national crisis occurs, time moves more slowly, anxieties rise and people become hyperconscious of everyday activities (see also Bryant 2016). We can see the similarities here between collective and individual Times of Crisis, timespaces home to altered temporal rhythms, Kierkegaardian anxieties and de Martinian lapses in presence. It is this scaling from how the individual subject experiences the world to comparable collective affective atmospheres and shifts in temporal momentum that remains at the heart of this study.

The abductions were not part of a single event; more a wider spatiotemporal bubble was opened with a porous lining that was infused with pasts and futures. Akin to the Greek case to which Antonis refers, the crisis event is torn from the timeline of successive 'nows' to encompass multiple pasts and futures simultaneously existing, with technologies intensifying potential temporal orientations. Dalsheim, drawing on Bergson, would have us believe that spatialization of time is primarily the result of our preoccupation with trying to order our present reality and that multiple times in fact coexist within what McLean has termed the human ambition to 'carve out a

knowable and thus seemingly manipulable world from the flux of becoming'
(2017: 135). De Martino might have simply said that temporal ordering is
a way of trying to avoid a crisis of presence at the moment our knowable
world ruptures.

In the southern Israeli city of Beer Sheva, Dafna Shir-Vertesh and Fran
Markowitz discuss the existential 'tension between the normalcy of the everyday and an ever-present war-like atmosphere' in what they term a permanent state of 'almost-war and almost-peace' (2015: 209). These mutually
constitutive contexts underwrite everyday life, with violence either receding
into dormant potentiality or rising to the fore as penetrative expectation and
imminence. With similarities to Masco's (2006: 28) observations on Cold
War nuclear warhead programmes where he argues that people reside in
a temporal space where missiles have already been launched and annihilation penetrates the present, in Shir-Vertesh and Markowitz's work, it is the
Hamas missiles and rockets providing the technoscape to advance or settle
states of existential anxiety and temporal confusion. The changes in everyday life provoked by missile launches are traced through chronotopes –
the embodied physical and temporal space – inhabited by citizens of Beer
Sheva. 'Withdrawal and convergence, fleeing, reaching out, and anxiety and
vigilance' (Shir-Vertesh and Markowitz 2015: 210) are themes identified by
the authors as overlapping modes of life structured by the perpetual chrono-
tope of almost-war/almost-peace; a 'hallucinatory reality' or schizophrenic
landscape of almostness and not-quite that causes people to question their
temporal trajectories and belonging to vernacular perceptions of First World
modernity. Elsewhere, Markowitz questions the inbetweenness of Beer
Sheva, on the fringes of the Negev Desert, as suspended between commonly
held stereotypes of Bedouin backwardness (parents call their children 'little
Bedouins' when the children behave in an undignified way) and pretences to
American modernity. The visitor, she suggests, might be struck by the visual
contrasts between the 'Third-Worldish ethnoscape' and 'a future-oriented
yearning for prosperous First World ... hypermarkets' (Markowitz 2018: 154,
157). This begins to sum up what I was experiencing when I was in town to
deliver a keynote lecture in a science park that was next to Abraham's Well,
and what I felt when warplanes thundered over my Ottoman-era apartment.

It would be going too far for me to proclaim that people embroiled in the
contexts discussed by Hermez, Dalsheim and Markowitz would be experiencing vertigo (although I expect this to be the case), but the authors all
point to situations where their research participants are being directed towards competing trajectories, often caught in a suspended state, an lengthy
hyperconscious crisis of presence that Markowitz terms 'almostness' and
'not-quite' (2015: 8). In these Middle Eastern contexts, a Time of Crisis
(or condition of pending almost-crisis) might make it feel as though time

is slowing down, provoke over-awareness of existence at a critical moment in individual and collective history, the world being held in suspension. The suspension encourages people to question almost/not-quite peacetime, modernity and trajectories of progression/regression, as in Markowitz's informants' references to categories of Third and First World existence. The muddying of pasts, presents and futures, as well as senses of temporal belonging, are moderated through encounters with the material environment. Generators, missiles, bomb shelters and shopping malls provide material accompaniment to temporal displacement.

Throughout my short visit to Israel/Palestine, I encountered on three separate occasions a variant of the following question: 'So, is Israel part of the modern Western world?' I was put on the spot, feeling that I needed to reply, but reading in the faces of my interrogators that the question was unanswerable. The first thought that crossed my mind was 'well, they are members of the Union of European Football Associations (UEFA)', but these words, tinged with more than a little irony, did not pass my lips. In the question there was always an element of wonder, a search for self-reification that would seem to align with the idea of suspension between almostness and not-quite as argued by scholars of the region. On one occasion, the First World issue was posed as an ironic statement on the discussion of the cancellation of trains in Haifa leaving me and my family stranded. 'And Israel is part of the First World!' came the words of a local non-anthropology professor, the facial expression and lip-biting of my colleague implying a 'and what do you think about that!?' subtitle. Her point was that a purportedly civilized country rapidly descended into chaos with no contingency plan at the slight hint of crisis – on this occasion, forest fires. Signs all in Hebrew, no English, no announcements over the public address system, pushing and shoving, an inadequate public transport service ... mayhem, she suggested. The labels of 'First World' and 'modern', she claimed, were a pretence, political ploys to hoodwink the West.

More emphatically, on discussing the policy of Benjamin Netanyahu's government, I was asked to pass comment on whether his controversial posturing towards foreign powers in the Middle East was that of a 'civilized, modern' country or of a 'backward nation, trying to prove that it is up there with the West'. Finally, on the reaction of a Jewish bus driver getting extremely nervous when asked to drive into central Jerusalem during Ramadan, a friend from the region commented: 'They will tell you that Israel is modern but look at this guy. This is the everyday Jewish guy who has been fed a lifetime of political rhetoric about the "enemy". He is terrified by anybody who is different from himself. This is Third World stuff, man.' The driver was frantically scurrying around trying to offload suitcases while coachloads of Muslim prayergoers were alighting along the narrow streets skirting Old Town Jerusalem. Visibly shaking, he shouted demands for our assistance while haversacks were tossed in the general direction of the sidewalk. In my friend's comments, modernity or First World membership was inherently indexed by cosmopolitanism, cultural tolerance and the ability to see beyond political spin-doctoring that creates chaos through a lifetime of brainwashing (let's not mention Brexit or the Trumpocene).

My point here is by no means to reduce and oversimplify the temporal politics of the Middle East, which is politically, culturally and historically one of the most complex regions on Earth. Rather, it is to say that I am not surprised that such questions of belonging to categories of 'First World' and 'modern' that have political and temporal connotations are so prominent; the uncertainty reflects the vertigo I experienced bouncing around between pasts and futures in my own observations presented in the opening to this chapter and those advocated by Hermez, Dalsheim, Markowitz and others. The sensory experience of contrasting technoscapes is haunted by 'the uncanny weird ... that is often informed by outmoded cultural forms, beliefs that are supposed to have fallen away in the age of industrial modernism' (Masco 2006: 28). Life is being lived between glorious if disputed pasts and projections of glorious yet disputed and haunted futures. There is a consistent sense of lost or contradictory trajectories, space-time topologies, amalgamations of overlapping elsewhens mediated through the technical landscape. For Dalsheim, this would constitute the duration of events as assemblages of multiple pasts and futures not accommodated in classic Heraclitean theories of linear temporal succession (see also Knight 2012a), Markowitz may pin the existential *ilinx* of simultaneous elsewhens to the chronic context of almostness in which Israelis reside, while following Hermez, the absent presence of violence creates a form of uneasy suspension where people are unable to invest unreservedly in one version of the future.

Moving away from the Middle East for a moment, the second context of a Time of Crisis provoking an interrogation of categories of belonging comes from Stavroula Pipyrou's research on secondhand clothes markets in South Italy. At the onset of the financial crisis in the eurozone and accompanying austerity politics in Italy, secondhand clothes markets appeared on the streets of Reggio Calabria. Despite diminishing economic means, people still wanted to maintain their *bella figura* (beautiful appearance), which is directly linked to social status, with designer clothes a particular marker worthy of public recognition. Pipyrou follows how people began frequenting secondhand clothes markets away from their own neighbourhood so as not to pollute their public image by being seen. Their engagement with clothes donated to charity in Northern Europe and destined for what her research participants termed 'Third World' and 'African' countries was not unproblematic, raising questions of 'waste management' and 'colonial domination'

(Pipyrou 2014a: 533). People's ironic engagement with secondhand clothes during the financial crisis, Pipyrou argues, led to them feeling like *africani* (Africans), secondhand citizens, part of the Global South, and internally colonized by the wealthy Italian north (2014a: 538). It was further part of an endemic 'geopolitical anxiety pertaining to the precariousness of South Italy on the fringes of the global North' (2014a: 543). Participating in secondhand clothes shopping transported people to other timespaces, elsewhens of backwardness, colonization and pre-modern life similar to what Antonis reports upon his interaction with what he terms 'archaic' energy technology. For Pipyrou's informants, it is worth noting that the geopolitical question 'where' was as important as 'when'; people described feeling confused and angry as to their perceived demotion to categories of subordination and inferiority linked to the past and the African continent.

In both the Israeli and Italian cases, there are multiple temporal trajectories simultaneously at play in a Time of Crisis, leading to classificatory questions about where and when people belong, adding to a sense of being lost. In the post-Enlightenment West, people attempt to jostle the world into contrived classificatory categories (McLean 2017: 133), and here competing elsewhens are labelled with specific affective and identarian characteristics, with 'Third' and 'First' World becoming markers on a quotidian timeline of social and material progression. A characteristic of vertigo in a Time of Crisis in Greece and beyond is temporal displacement mediated by new artefacts or policies that plant uncertainties of categorical belonging. The partial cessation of the old world order and the as-yet unformed emergence of the new brings questions of belonging to the fore, with people overtly comparing the historicities and temporalities embedded in artefacts and policies that incite vertigo.

During the winter of 2013–14, my landlady, Giota, a retired 68-year-old widow, would spend each evening sitting next to her open fire installed by Antonis. Giota has lived through many social crises in her lifetime and believes that the 'return to the past' is symbolically captured through the installation of open fires. She also raises questions about how time and modernity do not equate to knowledge. 'Knowledge has been lost because we thought we were modern', she says. 'Back when I was a child, we all used to have wood-burning fires, the whole village, but we knew what to burn and there wasn't the same feeling of desperation. But we thought this time had passed, we are Europeans now.' Repeating a line regularly heard among retirees in Trikala, Giota feels that open fires are symbols of the past and of poverty, 'unless you are a very rich person from Athens who thinks it is fashionable'. Discussing her current problems heating her home with a group of fellow pensioners in a local coffee shop, the ladies agree that they have been 'forced back in time to another era of Greece, an era before the dictatorship [1967–74] when Greece was cut off from the world'. This event is often referred to in quotidian discourse as the imagined boundary between pre-modern, pre-European, 'poor' Greece, and modernity, Europeanization, Westernization and prosperity (Greece joined the European Community in 1981). Giota and her friends say that although Greece is now supposedly in 'Europe' and all the 'ridiculous political voices on television' tell them to look forwards to the future, it cannot be denied that they are now in freefall 'back through the decades'. She claims that she is freezing to death in her home while her government pumps billions into an energy programme (photovoltaics) that is designed to line the pockets of multinational corporations and foreign politicians, highlighting the complex power games played over energy (Boyer 2011, 2014). Explaining how disorienting she finds the engagement with technologies embedded in what she insists is conflicting 'information' about how people should prepare to live their lives in the midst of crisis, Giota is bemused: 'I don't know *when* I live anymore. Are we modern or peasants again?'

It would seem energy technology is a productive lens for exploring orientations towards elsewhens. In contrast to Giota's musings on falling back through time into pre-modernity, the ethnographic record provides instances where technology has grassroots impact for igniting futures to be folded into the present. A clear example of promises of material change embedded in energy paraphernalia is presented by Gisa Weszkalnys (2015) in the context of oil exploration in Saõ Tomé off the coast of West Africa. Here, locals were taken in by rumours of potential futures based on the discovery of oil, duly investing in roads, website domains, resorts and hotels for oil workers. The speculative futures based on oil never came to fruition, with the infrastructure today still unused. Committing to speculative futures suggested by technologies surveying the east Atlantic seabed led to life already being lived in a future elsewhen, draining the islands not only financially but also emotionally, as stories of dry wells that harbour 'no oil' continued to be transformed in public rhetoric to 'no oil yet' (Weszkalnys 2015: 630).

In Saõ Tomé, people have invested 'hard faith' in technoscience (Battaglia 2005: 149). For Weszkalnys, 'speculation about resource potential thrives at historical junctures characterized by the foreclosing of previous material possibilities while it opens others alongside new markets' (2015: 621). The will to live in a futural elsewhen – another timespace – regardless of the sacrifices in the present is dependent on 'a tangle of things', including major socioeconomic events like financial crises, ideological struggles, technological innovation and human actors sensing new commercial opportunities. Similar to Weszkalnys' observations in Saõ Tomé, Greece is at a historical juncture where markets have been closed and material possibilities redirected. The present status quo offers nothing to people submerged in crisis, leaving them willing and susceptible to conceptual relocation to a past or future elsewhen. For complex historical and political reasons enmeshed in arguments about occidental/oriental belonging (Clogg 1992; Herzfeld 1987), Europeanization and land ownership, energy technology has been the catalyst for this vertiginous journey.

As Rebecca Bryant and I have argued (Bryant and Knight 2019: 100), natural resources, like other objects, acquire a power to reshape, invert, or mix temporal orientations owing to their different 'lifespans' from the human. Photovoltaics are associated with futuristic technology and ultramodernity, while gas and oil infer geological time (see also Irvine 2020). Interaction with energy technology, Antonis and Giota suggest, leaves one feeling 'lost' – a theme of Chapter 4 – not knowing whether life belongs among promises of sustainability and ultramodernity that are perceived as part of a European First World project, or contradictory dependence on technology with decidedly pre-modern connotations. Technology transports them on journeys into overlapping elsewhens, timespaces indexed by classificatory categories of belonging that people would not usually expect to simultaneously exist. The almostness but not-quite of intersecting elsewhens, life partially taking place in disparate timespaces, causes vertigo. The topological experience of life in suspension, betwixt and between, is intensified by the schizophrenic technological landscape that often proves to be the material mediator of temporal displacement.

FALLING

'Are we in the Balkans or Botswana?', Antonis asks rhetorically. 'We are certainly not in Greece ... The photovoltaics would have you believe that we are like France or Germany or you guys in England.' He pauses and flicks away the stub of his cigarette: 'What bullshit!' On the opposite end of the spectrum from bullshit, in 1987 Herzfeld brilliantly captured the feelings of Greeks six years after they entered the EU in the aftermath of a heated public debate on the nation's (past and future) belonging to the West:

> The Greeks of today, heirs – so they are repeatedly informed – to the glories of the European past, seriously and frequently ask themselves if perhaps they now belong politically, economically, and culturally to the Third World. Whether as the land of revered but long dead ancestors, or as the intrusive and rather tawdry fragment of the mysterious East, Greece might seem condemned to a peripheral role in the modern age. (Herzfeld 1987: 3)

At the turn of the millennium, Herzfeld's perceptions of ambivalence towards Europeanization and modernity would have seemed unconvincing to an anthropologist visiting Greece. Futuristic technologies, such as the internet, EU-supported infrastructure schemes, European fiscal unity and the impending Athens Olympic Games were opening even the remotest areas to everything the West had to offer. Yet now questions of First or Third World belonging have resurfaced and energy technology has provided the ideal lens through which to interrogate trajectories, with the Balkans being a regular comparative against which many of my informants suggest that Greece should be judged (Knight 2017a, 2019b).

Alongside Antonis on the agricultural plains one pristine early summer morning in 2015 is Vassilis, a high-school friend of Antonis and an acquaintance of mine of some ten years. Educated at a Romanian university in the 1990s, Vassilis says that he has witnessed first hand the positives and negatives of life in other parts of the Balkans. He has taken a job assisting Antonis on the larger solar installations since being made unemployed from his public sector job in 2012. Over the years, he has regularly recited his often-wild stories of life in Romania – corruption, female conquests, raucous football riots, but surprisingly very little about his university education. In many narratives Vassilis takes great care to paint pictures of the immense poverty he encountered while abroad, declaring his sympathy for the 'poor bastards' while delivering the stories with an enthused sense of superiority that exoticizes his Balkan neighbours. In the early years of our relationship, one recurring theme was his relief at returning to 'civilization' in Greece, where, he assured the listener, 'things were done properly', corruption was not so widespread, there were 'street lights and smooth roads' and women 'didn't have to sell themselves'. During the 1990s, Vassilis would insist, there was a cavernous social and political distance between Greece and the rest of the Balkans, at least in terms of the public imagination.

On this summer's morning, Vassilis starts a conversation about heating and electricity in Romania and his struggles to keep warm on a winter visit in 1992: 'The locals would often shiver at night, having to wrap layers of blankets around them and sleep together in the same room in their apartment ... I would lie on the sofa watching my own breath and thinking "ah mother, where are you, tucked up warm home in Greece?"' He continues with a double tap of his spanner on a metal bar protruding ominously from the base of a 'tracker' solar panel: 'You know, Greece was wealthy, people had jobs, there was democracy and the country was stable in Europe. Greeks were sure about their future.' He says that he could never have imagined back then that he would be worrying about his energy bills in Greece in the 2000s or, as was the case now, being anxious about how he could heat his home: 'Romania, Bulgaria, Albania. They were the opposite to Greece, struggling after communism, people didn't know what their future would be like. Insecurity and anxiety.' Kneeling down on the scrubland and motioning towards a bracket at the base of the metal stand, he returns to the topic of energy:

'Living there, you didn't even know if you would have electricity when you went home and flicked the light switch on or drove into town after dark. The everyday things were full of anxiety, but you just had to expect that. In Greece there was certainty, you could relax about the basic everyday things ... Huh, but not now [with a shrug and upturned palms], look at us!'

Over the next ten years, Vassilis' excursions into the Balkans consisted of short trips across the border to Bulgaria to stockpile cheap food and alcohol around Christmas and Easter or to fill up large canisters with petrol. Things changed for him in 2014, when he headed to Bulgaria in a privately hired lorry to purchase firewood for his newly installed wood-burning stove. That trip to Bulgaria in 2014 really got Vassilis thinking, for he was going over the border to buy cheap firewood because he had been forced by the economic crisis to stop using his more expensive petrol-fuelled central heating, which he could no longer afford. He had to heat his home with firewood, which he describes as an 'archaic', 'peasant' method. 'I was going backwards, on the road to some other time', he states. 'Greece was going backwards into the past, passing Bulgaria and Romania, all those countries, on its way down.' Although Greek politicians and the mass media regularly emphasize Greece's important role in the modern European political project, Vassilis can't help thinking that soon 'Greece will become just another Balkan nation, at the bottom of the [political] food chain'. He believes that the roles have already been reversed: 'Now Bulgarians look at us and think we are backward. They buy second homes in Halkidiki [in northern Greece], sit on our beaches and flirt with our girls. Shame on them ... No, well done them, shame on us.' For him, Greece has fallen from the cliff-edge into the whirlpool of history-making, yet the new history is not one of creative futural momentum, but rather of reliving past sociopolitical orders he associates with the backwardness of the Balkans. Greece has well and truly spiralled into the abyss.

Our conversation turned to how Greece ranked below Botswana in recent press freedom and corruption indices, and how only African nations usually miss International Monetary Fund (IMF) payments. Vassilis continues: 'When I studied in Romania, modernity was a distant dream, local people had no home comforts and they certainly didn't feel European.' He says that people he lived with, fellow students at a university in the east of Romania, had aspirations to be part of the West and join the ranks of 'modern', 'democratized' and 'free' nations, but they also felt 'held back by their past', which, similarly to how Dalsheim speaks of duration in Israel, they 'dragged with them throughout life'. Vassilis believes this was because: 'Once you experienced life under communism and all that anxiety every day you couldn't just shake it off.' His friends, he insists, had many dreams, but were caught between their past and their future. Antonis cuts in: 'I think that now Greeks are feeling similar emotions. I don't think that we are truly European anymore, not in the way of Germany or England [ironically, as it would turn out], like I said, isn't that right, Vassilis?' Vassilis agrees – he too does not really know where or when Greece now belongs: 'It cannot be denied that we are falling backward through the years. Greece in 2015 is like life in 1960, before the dictatorship when my grandmother was still living in her village in the mountains. Third Worldly. That is the time we are living in. Don't let these things [he taps a solar panel with his spanner twice more] fool you.' Antonis adds that his friend in New York was recently the butt of a joke about crisis and corruption directed at him by an Eritrean. 'An Eritrean!', he repeats emphatically. 'What does that tell you about how far we [Greece] have fallen? ... Eritreans take the piss out of us!'

The life of a 'normal Greek' in a Time of Crisis, Vassilis concludes, consists of flitting between everyday anxieties that leave one 'out of breath and with no sense of direction'. With their 'head in a spin and going crazy', the Greek does not know where to turn to next. 'Running all over the place to keep up with demands from the politicians, the foreign creditors, the taxman, and the wife and kids.' All this, he suggests, while 'all the hard work to make Greece a great Western, democratic, civilized nation is stripped away and we are left falling ... freezing to death in my home, queuing at empty ATMs ... reading about food banks in the urban centres'. He emphatically proclaims: 'This is the Greece of the future, the most Balkan of the Balkans.' For Vassilis, with spanner in hand working on hi-tech photovoltaic panels promising long-term sustainability, the future is in a timespace of the past, something that makes his 'head spin'.

ELSEWHENS

In crisis Greece, encounters with energy technology orient lives in seemingly contradictory directions, towards vernacular categories of (pre-)modernity, (pre-)Europeanness, prosperity/poverty associated with heterogeneous yet overlapping elsewhens. Suspension in an elongated epoch of crisis has led to feelings of existence in almostness and not-quite, as proposed by Markowitz in Israel – almost but not-quite futural momentum, almost but not-quite returns to the past. Resemblance, repetition, echoes that tear at the seams of existence, leaving people feeling lost and confused as to, quite literally, the direction of their lives.[2] Technology facilitates, enhances or inverts orientations, harnessing affects that push or pull between elsewhens, in the sense of interconnected timelines of partial familiarity and incomprehensible alienation explored by Heinlein, and induce vertigo.

When produced, technology captures the dynamic rhythms of its epoch and, in most instances, will long outlive the human. More importantly, engagement with technology provides trajectories towards other timespaces. In an example from Zanzibar that resonates with my observations of technological interaction in Israel causing vertigo, Nir Avieli and Tsahala Sermoneta (2020) explicitly identify 'modern material objects, namely mobile phones, sunglasses and souvenirs' as disruptive objects adorning Maasai men who, in traditional dress, are observed as tourist attractions as part of the 'authentic African' experience. The clash of perceived ultramodern and traditional technologies sets tourists on confusing trajectories. The result is a combination of the extraordinary and the trivial: the Maasai are at once fantastical and mundane (they use the same technology as us!), a porthole to the human past and a reminder of accelerating global modernity. In Greece, clashing technologies might transport people to elsewhens of a time of internationally endorsed ultramodern sustainability, a utopian cloud when we will all be carbon neutral and energy prices miniscule. Equally, the return to open fires might suggest a future based on the recurrent past, one of poverty and peasantry, of cyclical structures and repetition. These are the multiple simultaneous orientations of crisis that are topologically connected to past and future elsewhens based on perceived resemblances, proximities and social circumstances (Heinlein 2012).

From Antonis' experiences in Greece to my own observations in Israel, technological encounters and their backdrops amplify vertigo, situations where people look twice in momentary second-guessing of where and when they belong. The rhythm and trajectory of mundane everyday lifeworlds are fleetingly interrupted as sights and sounds that would not normally reside side by side exist in the same timespace – Facebook and Ramadan, drip irrigation systems and camels, Maasai and mobile phones, solar panels and open fires, toxic smog and sustainability, and Bulgarians buying up cheap Greek property. Antonis mentions that when working on photovoltaic systems, he sometimes pauses to take stock of what he is doing: 'My heart skips a beat and I become acutely aware of my own existence and my feeling of displacement, of not belonging anywhere.' He says that he is conscious that he is 'doing something for the future of the world [working on renewable energy installations]', but at the same time 'slipping back into the lifestyle of my grandparents' by resorting to wood burning to heat his home. He feels 'pulled in different directions' on the temporal compass, leaving him 'lost' as to when and where he belongs.

Technology could be said to warp or braid time, drawing disparate elsewhens into simultaneous being, affecting lives already in an uncanny state of suspension. The technoscape aggravates sensory confusion provoking contradictory cognitive orientations to everyday life (Masco 2006; Avieli and Sermoneta 2020). This topological experience of spacetime is facilitated by the materiality of technology, leading people like Antonis to be overcome

with vertigo, living pasts and futures through the tangibility of the material environment. The perpetual juddering, stuttering, stop-start of 'going
somewhere'; grandparents' peasantry existing next to space-age promises.
His subjective experience of onrushing elsewhens can be scaled up to comparable collective encounters with almostness and not-quite on the level of
regional (South Italy) and national (Israel) crises. Vertigo during a crisis of
presence related to locating the Self on timelines of semi-familiar pasts and
futures is a characteristic of the affective structure of individual and collective Times of Crisis. Categories of belonging (First World, European, cosmopolitan, African) associated with the perceived existential qualities and
social hierarchies of timespaces of the past are interrogated as people are
relocated to elsewhens outside of the expected linear progression towards
European late-capitalist modernity. The following chapter goes some way
towards unpacking the theme of suspension and the feeling of being lost in
time through lives that are stuck between multiple Times of Crisis, namely
austerity Greece and Brexit Britain.

NOTES

1. Avieli and Sermoneta (2020) note that: 'Double decker busses in London, New York
   Skyscrapers, cows walking freely in congested Indian towns, or ultraorthodox Jews
   in Jerusalem, are all mundane and taken for granted components of everyday life for
   the dwellers of London, Manhattan, Delhi, and Jerusalem, but totally extraordinary
   for tourists visiting these places.' During my time in Israel, I often felt like I was inadvertently falling into the category of tourist in awe at the extraordinary ordinary.
2. On repetition and return, see a special issue of *History and Anthropology* edited by
   Andreas Bandak and Simon Coleman (2019).

CHAPTER 4

ALEXIA

Life in Suspension

❦

'That morning when I woke up and turned on the television it felt like the end of the world. My stomach dropped to my toes, I forgot to breathe and was left gasping. It was unforeseen, like living an alternate reality where the world was out to get you, personally.' The morning in question was Friday 24 June 2016 and the British public had just voted by 51.89 per cent to 48.11 per cent to leave the European Union (EU). Alexia was left glaring at the television set, not so much listening to the reporter reflect on how the country would digest the enormity of the situation, what the audience was told would be a 'once-in-a-lifetime event', but rather transfixed on a void enveloping her world. In haste, she started to search online for information on how to secure her status in the United Kingdom. 'I had felt sure that Remain would win' she says, still with a wisp of disbelief nearly four years on. 'All the analysis and media coverage leading up to the vote led me to believe that there was no danger [that the Leave vote would prevail].' In her own words, Alexia 'fled' Greece in 2014 to 'escape the crisis'. She was a university student living in the United Kingdom while taking her second degree at the time of the referendum on EU membership, but was anticipating future problems with residency rights, an atmosphere of fear and uncertainty, and increased xenophobia: 'I just knew that this was the start of another crisis, the beginning of more difficulties ... another carpet being ripped from under my feet, leaving me hanging on to life.'

I first met Alexia in 2003 when she was twelve years old playing on the street corner outside her mother's bakery in central Larisa. Even then, she was top of her class, outperforming her peers in science, mathematics and the humanities. Her dream in those early days was to become a lawyer or maybe a doctor. On returning to central Greece for my doctoral fieldwork in 2007, Alexia, whose father left the family home when she was four, was a person of great expectations. During our regular tennis games on private club courts, we would discuss revisionist versions of modern Hellenic history and the pressures for a materialistic lifestyle brought about by globalization and neoliberal markets. I remember remarking on the irony of such reflection when she insisted on playing our matches at the club rather than on the modest, tatty public courts closer to her home. She responded that she knew someone at the club, a regular customer at her mother's bakery who was a lawyer who regularly took on cases in Thessaloniki, Greece's second city to the north. She thought it wise to utilize this contact and play at the club, mixing with the 'high society' of town. This is why, much to my ridicule owing to her poor standard of tennis, she had invested the pocket money given to her by her grandparents in tennis whites, a pair of Ray-Bans, Nike tennis shoes and a Wilson racket. She insisted we hide our dilapidated bicycles behind the bushes near the pedestrian entrance to the park and stroll into the club as though we had driven there. These were the things, she stressed, that matter – first impressions, moving in the right circles, seeing and being seen (Knight 2015: Chapter 8). She was going to climb the social ladder and make a success of her life, and our tennis games were more than simply friends enjoying a pastime – as she once remarked, 'life is not a hobby'.

Alexia was going places, with aspirations of class mobility based on education. After sailing through her exams, she enrolled in the University of Athens to study economics, graduating four years later with a first-class degree. 'Then came my first experience of suspension', she says. 'So, OK, I have a degree. It's 2013 and I have worked by butt off all through my youth, no partying, no boyfriends, just study. And now I'm sat in a coffee shop every day, or killing time in the public library, just letting my life go to waste.' With no political contacts or family business connections in the field of accountancy and no chance of applying her degree to a career in the education sector, despite her constant pursuit of interviews and opportunities, Alexia was left waiting in anticipation for a future that was not forthcoming: 'My life was empty, stripped of meaning. The waiting around every day, the lack of opportunity was sapping the very life out of me.' She describes being 'trapped in suspended animation', each day 'repeating itself, over and over': 'First, my world was slowing, but I kept pushing forward thinking that if I fought hard enough, even in the years of deep crisis, I would prevail. I was different ... then the slowing became a complete stop. I was trapped, with nowhere to turn. My life jacked up on blocks.'

Speaking from Scotland in 2019, Alexia recalls: 'In those years after university in Greece, 2013, 2014, I was at a dead end. Everyone I knew was in the same position. I eventually thought to myself, "Where does one go to escape crisis? How about the land of liberal multicultural luxury that is the United Kingdom? The land of milk and honey" ... How wrong was I!' She made the remarkable decision to move to the United Kingdom not only as a labour migrant, part of the infamous 'brain drain' that characterized youth mobility away from Greece during the crisis years (Chalari and Serifi 2018), but also to enrol at the University of Glasgow to study law. She maintains that the decision to leave her country, her mother and her training in economics was heart-wrenching, but it was 'the only choice' to 'jump-start' her life: 'I had to kick myself out of that constant cycle of failure, I had to re-ignite my dreams. And my dream had always been to become a lawyer. So, I took a deep breath, got a little money from my grandparents, and decided to start again.' Since tuition for undergraduate degrees in Scotland is free for EU citizens (unlike in England, where EU students are charged around £9,000 per year), Alexia calculated that if she could work a part-time job and stretch her grandparents' contribution, in four years she would be ready for her practical training to become a barrister: 'Suddenly, I was no longer suspended, my life was not empty, no longer on pause. I was running at full speed, such excitement and trepidation. Yes, there was guilt and sadness about leaving my home and my loved ones. But I knew that the UK was the right place for me to become that somebody I had always planned to be.'

Alexia worked up to three part-time jobs to pay for her living expenses and accommodation while in Glasgow, graduating with her second degree at the age of twenty-seven in 2018. By then, she had met her partner, Fotis, an older Greek man precariously employed in the arts sector. Fotis had been back and forth to and from the United Kingdom since 2001, spending time in Germany and Denmark working for friends and relatives in art and design businesses and with side-jobs as a mechanic, for which he originally trained. Alexia and Fotis became well-known figures in the Greek community in Glasgow, hosting art events and running private language lessons. 'We decided that this would be home', Alexia explains, 'so much so that we came to the conclusion that we needed a clean break from Greece.' In 2016, Alexia's mother passed away and Alexia decided to decline the inheritance (see Knight (2018) on the desire for disinheritance), instead passing all her assets to her younger brother who still resided in Larisa: 'I know it sounds harsh, but after a lot of grieving I felt that a weight had been lifted from my shoulders. I had a new home, with new like-minded people, and I could now focus on that.' The Greek community in Glasgow, she says, would often mock the populism of their country's government (both left and centre-right) while feeling secure in the age-old political system of the United Kingdom that was stable and would never change.

Then, 2016, the EU membership referendum. 'Tears. Anxiety. Weight-loss. Desperation ... those have been the Brexit years for me', Alexia recites.

'A new life, new opportunities, some form of stability and a sense of liberal freedom wrenched from under our feet.' Fotis was declined settled status allowing permanent right to remain in the United Kingdom in late 2019 owing to his mobility over the past five years and his precarious employment that included gaps where he did not officially 'work' at all, choosing to focus on his art. He is now caught between a country that will not recognize his legitimacy and a country in which he has not lived for almost two decades. 'He has disowned one and the other has disowned him! Where to go, what to do?' exclaims Alexia. Out of the frying pan and into the fire. Alexia spent her final two university years frantically networking, chasing – and eventually finding – unpaid internships in the hope that this experience, coupled with meeting people in influential positions, would secure post-university employment. Her four years studying in the United Kingdom do not count towards her settled status or citizenship application since, among other things, she did not have private medical insurance, even though it was not required at the time according to EU law: 'It's all there in the fine-print of that 85-page UK Permanent Residency application document [as it was titled at the time].'

Like many EU citizens in the United Kingdom, the first days and weeks after the 2016 referendum were marked by panic, tears and an eerie silence on the streets (Knight 2017d). Little has changed in the years since: 'We cried regularly over that document. We knew that the government would make it as difficult as possible for foreigners from that point on.' But it was not simply the bureaucratic complexities that bothered Alexia; there was an ideological aspect attached to what she saw as a 'shift' in the atmosphere of life in the United Kingdom, a collective – although some may say a naïve and essentialist – acknowledgement that the EU membership referendum was a rupture between multicultural acceptance and intolerance of alterity: 'The sickness I felt was not just that fear or the uncertainty of where I would go or what I would do after university. I mean, I knew I would be nearly twenty-eight years old on graduation, which is not young to be starting out again in the business world ... it was that everything I thought the UK stood for had been put on hold. Paused. Deleted.'

After graduating, Alexia managed to secure two successive short-term contracts as a paid trainee at two UK-based law firms. But with her partner's status in limbo and her own mid-term employment future uncertain, she describes living in a second stage of suspension: 'I cut myself free from one crisis and ended up in another. The feelings are similar – of hopelessness, of physical sickness with constant anxiety, of not knowing what my future will look like, of endlessly having to fight the system, of being trapped by forces I can't control.' She once again describes her life as in 'suspension', 'caught between crises', and her teetering precariously on a tightrope above a canyon. Her existence in a timespace of suspension is characterized by 'emptiness'; empty life (*adeia zoi*), empty person (*kenos anthropos*), empty future (*keno mellon*). This chapter explores emptiness that haunts a life in suspension, where people like Alexia are caught between the destruction of one world and the not-yet-visible possibilities of another. As such, it deals with a broader sense of an uncertain world in twenty-first-century Europe, explicitly detailing the vertiginous affects of being tangled in multiple crises. Notions of being trapped in a timespace without recognizable futural momentum and of living in a state of captivity that has been designed by global forces beyond one's control are introduced as distinctive to twenty-first-century crisis life, themes that will be taken further in Chapter 5. Engaging further with what Vyjayanthi Venuturupalli Rao (2013) terms 'schizophrenic landscapes' filled with anxiety and confusion, the chapter interrogates the transitional timespace between eras of destruction and emergence, placing emptiness and suspension as constitutional aspects of European late modernity. The gap between the destruction of the old and the emergence of the new is haunted by traces of futures past, residues of expectations, broken promises and fading dreams. In the schizophrenic landscape, vertigo is king.

EMPTINESS

After the destructive rupture of financial ruin and a decade of aggressive structural reform, my argument in this book has been that Greece has entered a timespace of chronic crisis marked by suspended futures and intense temporal disorientation. One vernacular holding together life in limbo is emptiness, connecting disparate domains of social life, becoming an integral part of the affective structure of crisis. People talk of empty state coffers, workplaces desolated by a brain drain (of which Alexia was part), hollow political promises of emergence, social and material dispossession, and hopeless futures. Scaling up from individual stories of defeated expectations and tangible material absence, emptiness has become part of the affective structure of a Time of Crisis, a vernacular of the epoch that runs through daily life as people make sense of the tapestry of destruction that shapes their experience of European late modernity where spatiotemporal arrangements of power, capital and state increasingly abandon people and places (Dzenovska 2020: 10).

In Greece, emptiness frames and classifies seemingly unrelated realms of anthropological enquiry, being spatial, temporal and existential, thus allowing for topological comparison of the general structure of the era. Topology – the 'science of nearness, connectedness and distortion' (Serres and Latour 1995: 60) – speaks of potentialities and possibilities at the 'thresholds of transition' (Gros, Russell and Stafford Jr. 2019). At the threshold of the 'new normal' – routinized crisis, which is discussed further in Chapter 5 – we find emptiness connecting and displacing previous orders and testifying to the violence of historical transformation (Argenti 2017). A topological analysis of emptiness underscores the distorted spatial and temporal connectivity between domains of a society stuck in suspended transition between rupture and emergence.[1]

Emptiness punctuates daily parlance in the guises *adeios* (empty) and *kenos* (empty, also void).[2] It references a 'before' of abundance and meaning, an elsewhen where neoliberal accumulation and European belonging were considered birthrights. It captures how the present *feels* different from the pre-crisis years, while emphasizing the prominent futural orientations of resignation and apathy brought about by endemic crisis: *adeia zoi* (empty life), *adeio tameio* (empty coffer), *kenos logos* (empty [political] speech), *kenos anthropos* (empty person) and *keno mellon* (empty future). Embracing the topological spirit of distortion and connection, in Greece emptiness is 'actively morphing, changing, and being recycled in the local imaginaries around displacement, suffering, and life-making' that denote a Time of Crisis (Rao 2013: 316). Emptiness facilitates the making sense of chronic crisis and precarious futures holistically, rushing through the veins of social life, connecting realms as diverse as inheritance law, psychoanalysis and rhetoric culture. The vernacular of emptiness is an affective pivot around which daily life unfolds.

Alexia taps into this vernacular to describe her life in suspension, comparing the emptiness of her years post-first degree in Athens with her experiences in Brexit Britain. In doing so, her analysis transcends national borders, connecting Greece and the United Kingdom, and merging two crisis narratives through one trope. Emptiness, then, seems to be the marker of an era that goes beyond a 'Greek crisis' or a 'national event', being intimately ingrained in the timespace of late capitalist modernity in Europe, something that is captured by a recurring vision that appears to Alexia when closing her eyes at night.

'I feel it rushing toward me, starting in the mid-horizon and rushing toward my face. I sometimes half-turn my head, flinching in anticipation of its impact. This is how it starts, some occasions more dramatic than others'. Alexia says that she envisions herself 'hovering' above a map of Europe. She implores me to imagine a multicoloured political map of the continent with a line drawn between Greece and the United Kingdom. And then, she later adds, tag on her partner's connections to Denmark and Germany: 'I see myself suspended above central Europe, trying to balance on this tightrope ... as I get closer to one end, I hit an invisible shield of sorts, something will not let me past, bouncing me back the way I have come ... I feel as though I am about to fall, wobbling over a void or cavern below.' As she looks down from this precarious place, trying to maintain her balance, she experiences 'a staggering emptiness, not just from the deep, dark hole I am about to fall into from my place suspended above Europe, but an all-consuming emptiness from within my body'. She puts this down to how crises shut down opportunities, dispossess people of dreams and aspirations, and curtail possibilities, 'tearing the soul' from people who have invested so much in their futures. In this 'cartography of time' (Rosenberg and Grafton 2010) or 'time map' (Zerubavel 2003), Alexia faces her fear of being stuck between crises, unable to fulfil her full potentiality owing to external forces repelling her off metaphorical walls, the ricochets between pasts and futures that leave her disoriented and unstable (Knight 2016: 41, Valentine et al. 2012: 1023). She is keen to emphasize the rhythm and speed of her life at different stages, now once again slowing to a stop for a second time. As life slows down, losing momentum, it is more difficult to keep her balance on the tightrope of life on which she is suspended somewhere between her country of birth and her adopted home.

Migrants caught in a net of multiple temporalities, Melanie Griffiths (2014: 1994) argues, can experience 'a long, slowing time of waiting (sticky time), one that can decelerate into complete stagnation (suspended time), a fast time rushing out of control (frenzied time) and tears in people's imagined time frames (temporal ruptures)' (Griffiths 2014: 1994, cited in Gutiérrez Garza 2018: 87). The time of stagnation or suspension that Alexia identified when sitting in coffee shops after graduating with her first degree in Athens and then again in the precariousness following the Brexit vote is marked by emptiness – of person (existential), of future (temporal) and of place (spatial, since she is trapped between homes). Her life was 'stripped of meaning' in both instances and – similarly to Mairi's existential struggle with a detached sense of Self – her person is plunged into a disoriented state that lacks trajectory or futural direction. A deeply ingrained stuckedness, in Ghassan Hage's (2009) sense of waiting out perpetual crisis, has led to what is portrayed in her vision of suspension above a map of Europe. Stuck between two timespaces of destruction, Alexia inhabits a liminal timespace, in Victor Turner's terms, being 'lodged between all times and spaces defined and governed ... by the rules of law, politics and religion' (1981: 161).

Alexia connects the emptiness of a life in suspension with what she calls the 'end of the world' that was brought about first by the economic crisis and then by Brexit (cf. Wolf-Meyer 2019). Crisis, which she believes should have been a once-in-a-lifetime violent schism, has actually torn through her world twice in the space of a decade, the impact leaving her dazed, grappling for balance and facing multiple forms of emptiness.

In a striking comparative ethnographic case, Dace Dzenovska (2019, 2020) argues for the structuring qualities of emptiness in rural Latvia, where emptiness has become an 'end of the world' trajectory that filters through various daily practices. Since the dramatic rupture that was the fall of socialism slipped into a permanent period of transition, people now 'expect to die as the world ends or the world to end when they die'.[3] As Alexia's narrative suggests for Greece and the United Kingdom, emptiness in Latvia is an integral part of the affective structure of crisis, a central plotline in the story of European modernity (Dzenovska and Knight 2020). Dzenovska argues that emptiness marks the threshold of transition as people inhabit a space where the old world order has collapsed and the new has not yet taken shape: 'emptiness comes before civilization and after its retreat' (2020: 11).

The claim that emptiness is an important aspect of world-making in European late modernity is supported by works on the politics of post-referendum Britain where emptiness most strikingly references future utopias/dystopias. Emptiness is a catchword in post-referendum Britain and is constitutive of the contemporary political landscape. For instance, in her party-political ethnography of the Scottish National Party (SNP), Gabriela Manley (2019a) tells how Scottish independence is being sold as a future with creative emptiness. Reeling from the major blow of a triumphant Brexit 'Leave' campaign (citizens of Scotland voted strongly in favour of remaining part of the EU), SNP activists pushing for a second referendum on Scottish independence from the United Kingdom propose visions of an independent Scotland as empty, a blank slate onto which everybody can build a collective future.[4] Instead of promoting clear economic and welfare policy, which is the official party line, SNP activists from across the political hierarchy insist that only after the dramatic rupture from Westminster can futures truly be formed. This destructive tear in the fabric of UK politics will provoke an uncompromising destabilization of social knowledge (Greenhouse 2019; Roitman 2014) and thus a timespace of emptiness will arise where a new order can be built from scratch. Scotland will exist 'in a timespace of indeterminate potentiality and creativity', with emptiness marking the 'transition between the old and new political dynasty, a timespace of transition and transformation where speculation replaces concrete policy' (Manley 2020).

From a perspective of emptiness, the belief that the future will be radically, unimaginably different from all known pasts and presents is picked up by both Dzenovska and Manley. The unimaginability of the future is a feature of chronic crisis that intensifies vertigo (see Chapter 5), with only distant and rapidly fading residual affective resonances guiding temporal trajectory. Dzenovska poignantly reflects on the sensual dimensions of emptiness that punctuate the unfathomability of the future in an era of transition:

> The smell of damp basements in urban areas suggested empty apartment buildings; the sound of doors swinging in the wind, an abandoned house in the countryside.

> Some of my interlocutors said that passing by empty houses made them feel anxious, even a little nauseous. Often, it was precisely the affective dimension of emptiness – the feeling one got when seeing abundant apple trees by abandoned homes – that conjured the future as something radically different but not yet graspable in language. (2020: 11)

Alexia inhabits this timespace of transition twice over, caught between the ricochets of collapsing world orders, both financial and political. It is her suspension above Europe, being knocked back and forth until she becomes dizzy, feeling unbalanced (in the same way as Dzenovska cites anxiety and nausea above), and her slipping between dimensions of panic and apathy, that reveals to her a rapidly emptying world. Citing Martin Holbraad et al. (2019: 22) on rupture, Manley (2020) argues that the point of radical sociopolitical change carries a creative/destructive dynamic, where ruination has a prolific (although still speculative) potential immanent within it. This space, or gap, is a radical political category 'between the death and emergence of political systems ... brimming with affect and possibility'. This is the point in time that Runia (2010) refers to as holding destruction and possibility hand in hand, the cliff-edge moment where people may jump into the creative vortex of history-making. Yet, being stripped of recognizable points for competent and confident navigation evokes fear, disorientation and anxiety. In the meantime, people are suspended in a timespace between affective states of hope and bitterness (Driessen 2019).

Characteristic of a period of radical rupture and suspended orders, based on Manley's observations of the creative potentiality of the gap, one may justifiably ask whether emptiness is ever truly vacuous. To paraphrase Frank Kermode (2000: 45–46), Alexia's life is currently situated between the tick of rupture and the tock of possibility, or the gap filled with speculation between the destruction of the old world order and emergence from the rubble of the uncanny present.[5] As such, the gap that she and many of my Greek research participants characterize in daily discourse as empty might not be deemed empty at all, but rather filled with speculation, anticipation or the nausea-inducing vertigo of teetering on the proverbial cliff-edge of history. The gap between 'tick' and 'tock' points to the weirdness of the world in its current form and leads either to conjecture and fantasy or to apathy and resignation about the future (Bryant and Knight 2019: 82). As a manifestation of life under intense anxiety and stress, with no horizon in sight, one might argue that a Time of Crisis is conspicuous for the fullness of emptiness, at least in terms of affective orientations.

But it is, I believe, the absence of familiar markers by which to successfully orient life and navigate emptiness that induces vertigo for people like Alexia. There is a sensation of being lost and helpless that provokes intense anxiety. In pre-Brexit Britain, Alexia's markers were, broadly drawn, social liberalism underlined by multiculturalism and acceptance of difference, the security of an elite education system and the feeling that centuries of (or at least the façade of) moderate British politics would never change. In pre-crisis Greece, Alexia found familiarity in family support networks, a culture of materialism and consumption, public sector security, and definitions of European belonging rhetorically linked to Greece as the cradle of civilization and democracy (Herzfeld 1987: 3, Knight 2017a: 183–84), all of which have been suspended since the crisis that surfaced in 2009. To paraphrase Christos Lynteris (2019: 128) addressing post-pandemic imaginaries, emergence into an empty world, without the stars by which to navigate, strips humanity of its autopoietic energy.

STARS

Following the theme of navigation that I find highly productive for thinking through vertigo, and especially the contribution of emptiness to a vertiginous life, here I choose to indulge in further abstraction by citing two episodes of hit US sci-fi series *Star Trek Voyager*. These snippets facilitate further musings on emptiness as materiality, affect and orientation. Simply titled 'Night', in Season 5, Episode 1, while en route home to the Alpha Quadrant, *Voyager* encounters an expanse of space with absolutely no stars. Taking two years to cross, the crew hunker down for the psychological strain of living in emptiness. After just two months of staring into darkness, many become agitated, deeply self-reflexive and highly suspicious of one another. Without markers by which to navigate and with seemingly endless emptiness in every direction, the crew start behaving abnormally, conflicts break out and all start questioning relations on the ship. A chance encounter with a 'native' alien race responsible for dumping toxic waste leads to the discovery of a vortex that passes through normal spacetime and delivers the starship to the other side of empty space and back into starlight, an emergence that is met with rapturous celebration.

Tackling similar topics, 'The Void' is Episode 15 of Season 7 of *Star Trek Voyager*, where Captain Janeway's crew are once again drawn into a resource-scarce area of space. The search for a return from 'The Void' to 'normal space', they decide, can only be conducted through resource- and technology-sharing with other ships caught in its clutches. Although *Voyager* discovers natives of the void, inhabitants that have made emptiness their home, alas for the crew the fear of emptiness is overwhelming and they frantically search for a return to the comforts of the nearest star system. The void is not quite as empty as legend would have them believe, but the forms of life do not provide comfort to the crew, instead breeding suspicion about the allegiances and intentions of friends and sowing the seeds of panic that contaminate and consume all on board. In both episodes the sensory affects and temporal rhythms of emptiness slowly break down established social relations, with deep psychological consequences.

It is of interest that in these *Star Trek* episodes, emptiness topologically connects the spatial, temporal and existential realms. In both cases, emptiness in the first instance indexes a literal hole or gap in the map of the Delta Quadrant of the Galaxy, trapping many other starships that may remain lost in emptiness for decades (of Earth time). In addition to storylines built around the temporal weirdness of emptiness (time passing slowly, repeating and looping back on itself), often the resolution to stuckedness in seemingly permanent emptiness is through temporal manipulation, namely by creating vortices and portals that bend the laws of physics to deliver our heroes to the other side of the void. By this time, their characters have been tested and emergence into 'normality' allows them to reconnect with their 'real' selves on familiar spatiotemporal coordinates – much like in the rich anthropological literature on trauma and ritual healing – having explored the darkness of space, soul and society.

Certainly the cartographical aspect of emptiness in *Star Trek Voyager* resonates with anthropological studies of forbidden or magical regions on the edge of maps (Stewart 1991) or unincorporated spaces where 'there be dragons' at the frontier of known lands (Williams 2001 [1961], cited in Dzenovska and Knight 2020; see also Tsing 2005). In the pandemic imaginary of the COVID-19 crisis, Lynteris (2020) has shown how mapping emptiness through satellite images of China during lockdown offers glimpses of potential futures that may be desired by Western governments. He argues that images of 'empty skies' during lockdown provide short-term 'cures' to China's overpopulation and environmental problems, and become powerful mythemes 'in the incurably colonial pandemic imaginary of Western societies'. NASA's comparative cartography of the atmospheric impact of COVID-19 in China offers 'blue sky hope' of curing social and political ills, while concealing 'the thousands of people dying as a result of COVID-19 and the millions of lives disrupted by the anti-epidemic measures' (Lynteris 2020). Cartography here is a portal to the future, or more appropriately *a* future where temporal speculation portrays a utopia of a 'clean' and empty China as desired by Western powers. In *Star Trek Voyager*, temporal manipulation – vortices, shockwaves, funnels that bend spacetime – and speculative portals destroy the state of emptiness and deliver emergence from a place of undesirable stagnation, repetition and (potentially eternal) suspension.

Resonating with storylines in the *Star Trek Voyager* episodes, for Alexia, emptiness spreads fear like a contagion among her close friends and family.

She is not alone in the timespace of dual crises; indeed, probably thousands of Southern European citizens find themselves caught between the financial ruins of the northern shores of Mediterranean and the political shenanigans that have come to characterize Brexit Britain. However, the navigational markers, stars if you will, she has grown accustomed to have faded, no longer burning bright enough to guide her life. As they fade, so their gravitational pull weakens and she begins to wobble on the tightrope of life, no longer held in place by their stabilizing force. As her stars disappear, emptiness takes over, a timespace of spatial, temporal and existential transformation and transition, of seemingly infinite waiting and self-questioning before the new world order dawns, new star systems are born and light once again shines on her darkened existence. Living in emptiness, losing all familiarity and gradually becoming accustomed to the new normal while searching for escape, Alexia explores the dark edges of soul, society and geopolitical power games.

So it is that the vernacular of emptiness is part of the affective structure of the timespace of crisis, inducing vertigo in a gap between the destruction of old and emergence of new social, political and economic orders. At this moment, life is held in suspension, bounced between the forcefields of the past and the future. The absence of familiar navigation markers means that people fail to situate themselves within a trajectory (Kirtsoglou 2010: 2). Omnipresent in local discourse on crisis, emptiness topologically indexes spatial change, temporal disorientation and existential quandaries. At this (elongated) threshold of transition, emptiness is woven into conversations, practices and feelings that identify radical changes and then eventual routinizations of new world orders, whether with the green shoots of creative potentiality as suggested by Manley, as an end of the world orientation argued by Dzenovska or in the uncomfortable comfort associated with the normalization of chronic crisis that is the subject of Chapter 5.

SUSPENSION

Continuing the cartographic theme, as mentioned, Alexia's describes her life as suspended above a virtual map of Europe, stuck between two crises, plunging her into a multiplicate condition of topological emptiness. While emptiness is the vernacular through which she expresses her vertiginous life, particularly in the affective register, it is the state of suspension that provokes reflection on emptiness in various existential, material and temporal forms. Alexia mentions being 'caught in suspended animation', implying a stuckedness or slowing down of time, being trapped or frozen in an inescapable elongated timespace of the present. This reference to captivity spills over into the notion that she is suspended in a period of transition, between two crises that have destroyed her respective world orders in Greece and the United Kingdom. Unlike Kierkegaard's (1980: 61) reading of anxiety-inducing suspension as freedom from the cultural structures of nations, a laudable position of unbounded possibility, Alexia cannot or does not want to participate in these crisis worlds that are lived through desperation. In a palpitating state, she feels a deep sense of loss and of being lost. Again, by invoking a metaphor of being suspended on a tightrope high above Europe, being repelled at either end by life-shattering events, Alexia suggests she is physically trapped in this condition of suspension that leads to all-consuming emptiness.

Suspension, Akhil Gupta (2015) asserts, needs to be theorized as a condition of being in its own right, detached from concepts of beginnings and endings. In other words, for Gupta, the temporality of suspension constitutes its own ontic condition, separate to ideas of rupture and completion, placing import on the *holding action* of suspension (Battaglia 2017: 281, original emphasis; see also Choy and Zee 2015) – how people, places and things are held in space and time. Indeed, Alexia explicitly mentions that her life has been 'put on hold' by Brexit as it once was by the Greek economic crisis, signalling a new era of suspension. Here I wish to dwell a while on what Rao (2013) calls a 'time of suspension' marked by a 'schizophrenic landscape' of temporal withdrawal, distortion and contradiction.

It is time being frozen or, more pertinently, the withdrawal from time that a young Italian woman, Giovanna, communicates to me in the days immediately after the Brexit referendum.[6] Her narrative, alongside that of Alexia, adds to the argument that emptiness and suspension are facets of crisis in European late modernity that transcend national borders, assisting in the formulation of more general theories of affective structure in a Time of Crisis. For Giovanna, the Brexit vote has suspended – taken hold of – her previous assumptions about the core values of British society, her momentum towards forging a future in the United Kingdom, and has brought into sharp relief the historically embedded political differences between England and Scotland.

A 35-year-old mother of two, married to an English retail manager, Giovanna had been living in the United Kingdom for eight years prior to the 2016 vote, the last four of which were spent in Scotland. Like Alexia, she reports that she felt secure in the multicultural outlook of the United Kingdom and what she describes, with an obvious hint of irony provided by the benefit of hindsight, as the 'stable political situation'. The referendum result left her feeling 'empty', 'disorientated' and 'as if being hit by a bus'. 'My world just kind of stopped', she says, 'like someone pushed the pause button on their fancy television. The actors, us, frozen while going about our normal lives ... there was a sudden jolt and then ... [she fails to complete her sentence] ... or you could say that someone has just cut our [climbing] rope and we have just discovered the frayed end.' For Giovanna, her family was ripped from their normative timeline, from time's arrow that scandalously provokes the fantastical idea of lineal progression, evolution and accumulation (see Hodges 2008). While life seemed to be continuing as normal for the people around her who were still caught up in the currents of time's flow, Giovanna's world had stood still, left hanging in temporal suspension.

Living in Scotland, the withdrawal from 'normal' life hit doubly hard, Giovanna recalls. She, like many citizens north of the border, already felt that Scotland was slightly politically detached from the rest of the United Kingdom given the SNP's focus on Scottish independence and the presence of much anti-Westminster and anti-England rhetoric from the regional government (Manley 2019b). Her narrative strikes a chord with Gupta's allusion to suspension of place: 'Somebody else, down there in England was having a party ... we were being made to come along, kicking and screaming in protest.' Not only were Giovanna's personal beliefs in social liberalism, cosmopolitanism and multiculturalism being challenged, frozen, paused, but the nation (Scotland) in which she resided was also more detached than ever from the euphoric political tidal wave sweeping other parts of the United Kingdom.

'Those days are a little hazy now', Giovanna reflects. 'I do remember my husband weeping over the really long and convoluted residency documents that he had spread out on our dining room table the morning after [the referendum result] ... There was so much small print.' When she realized that after eight years and two children born on UK soil, she did not yet qualify for permanent residency status, which is required after Brexit for a person to be able to live and work in the United Kingdom, she described how 'life drained out' of her body as if someone was 'sucking' her world away. Everything was put on hold: 'Suddenly there was no future that we could see. Everything had changed. We couldn't plan for anything beyond the immediate needs of the family. Like I say, we were frozen, put on hold ... the best way I can describe it is hitting that pause button on your TV or DVD player.' She describes a 'deep sickness' at losing her future in a 'personal attack on family and beliefs about what is right and wrong in this world'. She did not know where to turn. Her not knowing whether she could even stay in the United Kingdom was a near-future concern that consumed every aspect of her daily existence for the next three years, until she finally qualified for permanent residency, or what had by then been renamed by the UK governing Conservative Party as 'settled status'.

With half their family in Italy and having recently secured employment in a sector heavily reliant on EU trade deals, Giovanna and her husband saw their immediate future as quite uncertain, in what Alexia has described as 'suspended animation'. 'We just didn't know', Giovanna continues, 'everything had been cleared out [of our future] ... the world felt empty, my soul felt empty ... we didn't know in what direction to turn. To leave? To stay? To run or stay put to fight? We were deer caught in the headlights, as you say, losing our mind.' The United Kingdom's withdrawal from the EU led to Giovanna's husband withdrawing from his English identity. Expressing a deep shame, he tried at every turn to disassociate himself with what was commonly perceived in Scotland as 'the English vote' (62 per cent of Scottish citizens voted to remain in the EU and every constituency returned a 'Remain' majority). 'The delusional English believe once again that they are a great imperial force', he once told me, an empire that 'continues to rule the waves'.

'Decadence begins when a civilization falls in love with its ruins', Derek Walcott wrote. By his account, Stoler comments in an almost prophetic tone, 'England is doomed' (Walcott, cited in Stoler 2013: 27). Giovanna follows her husband's lead in repeating the line that England has fallen in love with the idea of its past grandeur, living in past times of 'the Raj, slavery, and pretences of global domination'. 'This is exactly what would happen', her husband told her, 'if the voting public were persuaded by Boris Johnson and Nigel Farage [leading figures in the 'Vote Leave' campaign]. Their words of intolerance toward different people, migrants, anyone with an education when really they [the political class] were the artists behind austerity Britain and all the social ills that entailed ... they wooed people with stories of England's glorious past.'

Giovanna's immediate future had been cleared out (Guyer 2007). Previous certainties for the coming days, weeks, months and years had been replaced by what appeared to be a singular monolithic event: Brexit. Like Alexia, Giovanna did not know where to turn; she was frantically searching for direction, her life left dangling by a thread for what, she said, felt like an eternity. The authorship of her life story, what she had once considered her birthright (Rapport 2019), had been interrupted and she was now experiencing writer's block. Emptiness was present as an expressive trope that helped Giovanna describe the physical and conceptual impact of the world-changing Brexit vote, a timespace packed with unfamiliarity, uncertainty and the general unabating whiff of imminent violence.

There are some connections to be made between the condition of suspension revealed in Giovanna's case and Antonis' allusion to suspended time made in Chapter 3. For both Giovanna and Antonis, life in suspension is accompanied by feelings of being lost, constantly searching for direction. The convergence of collapsing timespaces, all just out of reach but equally onrushing, is what Rao terms a 'schizophrenic landscape'. Living in the ruins of abandoned material and temporal projects leads to a profound questioning of belonging. For Antonis, interacting with energy technologies with contrasting temporal orientations – hi-tech futuristic solar panels and archaic traditional open fires – led to him experiencing crisis as a timespace of 'almostness' and 'not-quite'. Being tossed and turned between competing trajectories that promised futures based on different social and material relations, Antonis' head was in a spin, leading him to question *when* as well as *where* he was living. Which way was he travelling and where/when would he eventually arrive? Almostness and not-quite are part of the ontic condition of suspension where people articulate how they are trapped between worlds in rapid destruction. The striving associated with almostness and not-quite means that the horizon is always just out of grasp. Alexia, Giovanna and Antonis are living in a betwixt and between timespace, residing in the gap, in Kermode's terms, between two world orders, filled with speculation and suspense, anxiety and sometimes outright panic. The familiarity of past comforts and expectations has not yet been replaced by the navigable familiarity of emergent social orders of the new normal and it is in this gap where recognizable lives are in suspension that emptiness prevails. In research following the construction progress of a hydroelectric dam in Srisailam, India, Rao (2013) introduces what she terms a 'time of suspension', where locals are trapped by the archaeological remains of a bygone era and the defeated promises of a modern future. In an ethnographic case that strikingly resonates with Antonis' experiences of vertigo while working with the contrasting temporal trajectories of photovoltaic installations and open-fire systems in central Greece, in Srisailam promises of prosperous futures that include job security, financial relief and energy sustainability are dashed by project delays and heritage disputes. A time of suspension indexes vertiginous captivity where a sharp contrast emerges between a modernist sense of the future, expressed implicitly in the hopes of progress and modernization through development projects on the one hand and, on the other, in a sense of being arrested or imprisoned in a space that is neither progressive nor evidently continuous with the past. The time of suspension is engendered with powerful imaginaries of the future exerted by projects of modernization, their ongoing and constantly deferred temporal effects, and the ways in which these effects continue to be vividly entangled with the colonial and precolonial past (Rao 2013: 291–92).

Similar to arguments posed by Dzenovska above, emptied futures (and pasts) and life in permanent suspension, lost in an aimless present, are for Rao characteristics of the abandonment of projects of modernization. Instead of constructing futures in the guise of the green economy, the project of late capitalist modernity has destroyed both historical continuity and futural expectations – villages have been relocated and reassembled to accommodate the dam, livelihoods have been irreversibly altered by this physical displacement, and traditional landscapes obliterated, hopes and expectations have been shattered. After the dam's completion, villagers found that the 'future' promised by the state ironically 'converged, visually and materially, with the monumental "past" as the village became partially a museum' where the village was 'preserved' in the form of an archaeological heritage project (Rao 2013: 298).

In exploring the physical and affective landscape of the Srisailam Dam programme, inadvertently Rao makes reference to the same three pins of vertigo found in Alexia's narrative on emptiness and that have also been the foundation for individual chapters of this book, namely the existential, spatial and temporal aspects of life in suspension, which she aptly bundles together in the term 'schizophrenic landscapes'. The phrase fittingly denotes how lives are caught up and crushed in the convergence of collapsing worlds – whether you are being pulled towards futures of modernization and pasts of poverty and tradition (Antonis), are struggling to breathe as two crisis bubbles squeeze you from opposite ends of the continent (Alexia) or are feeling helplessness and panic when the carpet of familiarity is whipped from under your feet, leaving you dangling in mid-air (Giovanna). The time of suspension, a timespace trapped between other timespaces of destruction, is a domain of multiple personalities, competing voices and sensory confusion.

As discussed by Alexia and Giovanna, previous lifestyles, expectations and sociological beliefs have been confined to a bygone era and grandiose promises of cosmopolitan projects lie in ruins. There remains a desire to access these pasts, inhabit and engage with the remains of lives before crisis, and more than a slight sense of refusal to relate to or acknowledge the new normal evident in periods of transition following the destruction of modernity. There is a schizophrenic division in time between a time of promises and a time of deliberate abandonment. In the transformative gaps between spatiotemporal displacement of old and new orders, relational history, interpersonal relationships and the productivity of the landscape are held in suspension – the transformation of 'people, places and things' that for Gupta constitute the ontic condition of suspension. In Rao's case, the time of suspension stretched over the dozen years it took to build the dam and indefinitely beyond. The waste produced by modernization projects, she concludes, generates historical, societal and material fragments that are 'permanently withdrawn from time' (Rao 2013: 315; see also Gille 2020; Navaro-Yashin 2012). It is precisely this withdrawal that Giovanna references when she says that Scotland has become spatially and ideologically detached from the rest of the United Kingdom, and it is implicit in her claim that her life has been put on hold and she has stepped outside of the 'normal' progression of time, which in her world has been frozen like a paused television show. In this gap, speculating about her future in Britain has become Giovanna's all-consuming pursuit – a crisis of presence.

Rao's use of the term 'schizophrenic' is of interest here since it aptly captures the disorientation and struggles with the Self that characterize vertigo that we have witnessed throughout this book. People are being torn in multiple directions, searching and sometimes scrambling to locate themselves in timelines of pasts and futures, in the gaps between long-term promises and defeated expectations. This was certainly the case for Antonis in his struggle between affective histories and futural promises that were played out in an overtly tangible manner in his interaction with energy infrastructure. Alexia's emotional portrayal of attempting to access both place of birth and place of residence while suspended above Europe – a suspension that was both physical and metaphorical – but being repelled at both ends signals life caught in a schism between collapsing and emerging sociopolitical orders. Project Brexit has created multiple levels of unrecognizability for Giovanna, freezing her in suspended animation, trapped in what Nancy Scheper-Hughes has called 'dead time' where her family are 'waiting in fear and dread for the inevitable future to somehow miraculously pass over them and leave them alone' (Scheper-Hughes 2007: 470). Giovanna experiences withdrawal from the commonly shared timespaces of those around her, operating at different rhythms and speeds. In terms of directionality, while Antonis is torn between falling backwards and being pulled forwards on the commonly conceived Western model of temporal succession, Alexia is being ricocheted like a ball in an arcade machine between politically constructed walls of contemporary crises, and Giovanna is searching for trajectory, lost, left dangling and dispossessed of expectations. Her timeline has been cut and she is frozen like a cartoon character (let us say Wile E. Coyote) who, after overshooting a rocky outcrop, is suspended in mid-air anticipating plummeting to earth. Cue the 'Bye Bye' placard, the gormless facial expression and the gradually diminishing whistling sound effect. The schizophrenic landscape is thus characterized by 'momentary slips' between competing timespaces associated with different historicities, trajectories and affective structures (Jenkins 1991: 388, Sullivan 1953: 283).

These instances put more ethnographic meat on Rao's concept of schizophrenic landscapes, which indicates the messiness and incoordination of the ethnographic field and the vertiginous schism in relational history enforced by projects of modernization and neoliberal reform. In other words, in Runia's terms, a virtual cliff-edge has been created where a project of modernity has cut through historical continuity, causing people to lose balance, teetering on the edge while the earth continues to shake below their feet. Competing energies simultaneously occupy the timespace, a dynamic tension between what Mikhail Bakhtin (1981: 272) described as centrifugal and centripetal forces. 'You can be caught, captured, paralyzed, immobilized, stuck. You can be released, restored, redeemed, mobile, free. The tension between those opposites ... always contains both of its own ends' (Lepselter 2016: 29). Whether the rhythm of suspension is Antonis' Stretch Armstrong effect, Alexia's pinball action or Giovanna's cartoon character who is searching for ground that is no longer there, the schizophrenic temporal landscape leads to disorientation, anxiety and ultimately vertigo.

However, what may be more commonly construed as a classic rupture in a revolutionary sense (Holbraad, Kapferer and Sauma 2019) is not clean-cut and leads to a time of suspension between the destruction of the old and emergence of the new. This gap is filled with traces of futures past, residues of expectations, and material/visual reminders of loss and broken promises, discussed in the vernacular of emptiness. The traces, residues and reminders of muddled trajectories feed into everyday action, producing a schizophrenic landscape where vertigo reigns supreme.

TAPESTRIES

This chapter has shown that suspension and emptiness are constitutive of vertiginous life beyond the borders of Greece, being recognizable features of crisis experience embedded in European late modernity from the United Kingdom to Latvia, Greece to Bosnia and Herzegovina (on the latter, see Henig 2020; Hromadžić 2020). A time of suspension expands within the gap between the destructive dissolution of old orders – economic (Greece and Latvia) or political (the United Kingdom, Bosnia and India) – and slowly developing familiarity with emerging social and material arrangements (the so-called 'new normal'). The vernacular commonly employed to describe living in a time of suspension is emptiness. A timespace of eerie weirdness home to the unknown and unforeseen, a time of suspension between the tick of destruction and the tock of emergence is teeming with vertigo-inducing possibilities and latent potentiality. The disorientation felt with the loss of futural trajectory, the exposing and subsequent refusal of birthright expectations, and the inherent uncertainty about where the new political project is headed proves fertile ground for the affects of vertigo.

Emptiness challenges Alexia and Giovanna's navigational skills, stripped, as it is, of all familiarity, expectations and preconceptions. It is the absence of familiar markers by which to successfully orient life and navigate the emptiness of the great unknown that induces vertigo for Alexia and Giovanna. Like *Star Trek Voyager* characters adrift in the vastness of alien space, for Alexia and Giovanna, navigating the spatial, temporal and existential emptiness of suspension leads to critical self-reflection, suspicion of the new world and a frantic search for a return to normal spacetime. For now, they are trapped, incarcerated in an uncanny present with an affective structure of confusion, loss and breathlessness. Encountering and fathoming new frontiers of existence has seen life placed in 'suspended animation', implying a slowing down of time and the freezing of everyday future-oriented action. Captivity, and coming to know one's captors, is a recurrent premise of the narratives presented in this chapter and is the central theme of Chapter 5.

Alexia experiences vertiginous life caught between two 'end of the world' crises. Potentially denied futures in both her original and her adopted home, her being reverberates from the ricochets of defeated personal anticipations and shattered political assumptions. Fleeing one crisis, she hits the wall of another. Giovanna's life is similarly held in suspension, which she understands as amplifying existing geopolitical discontent between Scotland, the rest of the United Kingdom, and Europe. She has withdrawn from imaginations of future-making in the United Kingdom, just as she feels that Scotland has withdrawn from the timespace of mainstream British politics after the referendum on EU membership, and Britain as a whole has withdrawn from the once seemingly omnipotent European project. Both inhabit schizophrenic landscapes where multidirectional struggles with Self and World take place, culminating in a messy tapestry of conflicting temporalities, historicities and geopolitical conglomerations. People are torn in multiple directions at the convergence of collapsing timespaces, living in the ruins of abandoned material and temporal projects, left searching for answers as to when and where they belong.

NOTES

1. It would be tempting to include multiple disclaimers as to how emptiness differs from other proximate kin terms including ruins, rubble and vacancy. Although I find it more productive to focus on what emptiness *is* rather than what it *is not* or what it is defined *in relation to*, there are some pointers from the recent debate on distinguishing rubble from ruins that prove useful. Gordillo (2014: 9) argues that classifying objects as ruins emphasizes their pastness, detaching them from the present, underlining the Western obsession with preservation and heritage, and the 'abstracted veneration' of some material artefacts. Conversely, rubble commonly refers to shapeless and worthless debris rather than something to be protected and revered. Rubble primarily indexes destruction and failure. Emptiness is neither about venerating and ringfencing remains of the past nor reading the traces of failure in the present. The analytic goes beyond the site-specific indices of ruins and rubble to propose broader social coordinates of a specific timespace of European late modernity. Both ruins and rubble are infused with colonialist historicity and, despite attempts at transcendence, are inherently concerned with materiality. Emptiness better captures the multilayered sensibilities of the epoch of late capitalist modernity.

2. There are differences between the terms *adeios* and *kenos* that I have chosen to gloss here for the benefit of the narrative and to avoid confusion. *Adeios* usually carries no moral judgement, whereas *kenos* is often damning and a word indicating condemnation. *Adeios* can be positive, since it does not necessarily indicate the absence of something that should have been there, only of something that is usually there or that has been there. In some uses, *kenos* connotes an absolute state, something that could never be full by its very nature. Both provide slightly different 'flavours' of emptiness, but I have decided on approximations that best reflect the majority of uses in modern Greek.

3. There is a growing body of literature on so-called 'apocalyptic anthropology', from imaginations of global environmental catastrophe (Schneider-Mayerson 2015) and musings on the future of the Anthropocene (Scranton 2017) to policy-oriented scenario planning (Faubion 2019; Heemskerk 2003) and into the realms of speculative fiction (Wolf-Meyer 2019).

4. The first referendum on Scottish independence took place on 18 September 2014. A total of 55.3 per cent of voters elected to remain part of the United Kingdom, while 44.7 per cent voted to leave. After the 2016 United Kingdom referendum on EU membership, the SNP decided that the political landscape had changed sufficiently to warrant a second independence vote.

5. W.G. Sebald sets up his 1990 novel *Vertigo* in a way that the gaps and disconnects in narratives – and literary styles – provide a dizzying and often confusing read. However, the reader is left convinced that it is in these gaps, silences and deliberate aversions that deeper existential meaning is located. Writing-in gaps as part of the literary process provokes the vertigo that gives the book its title.

6. Of course, we are reminded that withdrawal from time resonates with de Martino's concept of the 'crisis of presence' and the 'dehistorification' experienced by an individual cut off from history and society.

CHAPTER 5

APHRODITE

The Captivity of Chronic Crisis

❧❧❧

On 27 March 2017, the conservative newspaper *I Kathimerini* ran an article on Greece's Stockholm Syndrome. The piece, published in the Greek economics section, discussed how living with crisis had become 'naturalized', the 'new normal', even at times 'positive', highlighting increased e-commerce, plastic (debit/credit card) transactions and reduced tax evasion (Papadogiannis 2017). Stockholm Syndrome has appeared regularly in the Greek print media to frame the experiences of a nation held captive by foreign creditors and inept political figures. Although authors offer politically nuanced opinions on accountability, Stockholm Syndrome as a trope to frame chronic crisis has adorned the pages of the national press and reflects grassroots narratives referencing the 'captivity' of crisis.[1] Captivity, I suggest, is the resonant aesthetic that propagates vertigo and signifies the suffocating inescapability of chronic crisis.

Captivity has become a recurrent theme in, and an overarching framework for, discussing life in a Time of Crisis, with characteristic affects of paralysis, nausea, suffocation and apathy. Within this book, we have encountered numerous references to captivity, imprisonment and inescapable containment. In Chapter 1, we met Mairi who, having lost her pension, having seen her business investments flounder and having partitioned her home to accommodate returning children, felt she had become a prisoner of crisis. In addition to the physical and material containment, she was being held captive by her Self, stripped of her essence to merely exist in her new role as housewife and caregiver. She discussed the violence of being torn from carefully made retirement plans and the alienation of the unknowingness of what it now was to *be* 'Mairi'. Popi, the avid gardener, was also said to be 'held captive', a slave of obsession to her vegetable patch in an atmosphere thick with fear and intimidation. For Mairi and Popi, unknowingness had become a condition of dependence, a relationship of captivity between the person, their social relations in worlds of receding horizons, and the condition of endemic crisis. Dispossessed of their previous lives, Mairi and Popi related their nausea and anxieties, the sense of an uncontrollable tailspin, to their captivity in a timespace of endless crisis. The inescapable was further textured with routinization – repetitive and obsessive behaviours. There was also an underlying tone to their narratives that suggested both women were starting to come to terms with a new normal, an acceptance that life would not return to times past.

A subtler form of captivity was raised in Chapter 2, where Dimitris described his vertigo induced by touching the old school wall. The rubble exerted a gravitational pull on him, a tractor beam from which he has never been released. He inferred that his relocation to Petrochori was a form a banishment from civilized society, somewhere he and his fellow villagers cannot leave even if they so desire. People like Dimitris felt compelled to inhabit a village that was abandoned as part of the government's dead zone policy of the 1940s, not out of desire but of necessity. At the same time, Petrochori was a 'safe place' where he could 'withdraw from fighting' the crisis, representing a modicum of comfort in captivity. He has become familiar with the space to which he was banished – a forced displacement – and has found security in his once-alien and intensely claustrophobic surroundings. On working with foreign technology, in Chapter 3, Antonis described how he trusted the structure of Troika reforms that had guided his life for nearly a decade more than he trusted his own Prime Minister's promises to rescue him from the hands of the foreign captors for which he had been forced to work. A little collaboration with the enemy, he suggested, was the best way to survive. The new occupation – this time by foreign energy companies – had detrimental consequences on his life, since renewable energy was an extractive economy, yet embracing the inescapability of the occupier-occupied, landlord–labourer, captor–captee relationship was the only way to survive the crisis years. In Chapter 4, Alexia talked of being held captive in suspended animation, blocked in by two crises from which she cannot escape. She tried to run from the Greek austerity years, only to fall into the clutches of the Brexit beast. She mentioned being imprisoned in the emptiness between two collapsing worlds, with nowhere to turn, trapped between old and new orders in a gap of destruction with crumpling temporal horizons. There was resignation that, for her at least, the world was in a state of endemic (political, economic and social) crisis and she deliberated the futility of fighting 'the system'. This had led to a paralysis feeding her sense of vertigo.

In all cases, captivity was part of the overarching framework of the narratives, while affective descriptions of suspension, collaboration and unknowingness either directly or implicitly referenced inescapability. This chapter brings the recurrent theme of captivity together with more instances where research participants communicate a foreboding sense of inescapability, of suffocation, being under surveillance, and immobilization – what Lepselter (2016: 5–7) has called 'hallmarks of captivity' defined against the 'glorification of freedom'. I ultimately argue for a scaling-up of individual captivity narratives to an overarching structure or atmosphere of societal captivity that exists in times of chronic crisis, providing the perfect environment for the proliferation of the affects of vertigo. Put bluntly, the captivity status quo produces and intensifies vertigo in multiple forms. Sometimes, routinization found in captivity provides a degree of comfort, or even generates identification, with the new normal, as suggested in numerous Greek media articles. At other times, the individual cannot move past the original rupture and remains in perpetual suspension, caught in the event horizon of the black hole of crisis. Captivity can also provoke a sense of urgency where people scramble around in a frenzied panic, searching for the exit door. Overpowered with anxiety, the desire to escape is manifested through anguish, claustrophobic palpitations and adrenaline bursts as the imminent future closes in (Anderson and Bandak n.d.). In Lepselter's (2016: 6) terms, those whose lives have been abducted by crisis experience an overspilling sensation of captivity and containment by something they cannot control, something that becomes inscribed on the body, movements and memory. The increasing familiarity with captivity (and the relationship between captees and captors) is explored here through what I have framed as Stockholm Syndrome; 'An expressive modality, a vernacular theory, a way of seeing the world, an intimation of the way *it all makes sense*' (Lepselter 2016: 4, original emphasis).

After more than a decade of structural austerity, Stockholm Syndrome as vernacular resource provides insight into how people locate themselves within the perceived permanence of crisis. On the ground, justifications for current living conditions are widespread and further illustrate how people have become accustomed to the current status quo, logicizing an era of significantly increased social suffering, vindicating the actions of the perpetrators and duly taking their deserved punishment. With crisis now endemic – becoming the 'mundane background' of daily life (Dole et. al. 2015: 7, Vigh 2008) – many of my research participants have established an intimate familiarity with living under the conditions imposed by their captors – once the so-called Troika of the European Commission, the European Central Bank and the International Monetary Fund, now unresponsive international markets and deep-rooted structural reform at the local and national levels. The strangeness of captivity has become ordinary (Lepselter 2019: 535), captivity itself proving suffocating and transformative where personal unknowingness is encompassed by a context of increasing familiarity. The individuals we have met in this book have been at different stages of identification and struggle with their captivity, the foreboding and asphyxiating atmosphere that provides coordinates for their vertigo.

We may remember that Runia poignantly argued that 'vertigo may feel like a fear of falling, but really it is a wish to jump, covered by a fear of falling ... Giving in to vertigo is a strategy for escaping from an unbearable tension by *doing* something – by breaking apart from what one used to cherish, by eating the apple, by committing an "original sin"' (2010: 2, original emphasis). Vertigo on the level of society, what Runia terms 'cultural vertigo', proliferates when the previous original sin has lost its capacity to anchor individuals in their everyday lives (2010: 18). For our purposes here, we can deduce that captivity forms the backdrop to vertigo, an atmosphere or aesthetic register. Giving in to vertigo is the acceptance of a condition of structural captivity rather than fighting for the glorified freedom that Lepselter mentions. Breaking away from the ultimately defeated life that one used to cherish may provide temporary comfort, but what about life in the *ilinx* at the foot of the cliff? There is a level of self-determination in continuing to fight the vertigo, of stepping back from the ledge or choosing to jump. In many instances in this book, the people we have met have still been fighting, perched on the clifftop making that decision. This is the condition of Mairi as she is being torn from her Self in super-slow-motion, of Alexia caught in suspension, paralysed between a rock and a hard place. However, in Petrochori, captivity provides Dimitris with solace and among the solar panels of western Thessaly Antonis has decided that collaboration with the captor is temporary relief from what Alexia referred to as 'fighting the system'.

Succumbing to vertigo, in Runia's line of thought, provides comfort when living in endemic crisis, a resignation to historical discontinuity, and in Kierkegaard's terms it is the expression of ultimate freedom, while for Serres it is a decision of the audacious individual. When leaving distant dreams of past lives to embrace what has now become a known quantity, emergence from crisis induces fear that something worse, more uncertain, the next unforeseen may be over the horizon. As crisis has become a perceived permanent condition in Greece, it has given rise to a form of societal Stockholm Syndrome as people negotiate lives without emergence, experience feelings of stuckedness, paralysis, futility and an intimate uncomfortable comfort with the captivity of chronic crisis. The vertigo-inducing captivity of being in crisis is beginning to become normalized, part of the daily routine. Here I explore how captivity is a register of vertiginous life in crisis and how some acquaintances have embraced the inescapability of the *ilinx*, however reluctantly, finding comfort in the familiarity of crisis. As such, the analysis moves away from single narratives of vertiginous life to build a wider framework for understanding affective structures of endemic crisis.

STOCKHOLM SYNDROME

In 1973, Jan-Erik Olsson attempted to rob Kreditbanken, a bank in Stockholm, Sweden. During the robbery, Olsson took four employees hostage for six days. When Olsson and his accomplice Clark Olofsson were captured and later taken to court, all four hostages refused to testify against them, instead launching a money-raising campaign for their defence. In analysing the condition of the former hostages, Swedish criminologist and psychiatrist Nils Bejerot identified a form of what has popularly been referred to as 'brainwashing', later coined by the mass media as 'Stockholm Syndrome' (Namnyak et al. 2008: 5). As well as feeling affinity or understanding for the motives and methods of the captor as a survival strategy, other characteristics of Stockholm Syndrome include wanting to remain in or later return to the place of captivity, maintaining a relationship with the captors, feeling extreme anxiety about life after captivity and futility for the hostage situation.[2] Stockholm Syndrome is existentially paradoxical, in that the sentiments captees feel towards their captors oppose the distain an onlooker might express.

Stockholm Syndrome, it has been argued, can be both a personal psychological condition and a societal issue shared by a group living through the same transformative conditions (Graham 1994). The primary concern in both cases is simply survival. Rather than talking about symptoms, Philip Pilevsky (1989) proposes in his influential work *Captive Continent* that the criteria of societal Stockholm Syndrome can be identified in groups, objects and nations enmeshed in a long-term relationship of dependence and exploitation. It is on these terms that I suggest that Stockholm Syndrome can be used as a 'vernacular resource' (Adorjan et al. 2012) to scale-up individual narratives of vertigo to a more structural attempt to frame societal reactions to, and relationships within, an endemic Time of Crisis.[3] The permanent state of crisis in Greece has fostered increasing feelings that resistance is futile to conditions of chronic austerity, creating an affective structure of Stockholm Syndrome marked by an intimate uncomfortable comfort with living in perpetual crisis, defeating hopes of futural change.[4] The personal unknowingness and the spatiotemporal displacement associated with life in chronic crisis is enshrined within an overpowering atmosphere of captivity. While providing a recognized reference point for the new normal of everyday life, the inescapability, routinization and even comfort and familiarity of crisis propagates an intensely pressurized atmosphere in which vertigo thrives.[5]

In the anthropological literature, captivity is often described as a transformative atmosphere or aesthetic that is difficult to define ethnographically (Berlant 2011; Lepselter 2019; O'Neill 2019; O'Neill and Dua 2019). Writing on Pentecostal drug rehabilitation centres in Guatemala, Kevin Lewis O'Neill (2019) employs the work of Gernot Böhme to better portray the situation of captivity: '[one] can be caught by an atmosphere', an aesthetic impression, a 'space with a certain tone of feeling' (Böhme 2017: 12). The atmosphere of captivity, O'Neill elaborates, contains 'affective, emotional resonances' that are 'nebulous and vaporous, that ... are difficult to grasp' for the onlooker. Yet the atmosphere of captivity surely 'grabs' those in its vicinity, enclosing them in an inescapable aesthetic (O'Neill 2019: 541). It is in precisely this atmosphere of captivity that my ethnographic analysis of vertigo plays out, among people gripped by affective, emotional, nebulous incarceration, in a situation that the outside world may find difficult to justify or comprehend. The outcome of entangled histories and social relations, the Stockholm Syndrome experienced in Greece refers to conditions not of a fortified location (see e.g. Reed 2003; Scheele 2019), but of the captivity of the mind as discussed by Mairi, of spatiotemporal displacement and trust found in unorthodox places as mentioned by Antonis, of Dimitris being banished to the rubble of an uninhabited village with an inescapable gravitational pull, of Alexia being trapped in suspended animation, mid-air, mid-life and mid-continent. In all cases, lives are at least partially orchestrated by an abstract punitive Other, while people attempt to maintain a degree of self-determination. In Böhme's words, it is the inescapable atmosphere of crisis that infiltrates the proverbial lungs, overrunning the body and providing the all-encompassing aesthetic that results in reports of dizziness, being lost, stasis, temporal displacement and physical sickness. Stockholm Syndrome is a vernacular that is part of the affective structure of the era, signalling how people relate to lives without emergence, feelings of stuckedness, futility and captivity; it is a way of seeing, making sense of and coming to terms with a radically altered existence.

FEAR

'I fear the future', Aphrodite tells me as we walk through the bustling streets of the Monday market in late 2017. 'Years ago, I could not wait to escape this crisis, the pressures of new taxes, the anxiety of constantly pending unemployment, the crazy political talk that surrounds us every day. But now we have all learned to cope.' A self-employed 38-year-old mother of two, Aphrodite echoes the views of an increasing number of my research participants when she states that people have become accustomed to living in

crisis: 'We are surrounded by crisis 24 hours a day, seven days a week ...
wherever you look.' A decade on and the latest episodes of the neverending
saga continue to be played out around the clock on television and in the daily
newspapers: 'The electricity bill on my kitchen table announcing the most
recent tax hikes, my son's secondhand clothes, when I ride my bicycle to
work [Aphrodite sold her car in 2012 as it was too expensive to run], these
are the everyday things that remind you that crisis is here to stay. They stalk
you at every turn.'

For Greek youth, a Time of Crisis is all they have known. The crisis
generation have been raised in a world where the vernacular is austerity,
memoranda, occupation, neocolonialism and Troika; the key affects being
suppression, nausea, disenchantment and, more recently, apathy and exhaustion towards the future. Everyday existence that once included promises of material accumulation, prosperous futures based on education, high
personal expectations and anticipations, all associated with life in twenty-
first century Europe, has disintegrated. This ruination is what Lewis G. Gordon, writing on the permanence of catastrophe in the post-financial crisis
age, calls a 'cultural disaster' that 'leads to a rallying of forces against the
future. It demands sacrifice of the young' (2015: 138).

In conversation with Aphrodite in 2014, she mentioned how she had
'given up' fighting the economic crisis that was infiltrating every aspect of
her daily life. For her, and many others, it was a choice between either accepting the status quo or, in her words, 'going mad': 'Eventually, if you listen
to all the commentators on the television, continue to discuss the crisis with
friends, or pay too much attention to the bills on your table, you will fall
sick, collapse, or contemplate suicide' (on suicide in the Greek crisis, see
Davis (2015)). She says that the crisis is permanent and 'singular', and 'the
Greek people have accepted that ... We are hostages to great forces that are
too abstract to fight ... we have adapted and learned to survive, however sick
that makes us'. She succumbed to the cliff-edge decision, no longer feeling
able to fight as her world was engulfed by the thick smog of crisis. But poignantly, she insists that she and her friends are now 'comfortable' with crisis,
that they 'know how to navigate' the suffocating consequences of austerity
enforced by their 'occupiers' that have 'suppressed' them for so long. She
has found what Olga Shevchenko (2009: 9) working in a post-socialist context has termed 'the competent navigation of a perpetual crisis'. Talk of a
post-crisis future, Aphrodite adds, 'only makes people more anxious to the
point of physically vomiting with the fear of the unknown', leading back to
the vertiginous state that 'wrecks you from the inside'. To stay put, she sol-
emnly looks me directly in the eye and shuffles to the edge of the couch opposite as if she is about to confide in me some deeply secretive and sinister

plan, 'is the best we can hope for ... we have learned to put the two pieces together, to connect our former [pre-crisis] hopes with our new reality'.

In the summer of 2014, the then Greek Prime Minister Antonis Samaras made a bold statement that got my research participants contemplating the potential futures of a post-crisis nation. That May, he triumphantly announced: 'There is growth ... we have come out of crisis ... Greece can once again borrow money ... we can get loans ... we did it together, we have officially emerged from the crisis.' Intended to encourage hopeful momentum towards a better future and speculation about what a society emerging from protracted crisis might look like, the Prime Minister's words on yet another false dawn instead provoked fear, anxiety and a feeling of being trapped in an endless cycle of broken promises. People seemed more ready to trust the current regime of Troika austerity than place their faith in the Prime Minister's pledge to rescue the nation.

The Prime Minister's claims that Greece was emerging from crisis stimulated talk about how local people had come to terms with living with the consequences of chronic fiscal austerity. 'We have just got used to it and we can't face change. There is security in staying put', Aphrodite explained, 'at least we have come to know the occupiers, the authorities that hold us captive, so well that we can guess their next moves.' She likened the atmosphere of chronic crisis to a box 'from which there is no escape ... there are four walls that you can lean against, peer out of, but there are no cracks to shimmy through'; Caillois' narrow door with a chink of light for future-making has well and truly been slammed shut. Aphrodite's words confirmed what I had been hearing from other friends and research participants in the field – that some Greeks had become accustomed and habituated to the idea of emergence as a repetitive cyclical process that feeds a sense of stasis rather than momentum and change. The intimacy felt with the crisis situation means that any discussion of emergence is met at best with apathy, often ridicule and sometimes remarkable fear as the future becomes an illusion that is difficult to sustain (Gutiérrez Garza 2018: 96).

On one of my regular visits to the cafeterias on Asklipiou, Trikala's Main Street, my long-term friend Athina, a 31-year-old barwoman with a university degree, elaborates on the apathy felt towards promises of emergence and the relative comfort in 'knowing' crisis: 'It is old news; we have heard it all before. Again and again they tell us that the crisis is over, that we are out of crisis. The economy is improving, and the rest of the world trusts us [economically] again. You feel like you are experiencing déjà vu, going round in circles, that the political speeches and people's everyday lives are stuck and continuously repeating, round and round in circles. It makes you dizzy. It's a neverending swirling pool.' Athina says that people now 'know what they

need to do to survive' in the 'permanent atmosphere of crisis' and, fearing
that 'one colonial program' of dispossession will simply be replaced by another, she insists that she is 'happy to remain in a state of suffocating delir-
ious dizziness' that she feels with the current status quo. She also observes
that the crisis 'happened for a reason', believing that 'we had it coming, after
decades of money, living the good life, we needed to be put back in our place.
This is our life now, living in the cage of a foreign captor'. She says that she
understands why Greece has been forced into a decade of austerity, but does
not believe that people have learned their lesson quite yet, 'if ever'. For her,
the permanent captivity of crisis does induce vertigo – she is suffocating,
dizzy and going round in circles, critiquing her life trajectory and in some
conversations even referencing her belief that she is living in an elsewhen of
wartime Greece. The visual image she projects is of an animal striding up and
down inside its tiny cage, repeating the same routine of pacing round in circles, going stir crazy. She finds it difficult to reconcile her life in the pre-crisis
years with her current everyday routine. But, she insists, the atmosphere of
austerity can also be pedagogical. Her greatest fear is that emergence from
crisis will lead to her fellow citizens reverting to their old ways of excess and
abundance, resulting in a more hostile programme of dispossession by a new
captor.

   A poignant discussion with a privately employed travelling salesman on
an intercity bus service brought home just how resigned some people have
become to living out their lives in endemic crisis and how the landscape of
political subjectivity has been radically altered over the course of a decade.
During a five-hour journey between two mainland Greek cities, I met Apostolis. The precariously employed 55-year-old father of one who had once
joined anti-austerity protests on the streets of the Greek capital in 2010–11
explained how he had now 'calmed down' and learned to accept a protracted
crisis: 'It's OK. Not too bad. You might still hear moaning and anger from
some people, but this is generally a façade, in my opinion. Most people have
learned how to survive, to find their way, no matter what transformations
they may have endured.' Despite losing his job in the public sector and taking
a major hit on his pension as part of the structural austerity imposed by the
Troika, Apostolis seems most forgiving, emphasizing that: 'We can't blame
them really [the Troika]. We [Greece] were the bad boys of Europe and had
to be put back in our place.' He once thought that he would be able to bide
his time until the crisis passed 'like a blustery storm rocking the ship'. He
went through the stage of fighting the inevitable, desperately trying to cling
to his past life, his futural desires and battling the riptide of deeply engrained
structural change. Now, a decade in, he has resigned himself to the fact that
he will spend all his life inside the *ilinx*, 'with somebody else dictating' what
he can and cannot do: 'And my son and daughter-in-law will [spend their

lives in crisis] too. But it's OK, I mean, what can you do? I understand the reasons why it has to be like this.'

These stories may sit uncomfortably with the reader and it is not my intention to act as advocate for the pedagogical qualities of austerity politics. Yet the vignettes provided by Aphrodite, Athina and Apostolis represent how people have become exhausted with a decade of crisis talk and are trapped in a perceived permanent present with an increasing inability to project imaginations for potential futures. Their narratives attest to how endemic crisis has bred an uncomfortable comfort with the present and a fear of what lies over the futural threshold – in the words of one of my Greek relatives, 'most people have now found their nest and are quite comfortable with what they have and don't want it to change'. The obsession with the present, the stuckedness of life with no trajectory, is itself vertigo-inducing. The repetition of the same timespace, something Athina describes as déjà vu and Aphrodite likened to living within the four walls of a glass box, hint at the affective vexations of captivity – familiarity and normalization are not remedies, but often intensify a sense of mounting suffocation. Yet, in the manner proposed by Runia (2010: 1), they have given in to the 'unbearable tension' between desires and reality that create vertigo, breaking away from the point of unknowingness that has so ravished many characters in this book. Now vertigo is not so much associated with decision-making while teetering on the edge of the abyss, but more to do with negotiating life inside the *ilinx*.

Justifications for current living conditions are widespread and the level of acceptance for the state of permanent crisis further illustrates how people have become accustomed to the chronic state of affairs, logicizing an era of significantly increased social suffering, vindicating the actions of the perpetrators and duly taking their 'deserved' punishment. Although as an author and anthropologist I do not necessarily condone the stance that Greeks are taking their deserved punishment and that austerity rightfully put the bad boys of Europe 'back in their place', the drip-dripping of this didactic narrative over the course of a decade has noticeably affected how people relate both to the foreign creditors and to their own past lives. In this respect, perhaps one can understand Bejerot's stance on how elongated crisis acts as a form of brainwashing. Athina is 'happy to remain' in the 'cage', caught in the affective, emotional but also pedagogical clutch of her captors. Aphrodite says that 'to stay put' is the best that she can hope for the future. All three express a level of understanding for why the structural austerity that led to the current circumstances had to be enforced upon their nation. All place more faith in the knowable lives of crisis imposed by foreign captors than in promises of emergence pledged by their own democratically elected government.

The disillusion with the concept of emergence from crisis is closely linked to the public acknowledgement of crisis not as a rupture in the normal progression towards late capitalist modernity, but rather a chronic, endemic, ever-present state of existence (Vigh 2008). Regardless of their political persuasion, people report that austerity is now permanent and something that they have learned to live with. We have seen that in the timespace of crisis, there is a collective sense of living in an era that has a particular temporality with a set of ways to express experiences of the period. Stockholm Syndrome, I suggest, can be employed as a resource or trope to further define the affective structure associated with the perceived permanence of the timespace of crisis.

VERNACULARS

A Time of Crisis in Greece is marked by a sense of permanence and inescapability, discussed by many people in terms of uncomfortable comfort, coping and intimate familiarity. Paralysis and stasis mark the temporal rhythm and speed. As futural orientation, the epochal paralysis is at odds with the momentum associated with hope, for instance. Hope is a form of futural momentum, vehemently pressing into the future when people imagine how potentialities can become actuality. Hope helps people cross the futural threshold, drawing into the present that which does not exist, but potentially could (Bryant and Knight 2019; Manley 2019a). Whereas hope provides momentum towards an indeterminate something, towards the actuation of aspiration, a Time of Crisis is defined by stasis, presentism, stuckedness and captivity. Suggestions of emergence from the epoch of crisis, as proposed by former Prime Minister Samaras, induce intense anxiety as to what is over the futural horizon and on occasion entice people to defend their hardship – and lack of future – as justified and somehow deserved. This has led to the narratives of people like Aphrodite, Athina and Apostolis that speak of a societal Stockholm Syndrome, a potent atmosphere of familiar captivity.

The future is unimaginable outside of crisis, or at least is perceived as a place of emptiness or filled with fear. The future is more dangerous than now familiar crisis that somewhat paradoxically offers a place of security in the known world. The Time of Crisis in Greece is a place of coping, familiarity and maintenance, where people have fashioned a space of self-determination from the ashes of international bailout programmes and personal financial turmoil. Learning to live with drastically decreased household income, policy attacks on healthcare, energy and property rights, and yet slowly being able to justify the actions of the oppressors is central to the analysis of the affective structure of a Time of Crisis being likened to Stockholm Syndrome.

Crisis now commands a monopoly over every possible future, such that the idea of a future catastrophe has become a real force in the ordering of lives and worlds in the present. Crisis has taken hold as both a backdrop to and a condition for the intimate terrain of everyday lives. 'Crisis time' orders everyday life beyond the original event,[6] becoming a form of governance (Dole et al. 2015) and a narrative tool driving the era (Roitman 2014). Crisis here breaches the classic event-driven reading of history (Ahmann) to order the mundane as a form of background noise (Serres) or atmosphere (Böhme) that continues to prey on its subjects. One of my research participants, a left-leaning 48-year-old public sector worker named Christos, says that he feels Greece has been 'suspended in time' by the economic crisis, caught in a perpetual present in what he refers to as 'a crisis that has lasted a lifetime' that has left him 'spinning on the spot, like a top'. A Time of Crisis is all that anyone under the age of twenty-five has ever known – there is no experiential reality of adult life outside of this epoch. The younger generation now report having written-off their future as based on 'more of the same' and express apathy, disillusion and often disinterest when asked to imagine a post-crisis Greece. The older generations have disassociated themselves with the future as, in the words of one informant in her sixties, 'we won't be around to live it [the future]. We will only ever live what we have now [the crisis], so there is no need to prepare for the future' (see Knight 2016). Lives have become depleted of futural imaginings (Gutiérrez Garza 2018: 96).

These stances invoke what Rebecca Bryant has called the 'uncanny present' – the feeling of being trapped in an elongated present where the 'succession of nows', in Heideggerian terms, never presses into the future. Instead, there is hyperconscious awareness of the continuous presence of the present (Heidegger 1972: x). For Bryant (2016: 20), at a Time of Crisis, 'we acquire a sense that what we do in this present will be decisive for both the past and the future, giving to the present the status of a threshold'. Crisis, she claims, becomes such precisely because it brings the present into consciousness, creating an awareness or perception of presentness that we do not normally have: the present becomes uncanny. The present feels distorted and disturbed due to the looming edifice of crisis leaking through its cracks.

At first glance, Bryant's argument seems pertinent to unpacking the extended presentism expressed in austerity Greece, yet on closer inspection of the above narratives, the decision moment seems not to hold as much importance in the manner Bryant suggests, because the present is no longer under stress from the past and future since crisis has ceased 'leaking through the cracks'; it has become all-encompassing and permanent. My research participants imply that in many cases, the present is elongated and inescapable, but there is no futural threshold to cross. The decision moment, the standing on the proverbial cliff-edge, is the rupture of disassociating with the pre-crisis past, rewriting life histories in Runia's sense. In some instances, people indicate that decisions in a Time of Crisis simply do not matter, since crisis is inescapable and authored by forces beyond the control of the everyday person. The post-crisis future is either not in sight or wholly undesirable. Christos, the public sector worker, insists that the inscrutable future is no longer a desired destination when considered alongside the knowable present – 'we have just learned to adapt', he says, 'to the radically altered way of life ... the future doesn't offer me anything. Even with all this suffering around me, today I have found my own safe place [in the world]'. He says that he is 'disinterested in the future' and that 'the world is stuck in crisis and I just have to get on with it, stop moaning, and accept it ... It must have happened for a reason and I now know that I have to accept it'. Like Alexia in Chapter 4, Christos discusses the future in terms of emptiness and exhaustion, as an undesirable timespace to inhabit. His focus is on maintaining the present, despite acknowledging the continued consequences of economic crisis that nearly all my informants believe to be imposed by the international community against the will of the Greek people. Christos concludes that 'the future doesn't have anything for me ... at least here I have my job, a few euros for the supermarket and a roof over my head. I have learned ... all Greeks have learned ... to be happy with that. To get by on what we are given and no longer ask too many questions'.

We can observe similar futural orientations expressed elsewhere in crisis-ridden Europe and, as Dzenovska has argued, an ethnographic focus on themes such as emptiness and maintenance can provide insightful critiques of how a Time of Crisis has impacted how people affectively invest (or not) in the future. For Dzenovska, during the economic crisis in Latvia, migration away from the deindustrialized, rapidly emptying countryside to work in rural England is an act of seeking futures past, namely of stable employment and small-scale financial prosperity. Remaining in the emptying Latvian countryside is a political act where people create the future as a little bit more of the present – a present of austerity and scarcity that is traded for 'the sense of making life go on for a little bit longer' (2018: 20). Her informants cling to the epoch of crisis and find comfort in its familiarity. The future-oriented action of migrating is undesirable and suffering the consequences of crippling internationally imposed austerity measures is understood as both a political and a pedagogical necessity. In a comparable case, this time set in the context of a post-industrial German city, Ringel offers critique of the past–present–future relation through the lens of maintenance. In some instances, he argues, future-oriented actions may include endurance, permanence and desires to maintain the present as future. People strive to maintain their current living conditions through endurance and sustainability in the face of unwanted accelerated change (Ringel 2014, 2018: 25; on accelerated change as a facet of modernity, see Eriksen (2016a, 2016b)).

Similar to Dzenovska's and Ringel's informants, Christos, Aphrodite, Apostolis and Athina are seeking to maintain the present despite the hardship of everyday life. They have managed to disassociate with the pre-crisis past, giving in to the unbearable tension between their lives then and now. Although perhaps difficult to understand for outside observers, the wish to continue in a Time of Crisis rather than invest in imaginations of an emergent post-crisis future is based on a decade of toil trying to negotiate how best to accommodate the everyday pressures of crisis into family and work life. Further, the acceptance of crisis as chronic condition is at least in part a lasting effect of a string of broken promises from Greek politicians and local councillors that has led to disillusion and apathy. 'The desire for cultural continuity in the face of a decaying capacity to imagine a future that resembles the present', Gordon (2015: 126) suggests, 'leads to the ossification of the present in the name of preservation.' In Gordon's view, permanence as a primary temporal aspect of crisis can be considered more devastating than apocalyptic scenarios of annihilation and extinction since the latter leaves nothing for reflection – in this scenario there would be no survivors left to comprehend its significance. As much as we might associate rupture and unknowingness with vertigo, the permanence of crisis is a vertiginous state, in that acknowledging the endlessness of a life in captivity emphasizes the utter futility of existence. One can never raise one's head above the suffocating smog of crisis. The permanence of crisis may also provoke frenzied urgency as the realization dawns that the timespace is inescapable.

How chronic crisis has settled into every aspect of existence is expertly portrayed by a precariously employed forty-year-old research participant Kostas, a car mechanic, when he says: 'When you realize there is no end to crisis, that you can trust the promises of nobody, you seek sanctuary in that which you know. I know how to live in the crisis.' Providing for a family of four during the austerity years, Kostas states that only he can 'defend' the family from further harm inflicted by 'those who have big ideas about the future of Greece, but we know that they do not care any more than our current occupiers'. When I quiz Kostas to further explain his desires to maintain current political and economic conditions even when politicians and bureaucrats are boldly claiming a bright future for the emergent post-crisis Greek nation, he says: 'I know that you [outsiders] might not understand it. It might seem strange. But fighting for our future now seems futile. We no longer know who to trust and who is lying. I laugh at them all and just say "I will focus on my own life" and for that I need security ... I have become familiar with crisis. I know it [crisis] and the rules [of the creditors]. What comes after is too uncertain. I don't know how to find direction outside of crisis. I do not believe that it is anything better [than what we have now] and I can't put my family through it.' He places more trust in his current captors – who he sees as 'northern European neoliberals … Germans and big banks' – than in his own government that offers promises of emergence. Further, he feels that in the atmosphere of crisis he can navigate his life, his ravished subjectivity, according to familiar trig-points, and cannot invest in the darkness of a future unknown.

This seemingly illogical preference to remain in a Time of Crisis, with the associated personal and collective anguish, decreased living standards, stresses and anxieties, is the vernacular of Stockholm Syndrome that marks the epoch. Within the timespace of crisis, people have managed to find a degree of self-determination and after years of struggle and protest, they convey a sense of security and stability in the familiar environment of crisis. The self-determination in reference to crisis helps people preserve some form of stability in everyday life (cf. Shevchenko 2009: 9). Stockholm Syndrome can thus be utilized as a vernacular resource to help unpack the affective structure of a Time of Crisis and pull together the narrative strands of people resigned to a life held captive in the coordinates of an apparently chronic condition.

SCALING-UP

In prominent cases of long-term captivity where confinement has become seemingly permanent, it is not unusual for an intimate bond to be formed between captee, captor and the physical space of captivity. Some examples from the literature on Stockholm Syndrome help identify the atmosphere of captivity and the affects, emotions and supposed pedagogies that can be scaled-up to describe nonpathological vernaculars of captivity on a societal level. Kidnapped at the age of ten, Natascha Kampusch was held for eight years and was submitted to physical abuse and mistreatment. After her release and her kidnapper's subsequent death, Kampusch kept a picture of her captor in her wallet. She later bought the house in which she was imprisoned, claiming that she wanted to protect it from dereliction, regularly visiting to clean the property. She recognized the role of the house in her formative years, during which she reports having managed to find space in her life for normal activities, such as reading to educate herself and listening to the radio (Kole 2006). In another example, twenty-year-old Colleen Stan was held captive in California for over seven years. On occasion, she was allowed to go out jogging and care for the family's children on her own. With an open door and a telephone, she made no attempt to escape, even when permitted to visit her family by herself four years into her captivity. The next day, she was collected by her captor, posing for a photograph together, before returning to captivity (Green 2009).

As I have suggested in this book, the physical and psychological effects of Stockholm Syndrome are not confined to individuals in hostage situations, but can be scaled-up to a societal level to be descriptive of relationships between groups, objects, nations and deities on whom someone may be dependent (Lepselter 2019; Pilevsky 1989: xi). Characteristics associated with societal Stockholm Syndrome that are pertinent to the Greek context include fear of life post-captivity, temporal disorientation, guilt for one's imprisonment, and dependence on and justification of the captor. In the need to prioritize survival amid drastically altered social conditions, it has been argued that captees displace the 'impulse to hate the person who has created the dilemma' (Adorjan et al. 2012). Coping methods are relatively quickly developed, including genuine feelings of commitment to the new conditions of life as the captee begins to convince themself that the only way to survive is to establish an attachment to the captor. In the international relations literature, Stockholm Syndrome as a trope has been used to define the relationship between Western Europe and the former Soviet Union in the late 1980s, where Western European governments were trusting their enemy (the Soviet Union) and questioning their long-term ally (the United States) (Pilevsky 1989). For Pilevsky, Western Europe became, in a profound way, a captive of the Soviet Union; a relationship based on fear and dependence where Western Europe began increasingly to identify with its captor at the expense of the United States.

In the context of the latter years of the Cold War, Stockholm Syndrome was employed as a vernacular resource that referenced societal relations during a transformative epoch, and it is in this manner that I believe it provides a useful discursive framework to think through the affective structure of a Time of Crisis. The perspectives described by my research participants – paralysis, justification for their punishment, security in entrapment, fear of life outside the timespace of crisis – echo the indicators of people involved in an intimate relationship with their captors, where survival is of foremost concern.

In a similar manner, the trope further resonates with Lepselter's (2019: 6) accounts of abductees who are stalked, tracked, silenced and paralysed, all the while being calmed and pacified by their abductors, making it nigh on impossible to break free. With endemic crisis, as with the experience of abductees, there is the 'overspilling sensation of captivity and containment by something you can't control ... unseen forces that inscribed your body and tracked your movements'. Yet, in our case, since the containment is being enforced by a bureaucratic arrangement and interstate governance, the story is shaded with overtones of suffering for a greater good, identified by Lepselter as civic benevolence, progress, enlightenment (2019: 49) and being held against one's will to 'be converted to the wonders of modernity'

(2019: 47). There is no one identifying trait that links all stories of captivity or Stockholm Syndrome, but rather an underlying resonance, a vernacular poetics, a pattern and structure beneath the surface of things (2019: 47).

Stockholm Syndrome is a useful tool in analysing everyday explanations of the crisis and desires for the future, furthering an attempt to populate the affects and orientations of a Time of Crisis. In employing the term, I do not intend to pathologize crisis in a way that detracts from agency and creativity (cf. Theodossopoulos 2014). On the contrary, coping with crisis under Troika captivity led to many people fashioning a space of self-determination within the confines of austerity; permanent crisis does not necessarily equal total destruction. With sovereignty removed, people have invested a great deal of emotion and energy into finding coping strategies that transcend the renegotiated living conditions of often extreme poverty and precarity. They have chiselled out a space within a Time of Crisis in which they can survive.

Epochal thinking is central to ethnographic observations of Stockholm Syndrome, in that crisis should never have been permanent. The event – the capture of Greece by international creditors – was supposed to be but a fleeting moment, a temporary digression from progression towards late capitalist promises of utopia. Instead, the rupture has become a chronic state of affairs, meaning that people feel that they have had to accept their fate, cease protest and adjust to the long-term prospect of, in Christos' words, 'a crisis that has lasted a lifetime'. Like a captor, the Troika created unparalleled stress through unending negotiations and manoeuvres, dressing up their most threatening deeds with a human face. The Troika carried out their mission by attempting to provide a human disposition to try to bury the fact that the international politics of the austerity years reflected very little humanity in the first place (cf. Pilevsky 1989: xiii).[7] To paraphrase Lepselter working with neurodivergent young people, the disorientation caused by the creators of crisis fed a 'public culture of captivity' forming a 'taste of containment' that has become popularized into a powerful ubiquitous vernacular, apparent both in the media and at the grassroots level (Lepselter 2019: 534). Captivity is part of the dramatically transformed political subjectivity, diverging the typical as defined by the world at large. For Lepselter, captivity is 'an atmosphere of the moment' with multifaceted affective levels: 'Sometimes you feel you are held captive by your own mind; sometimes you are held captive by the expectations and structures that never fit. You are held captive by the orientation of a mind to a world' (2019: 537). These complicated nebulous layers that form the atmosphere of captivity contribute to the epochal experience of crisis.

Once considered in epochal terms, permanence becomes a key feature of the timespace of crisis, increasing the feeling that one is held captive. The commonly held perception, Slavoj Žižek (2014: 4–5) tells us, is that the crisis event denotes 'the surprising emergence of something new which undermines every stable scheme'. The event is 'shocking, out of joint' and 'interrupts the usual flow of things' (Žižek 2014: 2). But in Greece, crisis *has* become the 'usual flow' and the 'stable scheme' that provides what Veena Das (1995) calls a 'reference point' for everyday life. It is true that when the economic crisis hit in 2009, the event shattered ordinary life, it was a rupture, 'a transformation of reality' (Žižek 2014: 2) that acted as a 'transcendental placeholder ... a means for signifying contingency' (Roitman 2014: 320). But now the event consumes all life and has been turned into a symbolic resource with which people identify and orient their worlds. Crisis talk now performs a permanent communicative function, allowing people rhetorical transitions between topics and a way to justify socially problematic scenarios associated with poverty and loss (Shevchenko 2009: 74).

Working in post-socialist Moscow, sociologist Olga Shevchenko has written a thesis on the routinization of crisis, or what she calls 'the permanence of temporary conditions' (2009: 62). Many aspects of life in Moscow after socialism are relatable to the Greek case. Expecting rapid change after the political rupture of the late 1980s, Shevchenko found that for the majority of Muscovites, the post-crisis era brought a continuation of a Time of Crisis. Akin to how Greeks discuss their concerns that emergence will bring another, perhaps more punitive politico-economic regime, Muscovites lamented that post-socialism offered no stability, no change: 'life was unfolding in crisis all the time' (Shevchenko 2009: 17). Shevchenko suggests that over previous decades, Muscovites had become intimate with a framework of permanent crisis within which they had managed to develop an entire infrastructure of coping whose 'permanence would match the permanence of crisis and prevent it from disrupting one's life' (2009: 63). Shevchenko claims that crisis had become the 'new habitus', since people reacted to its permanence by fashioning equally permanent ways of dealing with a life in perpetual crisis.

In the same manner that people in Greece talk of having learned to cope with a Time of Crisis in an intimate relationship that provides a sense of security and familiarity, in Moscow the chronic nature of the event had led to a normalization of crisis, and rupturing the status quo was undesirable. Within the total crisis framework, coping strategies had led to people finding their own spaces to determine life within the constraints imposed by outside forces. There were possibilities for life within the remit of a Time of Crisis. This is very similar to what people report when they discuss having 'learned to live' in the timespace of crisis in Greece, no longer 'fighting the regime', but 'giving in' and 'finding a way to get on with life, whatever that might now look like'. This is where the vertiginous affects of captivity cease being psychological, belonging solely to the individual, and also become a shared cultural phenomenon (Runia 2010: 17).

This leads back to thinking about the intimacy felt with the permanence of crisis in terms of Stockholm Syndrome. The normalization of a time of intense suffering – when the event loses its eventedness –, denigrating livelihood reforms imposed by outside forces, and the fear of change all resonate with this analytical category. Victims of long-term captivity, for instance, are regularly reported to be permitted a degree of freedom within the strict boundaries set down by their captors whereby they can participate in everyday activities such as housework, gardening, going to the supermarket or, in the case of Natascha Kampusch, being taken on holidays or to neighbourhood parties. Upon their release, some discuss how they had found small spaces for self-determination within a life of extreme suppression.

In Greece, Stockholm Syndrome captures the affective structure of a Time of Crisis, an epoch experienced as permanent. As a vernacular resource, it helps explain on a societal level the catchwords, affects and orientations that people embody and that have become signifiers of the era. Engaging in conversations with people like Aphrodite or Christos about their desires, their futural trajectories, perceptions on emergence, and understandings of how and why crisis came to be, one cannot but help draw parallels with the criteria of Stockholm Syndrome scaled-up not as pathology, but as an explanatory tool framing the shared experiences of endemic conditions shaped by inescapability.[8]

COMFORT

Captivity is the resonant aesthetic that propagates vertigo and signifies the suffocating inescapability of chronic crisis. It is the connecting thread, the haunting *something*, that links so many stories. In this chapter, vertigo has been not so much associated with decision-making while teetering on the edge of the abyss, but more with navigating life inside the *ilinx* once the inescapability of crisis has been recognized. Clinging to past lives has been replaced by an uncomfortable comfort of inhabiting the uncanny familiarity of the *ilinx*. Captivity in the *ilinx* of crisis generates an atmosphere of suffocation, as the violence of routinization plays out on body and mind.

It may be unpalatable to recognize that some people have found an uncomfortable comfort in living in a Time of Crisis and outwardly express a desire to maintain the status quo, often acknowledging the reasons behind their current torment. In Greece, a Time of Crisis is a timespace marked by the affective structure of Stockholm Syndrome – a set of feelings and beliefs that orient action for people living in a permanent state of crisis. Crisis is no longer a rupture, but a normalized routine in which people have fashioned some form of existence within parameters of drastically restricted income, decreased materialism, fragmented family relations and a public rhetoric emphasizing psychological warfare waged by Northern European creditors. Some see the Time of Crisis as pedagogical and many justify as reasonable the severe austerity measures handed down by international creditors given the preceding decades of financial indulgence.

It is common in the existing literature to encounter the so-called 'Greek crisis' as a timespace defined by protest, resistance and solidarity (Cabot 2016; Rakopoulos 2016; Theodossopoulos 2014); however, I suggest that these actions are not structural, but rather performative instances that often take place quite spectacularly in the public eye and detract from quotidian activities, pressures and the temporalities of everyday life. Put simply, for people like Christos, the primary concern is keeping a job and putting food on the table, 'not throwing Molotov cocktails' or even 'being my neighbour's best friend'. His priority is to maintain the daily rhythm of waking up, working an eight-hour shift and paying his rent at the end of the month. He knows that 'even if exploited ... even with a knife held to the throat holding me captive', it is 'essential to maintain the situation that offers my family security'. He states that he has 'fashioned a place in the world ... somewhere we have intimately come to know'. He quite powerfully declares that one should be 'suspicious of life outside of the crisis ... don't ever trust what they offer you' and proposes that 'collaboration with the captors, as the past has shown us, is sometimes the only decision'.[9]

Like Christos, Athina is proud of how she has learned to survive the oppressive consequences of a decade of austerity. 'You do feel trapped', she says, but 'we have found minor triumphs. We are survivors'. Athina and Christos are partaking in what Victoria Goddard, working in Naples, has highlighted to be 'the art of managing, of making do', the vital ways of 'keeping individuals and households alive' during crisis (Goddard 1996: 50). Part of the staying alive involves an everyday intimacy with captivity, a deep-grained fear of post-crisis, and justification for current conditions. The post-crisis future is viewed with suspicion, foreboding, a lack of trust based on the broken promises of the proximate past and a feeling that the next captors are just over the horizon.

Crisis in Greece now provides the background noise and directional apparatus for everyday life. Stockholm Syndrome is a vernacular resource that helps unpack the affective structure of a Time of Crisis, marked by permanence and inescapability. People express an intimate uncomfortable comfort with living in perpetual crisis and Stockholm Syndrome is a useful tool for scaling pervading explanations for wanting to maintain a Time of Crisis enforced by foreign captors in the face of promises of emergence. I emphasize that it is not my intention to pathologize a Time of Crisis, thus foregoing agency and creativity to navigate the social milieu. Coping with crisis under

Troika captivity, despite unthinkably restructured political subjectivity, has led to people moulding spaces of compromised self-determination within the confines of permanent economic and political suppression. It is precisely this familiarity, with its navigable star chart, that people seek to maintain, regardless of the asphyxiating circumstances.

We might recall how Kostas describes how he trusts the structure of Troika reforms that have guided his life for nearly a decade more than he trusts his own Prime Minister's promises to rescue him from the hands of foreign captors. We can pause for critical reflection on Athina's statement of how she believes that Greeks have 'learned nothing' from living in the destitution of crisis and 'had it coming' after decades of 'living the good life'. Aphrodite says that she has accepted the status quo of living under the thumb of 'foreign occupiers', while Christos describes having found his 'safe place' in the 'here and now', accepting that Greece is locked into permanent paralysis by powers he can 'no longer fight'. This is the vernacular of Stockholm Syndrome that populates the timespace of chronic crisis. In Lepselter's words, it is an expressive modality, a way of making sense of the world.

Captivity has been a recurring theme throughout this book and the intention of this chapter was to build on individual narratives to provide a societal account of the inescapability of crisis. The thick atmosphere of crisis that has been breathed for a decade contains inescapable affective and emotional reverberations. In previous chapters, we have seen vertigo-inducing unknowingness and the coming to terms with spatial and temporal breaks from past lives. Balanced on the cliff-edge, at the decision-making moment, the world is sent into a tailspin. Jumping into the *ilinx*, surrendering to the desires for familiarity and for the cessation of a nauseating existence should bring closure to vertigo. Yet often the acceptance of rupture leads straight back to vertigo, this time the structural endlessness of a critical present, a permanent frenzied reminder of inescapability. Chronic crisis perpetuates the spin cycle of everyday life with no futural horizon or possibility for change. Those who give in to the unbearable situation, by making the break, may find a space of relative comfort within the familiarity of crisis, yet, ultimately, they remain stranded in the stuckedness of a futile situation.

NOTES

1. News outlets carrying stories on Stockholm Syndrome span the political spectrum and include *I Kathimerini, Proto Thema, Times News, AlfaVita* and *left.gr*.
2. There is an excellent forum on the theme of captivity – covering topics as varied as international shipping, prisons, animal enclosure and neurodivergence – published in the journal *History and Anthropology* (2019, 30(5)). A recent publication, *Art of*

Captivity by Kevin Lewis O'Neill and Benjamin Fogarty-Valenzuela (2020), is also an excellent visual resource.

3. It could be argued that Herzfeld's (2002, 2016) concept of crypto-colonialism resonates with the idea of societal Stockholm Syndrome in that people have become so accustomed to societal structures and narratives of nation-building that they fail to recognize the underlying processes governing their everyday lives. In Herzfeld's case, captivity would be to the foreign architects of Greek independence that laid the foundations of the modern nation-state.

4. On futility, see the *Anthropological Theory* collection 'Futile Political Gestures' (2020) edited by Galina Oustinova-Stjepanovic.

5. Such contexts of negotiating the societal, psychological and emotional consequences of sudden captivity are plentiful in science fiction. For instance, in Stephen King's 2009 novel *Under the Dome*, residents of an American town come to terms with the calamity of being suddenly cut off from the outside world when a giant, impassable glass dome descends around the town (the book was transformed into a television series of the same name in 2013). The multiperspective story depicts the plethora of reactions to life in captivity, from servicing illicit demands such as drug-running, the search for truth through science, the making and breaking of romantic relationships, protest and violence of/against the political system, and the eventual routinization of the new daily reality often lived out in the local cafeteria, always with the overbearing potential for extraterrestrial beings to take control of an individual's body at any given moment.

6. Padraic Scanlan (2019) has argued that after emancipation former slaves of the British Empire were held captive by economic means. Imperial liberalism and the consolidation of global capitalism 'was also an ideological and economic regime that took captives and prevented escape'. Scanlan's inference that money be the means of enforcing captivity could also be applied to the Greek case.

7. At one point, Greece was offered humanitarian assistance for dealing with the potential social consequences of leaving the eurozone. For a discussion of the violence inherent in humanitarian action, see Fassin (2007, 2010), Pipyrou (2020) and Ticktin (2017).

8. The mass media has played a significant role in normalizing crisis; the rehashed daily conversations in 2019 are only superficially different from those on television screens in 2009. The economic crisis continues to be played out 24/7 in Greek media, giving the event a permanence on a scale of minutes, hours and days.

9. Here he refers to the Greek collaborationist government during the Second World War Axis occupation of 1941–44.

CONCLUSION
Parting Shots

❧⌘❧

I am a child once more. Maybe ten or twelve. On a family outing to the south coast of England. It is dangerously windy. I dare myself to get as close as possible to the cliff-edge. My senses are assaulted from all sides by an overwhelming compulsion to jump. This is it. What I came for. What I remember from last time. Vulnerability. A decision to make. I can re-create history. The possibility of possibility. As I approach, my pace slows from exhilarating carefree dash to deliberate placement of each shrinking step. With rain beating on my face and strong winds blustering against the back of my plastic raincoat, the raging sea entices me to join it, maybe 100 metres below. Small pebbles slip from under my feet. I watch them fall until they disappear into infinity, captured in the blurry horizon of explosive sea spray. It hits me that I will never see those same small stones again. I feel sad, a little disappointed that that was the limit of our acquaintance. Billions of years in the making, fleeting connection. Insignificance in vastness. I am separated from my parents, alone in this moment. Stillness. Thoughts and fascinations. They are oblivious to my calling. Then I hit it. That threshold I cannot cross. It was the same last time. A shoelace closer and logic will be overpowered by vertigo. I am dizzy (and writing this, I feel nauseous). I cannot trust myself. My God, this is the question of existence. I am opening a Pandora's box of imponderability, but I want to believe. This is why I push ever further, testing the boundaries, flexing the invisible point of no return. The family dog drops a stick at my foot and snaps me from my trace. Though seemingly oblivious, I cannot let her succumb to what I experience. That timeline is for someone else. I am not The One.

*****

I must ask, 'what is qualitatively different about my vertigo here? Why did I not succumb to the abyss? What in my social landscape pulled me back?' On the clifftop, I am not forced to cross that critical point and I feel a level of self-determination in continuing to fight the vertiginous urge. I step back from the edge. My ten-year-old Self is not in crisis. I am merely testing boundaries. I am not yet sure where my future lies and the persuasion to rupture history is not compelling enough.

In Greece, the sensory inscriptions and erasures of economic crisis sever factuality from actuality, fashioning forms of vertiginous life full of paradoxes and counterfactuals. Vertigo speaks to the tempos and rhythms of life in the tangled mesh of enforced rupture and desired continuity. The embodied actualities and material histories of vertiginous life are so often simply overlooked as the collateral damage of a decade of crisis (cf. Feldman 2015). The erratic tempos of life in contemporary Greece forge the vertiginous condition that overrides, displaces or disorientates the expected rhythms of established lifeworlds. The temporal landscape is frantically oscillating – backwards and forwards, histories and futures happening at once, tidal currents, inconstant connections that breach the realms of parallel elsewhens.

The economic crisis of 2009/10 set people along alternate timelines, defeating previously known histories and futures. The whirlwind of this dehistoricization uprooted people from familiar trajectories; a Kansas cyclone catapulting a nation of Dorothys somewhere and somewhen over the rainbow. The timespace beyond was as surreal as it was unforeseen. Back working on the solar panels in the fields of western Thessaly, Antonis reflected on his unnerving estrangement from time and place by remarking that 'this is not my time ... I am not living my time'. The feeling that the timespace of crisis is somehow detached from previous lives and alien to once-anticipated futures gives it a bubble-like epochal status. Antonis suggests that he inhabits someone else's reality.[1] Creating a crisis of presence that tenders a unique perspective on the world, the timespace operates on violent rhythms of suspension and inescapability, an atmosphere filled with lurking personal unknowingness and nauseating temporal disorientation.

Considering for a moment the hypothesizing of Runia, Kierkegaard and Proust on giddiness and courageous leaps, vertigo can be traced to at least two coordinates of the destruction/creativity scenario apparent in the crisis timespace. People like Mairi continue to scramble to hold on to the collapsing familiarity of the past, gripping the cliff-edge with their fingertips, dangling above the gaping jaws of the radically different future unknown. At this moment, life is in suspension, caught between the impossibility of return and the imponderability of the yet-to-come. Stripped of essence, existence becomes unbearable. The crisis world has people caught on the event horizon of the supermassive black hole of life – in apparent stasis as the universe rushes by. More than a calendrical decade later and violent rupture has become chronic condition – for younger generations, a Time of Crisis is all they have known. Here, instead of clinging to rapidly receding horizons of the past, life inside the crisis *ilinx* is clad with its own vertiginous veneer. Born into the crisis epoch, people like Aphrodite have resigned themselves to life inside the endless whirlpool of crisis, held captive by its seeming permanence. Once in the clutches of the *ilinx*, there is no escape, no way back or forward – a realization that elicits perpetual anguish.

The scaling of temporal duration and the problems raised by the bookmarking of history through critical events have been core concerns of this book, as has the relationship between individual and societal experience of crisis. Individual stories of people who have felt the full force of the crisis years have allowed, through the development of ethnographic theory, reflection on the societal consequences of a Time of Crisis. One of the most notable aspects of crisis is that it illuminates how and to what extent the Self is intimately tied to the social landscape and the manner 'in which deterioration in one aspect of our existence will, almost by definition, affect other areas of our lives' (Vigh 2008: 15). Pacing Vigh, crisis as chronic condition 'often results in individual or existential crisis, just as much as the latter, through the acts of the desperate or despairing can cause societal breakdown'. The relationship between the personal and the social is brought into sharp relief precisely because crisis destabilizes the way people constitute and construct themselves as parts of larger entities. Crisis corrodes the constructions of meaning by which the different timespaces – bundles of relations, affects and practices – of our existence are interwoven (Vigh 2008: 15).

Scaling-up from individual accounts of defeated expectations, torn personalities, temporal confusion and emotional torment facilitates commentary on the societal ramifications of more than a decade of precarity and allows us to contemplate other forms of crisis beyond Greek shores. Scaling of duration (from crisis confined to moments, hours and days to chronic crisis lasting years) and of people (individuals, local communities, the nation as a collective, global relations) reveals how individual unknowingness is inextricable from the consuming atmosphere of anxiety and captivity fashioned by international governmental organizations such as the Troika. In everyday situations, people relate changing material environments, such as relocating 'back to the village' or relying on wood-burning stoves to keep warm, to wider questions of belonging in the twenty-first century and to a timespace of modernity supposedly shared with Northern Europe. Such temporal and geopolitical anxieties are fostered, in part, through vertiginous relationships with technologies that are imbued with paradoxical trajectories and futural promises. Further, they discuss empirical qualities of participating in categories of belonging, leading to remarks that existential emptiness and un-knowingness are core characteristics of the epoch.

Crisis timespaces overlap beyond national borders when one considers the complexities of lives caught between Troika and Brexit, geopolitical disputes that hold within them innumerable personal tailspins. This leads to spatial and temporal inescapability from life in crisis with repetitive narratives centred around suspension and captivity. Societal Stockholm Syndrome – a theory most prominent in the international relations literature – connects grassroots accounts of inescapability with geopolitical structures that promote axiomatic violence and the curtailment of individual freedoms. This speaks to my overall attempt to stay true to personal readings of the imprint of crisis while offering comment on wider structural relations that perpetuate the crisis condition.

CRITIQUES

The diverse spatiotemporal contexts of crisis open a critique of whether any two versions of vertigo are the same, or even referencing similar phenomena. How can my personal Time of Crisis, confined to three hours at home waiting for news on my brother's health, share the page with a nation being ravished by over a decade of economic reform? Surely, not only are the durations, causes and quantitative fallouts incomparable, but the vertiginous shockwaves must be also quite different, right? It is distasteful, I hear the reader scream, for the fine-grained ethnographic description of shortened horizons provided by a newly diagnosed cancer patient to conceptually appear alongside a story of relocation to an ancestral village or a vignette on photovoltaic panels. Is it right to place a psychoanalytic theory of captivity once used to interpret relations between Cold War nation-states next to the words of Soula, Voula, Toula and Roula who, in their small-scale village lives on an agricultural plain or in a mountain hamlet, feel the inescapability of epochal crisis? And what about vertigo brought on by excitement?

I do not attempt to place the spatial and temporal scales into qualitative hierarchy. Part of the dizzying affect of what I have packaged as vertigo is precisely the palpations felt when zooming in and out of crisis timespaces. One may recall the shuddering camerawork of the *Hawaii Five-0* opening credits, Steve McQueen's Le Mans crash, the dolly zoom made famous by Hitchcock or even W.G. Sebald's radical literary style – pulsating rides where people try to correlate the fragility of individual existence with the vastness of time and history, often questioning their memory of the past and its connectivity to being in the present. Day-to-day livelihoods are navigated from amid the riptides of international politics and shifts in abstract global markets. It is precisely this zooming in and out that adds textured layers to vertigo – trying to maintain focus as the picture blurs, attempting to piece together how radical changes to the Self fit with the newly reordered world.

Considering individual experience within these polytemporal and multi-dimensional bubbles underscores the whirlpool effect – what I have called, following Caillois, the *ilinx* – that induces vertigo. In contrasting ways, for de Martino, Runia and Kierkegaard, at the very crux of vertigo as analytic is the realization of individual vulnerability at moments when decisions will potentially remake history – as I felt on the cliffs of southern England – often going against the perceived natural flow of time's arrow. For de Martino and Runia, the historical rupture of a Time of Crisis leads to a state of near-magical possession whereby the world is suspended and uncanny – 'crisis time' takes control of body and mind. At this point, the individual may decide to jump into the whirlpool, overcome by vertigo, or resist the force while holding on to remnants of dying pasts. It is crisis that forces people to cross this threshold and succumb to vertigo, the horizon that I could not traverse on the ferry or on the cliffs. In Kierkegaard's reading of the cliff-edge decision-making moment, the source of vertigo is the hyperconscious recognition that one has the freedom of choice, the (often misplaced) belief that jumping may not only relieve the vertigo, but may also create new history. Proust writes that people experience giddiness when standing on stilts of accumulated time and history. Most people start to wobble, not knowing how to connect the vastness of pasts with often shockingly uncertain futures. Yet stilts also offer a vantage point to survey the temporal landscape. If one can manage the accumulated knowledge of pasts and futures – to come to terms with it, to tame it, to recognise its pedagogical potency – then one can actualize the creative potentialities of the dizzying position. Successful navigation of unforeseen knowledge from atop the stilts, both Kierkegaard and Serres in different ways propose, distinguishes productive innovation in connecting old and new lives from entrapment in a quagmire of cyclical existential crisis. In all interpretations, the precarity of the individual lies against the supermassive onrushing storm of time and history, cumulating on that cliff-edge, the blustery winds knocking the unsuspecting subject perilously off-balance. The depressurization hatch has been opened in the cargo bay of the *Starship Enterprise* of life, threatening to suck all known beings into the vast abyss of spacetime.

Of course, no two times of crisis are structurally or affectively the same. Instead, I have sought to highlight the striking similarities and differences of the resonate *something*, the atmosphere and aesthetic, that runs through people's accounts of life in various incarnations of crisis. Often the repetition of words and phrases in everyday discussions of the crisis years points to how living through dramatic social change has problematized perceptions of Self and society – nausea, dizziness, the sense of falling or being held captive are recurring themes in crisis narratives. There is nothing to say that my dizziness is the same as yours. A 'how could I have been so wrong?' disorientation when futural expectations are not realized may not conflate with an 'I've been here before' sense of déjà vu associated with the perception of falling through time. The motion sickness nausea of my Brittany Ferries sea crossing *felt* and *meant* something different from the nausea awaiting my mother's hospital telephone call, as did the philosophical contemplation on rewriting history from the top of a cliff on the south coast of England. On the ferry, vertigo initially manifested as a motion sickness provoked by the side-to-side, up-and-down tempos of the boat, later to be confounded by my overwhelming desire to jump into the ocean abyss, leaving me short of breath as I attempted to supress the temptation. My waiting at home those three hours in December signalled a realization that my life was at a transformative intersection where existence would never be the same; the almost-end of the old world and the not-quite emergence of the new. That was a threshold that had to be crossed.

In all cases, vertigo was that of physical movement, of a change in temporal rhythm, of inescapable vulnerability and of a collapse in moral order. These forms of multidimensional transport had seized my person (Caillois 2001: 24) – was I to give in to my depraved desire to jump or my logical disposition to stay onboard? Could my shredded world of lost relatedness ever be reassembled? What are the boundaries of existence, knowing the Self in the vastness of the universe? These instances were crises in their own right, provoking out-of-body experiences, hyperconsciousness of the Self and the surrounding environment, indexed by an internal struggle of whether to fight or give in. The fact that I recall the minute detail of the sounds and smells of these landmark moments reveals the eeriness of the timespace, saturated in a struggle with the Self, a reflexive detachment from the 'normal' (de Martinian) world that now seemed alien to my being. In these critical situations, time operates at a different rhythm – elongated, stuck, twisted or counterfactual – as ruptures or slippages in perceived normal linear progression deliver 'heat' to temporal experience (Greenhouse 2019: 86–87).

Different though the structures and durations of times of crisis may be, in the Greek case resonant narrative strands weave together and connect tales of workplace diversification, forced relocation, divided households and engagement with the apparatuses of governmentality. Personal struggles with aspects of the Self and the maintenance of social relationships are linguistically repetitive and unpacking these through individual stories illuminates how a Time of Crisis effects identity formation and relatedness. So regular are the references to nausea and dizziness, as well as falling through time and historical repetition, that one cannot help but start to piece together how these contribute to the structure of an extraordinary epoch experienced by a significant collectively in Greece and further afield. Repetitive narratives of everyday affects inform a bigger picture of how, for a considerable number of people, vertigo is a significant component of crisis experience, contributing to the overarching structure or atmosphere of a shared timespace. The fine-grained details of how vertigo is felt, manifested or articulated may vary, but it is undeniable that it is 'in the air' as an orienting characteristic of the timespace of crisis. At this point, vertigo transcends words and phrases to become an uncanny resonant aesthetic of the epoch, often read through the gaps, silences and moods of 'living the crisis'.

Charting similarities in the individual experience of shared crises facilitates commentary on the affective structure of the timespace, the overlapping and entangling of people and objects that share an epoch, paying close attention to common vernaculars. This does not forego novelty or self-determination, or necessarily mean losing the nuances of individual experience. Importantly, however, an attempt to understand the overarching affective structure of a shared timespace leads to more detailed and comparable knowledge of the 'ends, projects, actions, and combinations thereof that participants ... pursue' in a Time of Crisis (Schatzki 2010: 52).

A comparison that helps elucidate this point comes from Ringel's (2020) work on the temporalities of the COVID-19 coronavirus pandemic. Here, Ringel acknowledges how a Time of Crisis is comprised of many *different* times that are at once personal and shared. 'Corona time' consists of the 'time of lockdown', 'quarantine time' and 'home office time', which overlap yet all have a slightly different temporal rhythm and affective texture for all of us. 'We have learnt to inhabit these new presents', he continues. 'These lessons are deeply personal and differ in each household. Still, they speak of an experience shared worldwide', often accompanied with a feeling of stuckedness and entrapment. This is precisely what emerges from a close reading of the economic crisis and its aftermaths in Greece. Crises within 'The Crisis' produce diverse representations of time and, layer upon layer, are mixed together under such intense heat and pressure as to create the *ilinx* that becomes overpowering. The multiple temporal speeds of life – from the initial sudden ruptures and breathtaking discoveries of redundancies, empty pension funds and even suicides to the drip-drip slow violence of austerity politics – denote an epoch affectively and materially different from what has gone immediately before. The multiple layers of individual and societal suffering and the cumulative multiplier effect of crises within 'The Crisis' exert an immense strain that pushes people to the cliff-edge. Overawed by the pressures of the unfamiliar, they peer down into the *ilinx*, feeling the desire to jump surge through them, to make a clean break from a most challenging moment in historical experience. Yet something holds them back: past lives, promised futures, the lingering fragments of previous Selves. The tug of war between pasts and futures while stuck in what Ringel calls 'new presents' creates vertigo, accentuated further by the belief that the *ilinx* is not opening portals to creative futures, but rather to undesirable bygone eras – the 'falling through time' aspect of so many narratives of a Time of Crisis.

The flooding of the Time of Crisis category with unfinalized structures of meaning and imagination exceeds individual experiences and produces a lingering and saturated atmosphere. The correlations in individual stories cannot be ignored, providing the lifeblood in the veins that sustain the complex body of epochal crisis. The reading of the parallels between stories over an accumulated period, as Lepselter and Masco prominently advocate, enables the sketching of master narratives. Vertigo is one of these master narratives, an expressive modality of making sense of the world, an ever-present *something* that grips life. In its persona-centric approach, this book has explored core themes that echo and multiply within the modality, unearthing ways that troubling times begin to *make sense.*

RECURRENCES

I have chosen to foreground the temporal textures[2] of vertigo running throughout stories of forced relocation, interaction with material objects, and individual struggles with unknowingness. This brings us full circle to where we started in the Preface and the original concept of '*temporal* vertigo' – the intense confusion as to where and when people are located on the usually unquestioned linear timeline of progression. Caught in the ricochets of defeated futures and returning pasts, the 'spin-cycle on repeat' as Charles Stewart once suggested to me, people often pose the rhetorical question '*when* am I now?' I have argued for the shared affects of a Time of Crisis, complete with accompanying vernaculars, feelings and orientations that feed an atmospheric *something* that connects disparate lives and worldviews. Falling back through historical time and returning to the past is most tangibly evident in the relocations to long-abandoned ancestral villages and in the installation of wood-burning stoves considered to be leftovers of peasant life from the pre-dictatorship, pre-European, pre-modern years. Vertigo here is triggered by materiality in the manner that objects and technological infrastructure operate as 'time capsules' (Stewart 2003: 487), with trajectories that explode, implode, twist or braid time (Bryant 2014: 684). Of course, in practice, the temporal, material and existential intertwine and cannot truly be separated, yet it has been helpful for the analytical endeavour to intensify investigations along these three pathways.

Suspension, emptiness and captivity are recurrent themes as people discuss their vertigo. The concept of navigation is also prominent; the ability (or lack of) to orient life via familiar markers on the spatiotemporal map. The struggle to navigate new bureaucracies and renegotiated futures has led to the unknowingness of the Self, the idea that crisis is empty of familiar 'stars' by which to guide safe passage and the belief that technology has inherent directionality. Indeed, for Kierkegaard (1980), the potentiality of vertigo as a creative force is dependent on the competent navigation of the frontier of destruction. Being located in a transitional timespace that might be conceived as a gap between familiar old and emergent new world orders, Kierkegaard proposes that vertigo can be harnessed through the education of the Self to accept the dizzying possibility of possibility. However, the option to leap into the *ilinx* is the most self-destructive of possibilities and seems to go against all that is known and logical. Hence, for most people, vertigo endures as a terrifying assault on the senses owing to its unusual and awesome temporalities and rhythms – it remains unnavigable. Vertigo experienced standing on the cliff-edge of epochal history-making is a tightrope moment, a double-edged sword, a tug of war between the yearning for familiar yet inaccessible timelines and usually repressed desires for disorder and destruction. Peering into the swirling abyss, vertigo becomes all-consuming, moving from the realm of metaphor or descriptive trope to physically, psychologically and socially infiltrate life in the crisis world. At the base of the cliff, the impending *ilinx* is inescapable, replicating a sense of frenzied urgency that defines the chronic condition.

OUR TIMES

Taking individual crisis experiences to then speak of collective atmospheres and affective structures offers quite a remarkable insight into conditions of life in twenty-first century Europe. The widespread implications of conceptual commentary through individual voices resonates with conditions far beyond the borders of crisis Greece. Each narrative may bear witness to the grassroots consequences of austerity politics very much in situ in Athens, Thessaloniki, Trikala or Larisa, yet ultimately the stories can be read as a conceptual critique of 'our times'. The existential crisis of unknowingness and the associated kin-terms of alienation and dispossession have been the subject of debate in dogmatic discussions on neoliberalism in late modernity (e.g. Harvey 2005; Klein 2007). Along these lines, Mairi's unknowingness in Chapter 1 is an intensified version of the affects of modern society writ large. Existential crises linked to concepts of emptiness and estrangement from the Self are familiar in common parlance about modern life, although claims that this is unique to our times may be countered by Rousseau's and Nietzsche's similar observations about the structure of modern industrialized societies, beating us to it by a mere couple of centuries. 'Unprecedented' is, after all, an over-used word in contemporary anthropology and the popular media to boot.

Antonis' questioning of belonging to First World trajectories and shared timespaces of 'Europe' and 'the West' in Chapter 3 is a concern not unique to Greece, but also prominent in crisis timespaces in Israel, South Italy and most recently the United Kingdom. Emptiness and suspension – the themes of Chapter 4 – have been addressed as analytics particular to the contem-porary moment on the European continent (Dzenovska and Knight 2020). Increased and more diverse forms of displacement (see Chapter 2) as a sym-bol of this century have been the subject of anthropological interest for over a decade. Perhaps the most radical proposal of my argument is the case for societal Stockholm Syndrome through repetitive grassroots narratives of captivity when everyday life is in the inescapable grasp of abstract Others – international banks, credit organizations and governmental bodies (cf. Bear 2015). Vertigo-inducing captivity has only recently come to the fore in an-thropology (O'Neill and Dua 2019), yet it should not be too much of a stretch for the imagination to envisage how the futility of a chronic condition could prompt uncomfortable comfort with the familiarity of crisis.

Ultimately, I hope that you, the reader, can relate to some aspects of ver-tiginous life presented on these pages. Perhaps you have experienced diz-zying occasions when time has become elastic or has seemed to be stuck. There has been a hyperconsciousness of existence, maybe an out-of-body experience or the feeling of anxiety-inducing entrapment. Perhaps there have been times when the world is spinning, apparently empty and eerily unfamiliar or unnavigable. You have been suspended in an elongated pres-ent with little idea of how the past connects to the future, if at all, falling through the once-archived and now onrushing past. Deaths, earthquakes, broken relationships, pandemics. Material objects, alien technologies, dis-jointed and uncanny sights and sounds. The scale and duration of a Time of Crisis is likely to differ, but many of the vertiginous affects and narrative keywords will resonate. There might be the sense, the feeling or atmosphere of epochal change – *nothing will ever be the same*. Destruction, transition, being knocked off-balance. Out with the old and in with the *something else*. The *ilinx* awaits.

NOTES

1. This feeling of an uncanny relationship with pasts and futures is not unprecedented in the crisis literature – the working definition of crisis is a point of recognition after which 'history could look entirely different' (Koselleck 2002: 243; Goddard 2006: 270; Serres 2014).
2. On the temporal textures of critical events, see Henig (2020: 93).

EPILOGUE

A Note on Crisis

∾⌣∾

It has not been my intention to provide a blow-by-blow account of the so-cial consequences of global financial meltdown. Neither has there been lengthy engagement with regional debates on the cultural characteristics that contribute to the protracted episode that has come to be known as the 'Greek economic crisis'. Yet, inevitably, the stories narrated here have been set deep inside the suffocating smog of prolonged austerity and structural reform. Here I provide a brief recap of how we got to this point of chronic crisis, as well as some signposts for the uninitiated who might wish to delve further into the thematic literature on financial collapse, vulnerability and crisis Greece.

Much anthropological ink has been spilt on breaking down the 2008 global financial downturn into fine-grained analysis of the dramatic life-style changes experienced by citizens of Greece and other nations that were bunched together by the media into the somewhat derogatory category 'PIIGS' (Portugal, Italy, Ireland, Greece and Spain – plus Cyprus). The 'Greek economic crisis' began in 2009 when the newly elected Prime Minister Giorgos Papandreou (PASOK) revealed that previous governments had underreported data on national debts and budget deficits, leading to a slump in market confidence, indicated by widening bond yield spreads and the rising cost of risk insurance on credit default swaps. Although Papandreou reassured his populous with the now infamous 'there is money' (*lefta iparxoun*) speech, Greece's credit rating was downgraded to 'junk' status owing to the high risks involved with its projected inability to repay loans. In 2010, Greece received a €110 billion bailout from the so-called Troika comprising the European Central Bank, the European Commission and the International Monetary Fund (IMF), followed by another €130 billion in 2012, and €86 billion in 2015 in return for stringent austerity measures.

Later in 2010, Ireland received €67.5 billion, followed in 2011 by Portugal (€78 billion), Spain in 2012 (€100 billion 'support package') and Cyprus in 2013 (€10 billion). In all cases, the consequences of financial strife have been severe and lasting for the local populations.

The crisis dragged on for a decade, spiking in summer 2015 when Greece became the first developed nation to fail to make an IMF loan repayment. A heated referendum on a third bailout package held on 5 July 2015 resulted in a resounding 'No' (61.31 per cent) to further international support, only for Prime Minister Alexis Tsipras (SYRIZA) to agree a three-year Troika bailout on 13 July with harsher austerity conditions than those rejected in the referendum. In popular discourse, the referendum was also dubbed a vote on continued membership of the European Economic and Monetary Union (the eurozone) and wider issues concerning Greece's place in the European sociopolitical project. Greece returned to international markets in 2018 with the completion of required structural reforms, and triumphant political announcements in early 2019 proclaimed the end of the Greek economic crisis. However, loan repayments will continue for decades, cuts to public spending have not ceased, and the consequences of ten years of social and economic turmoil will be felt at the grassroots level for generations to come. The transformative processes of 2009–19 have a permanence beyond the ten 'official' crisis years, constituting an elongated Time of Crisis where the effects of austerity and structural re-adjustment are embedded and embodied, and are unlikely to subside any time soon.

Countless tax hikes, consistent cuts to public spending, record levels of unemployment, the restructuring of haulage and tourism industries, opportunistic international investment in sectors such as energy and healthcare, the decimation of pension and personal insurance schemes (the list is seemingly endless) and the subsequent degradation of kinship support networks continue to have a dramatic effect on everyday life for the majority of citizens. Some of the prominent themes of academic preoccupation during this time have included the rise in solidarity and resource-sharing initiatives (Rakopoulos 2016), the role of protest and resistance in channelling social disquiet (Theodossopoulos 2013, 2014), the impact of prolonged crisis on mental health (Davis 2015) and cultural production (Papanikolaou 2011, 2021), the prospects for youth or the so-called 'crisis generation' (Chalari and Serifi 2019), questions of class and social mobility (Kozaitis 2020), the emergence of neocolonialism and extractive economies (Argenti and Knight 2015), and how the migration crisis that reached a crescendo in 2015–16 stretched already struggling infrastructure to beyond breaking point (Cabot 2019; Kirtsoglou and Tsimouris 2018; Rozakou 2017, 2019). Scholars such as Michael Herzfeld (2016) have taken analytical arguments beyond regional ethnography to reassess concepts of belonging, nationalism and colonialism on scales of global comparison. It is also worth pointing out that many concerns of the post-2009 anthropology of Greece have deeper roots identifiable in much earlier works on patronage and clientelism (Campbell 1964; Peristiany 1965), modernity and belonging (Faubion 1993; Herzfeld 1987), bureaucracy and governance (Herzfeld 1992), historical consciousness (Hirsch and Stewart 2005; Sutton 1998), *ethnos* and religion (du Boulay 1974, Stewart 1991), migration (Cabot 2014; Friedl 1976; Hirschon 1989), conspiracy theories (Brown and Theodossopoulos 2004; Sutton 2003) and gendered spheres of labour (Dubisch 1995; Kirtsoglou 2004).[1]

A prominent anthropological analytic arising from the 2008 global economic downturn, to which this book speaks indirectly but significantly, is precarity. With its roots firmly in economic anthropology, precarity has been discussed in relation to employment vulnerability and exploitation (Allison 2013; Molé 2010), neoliberal debt (Han 2012), dispossession (Collins 2012; Muehlebach and Shoshan 2012), household finance and gendered space (Davey 2020; Wilde 2017), the financialization of poverty (Kar 2018; Schuster 2015), and social class and welfare (Narotzky 2016; Standing 2011). The rise of the term 'precariat' – a portmanteau obtained by merging precarious with proletariat – conveys a condition of existence without predictability or security, affecting material and psychological welfare. Numerous collections have been published on precarity – Anne Allison's (2016) *Cultural Anthropology* forum, Clara Han's (2018) *Annual Review* essay, Andrea Muehlebach's (2013) 'Year in Review' *American Anthropologist* article and Sharryn Kasmir's (2018) *Cambridge Encyclopaedia of Anthropology* entry are of particular note for their breadth.

Part of the global culture of fear and perceived insecurity stemming from the multiple crises of the early twenty-first century (Neilson and Rossiter 2005: 6), the stories of vulnerable and precarious subjects in the Greek crisis could well be approached through the precarity lens. As Joseph Masco reminds us, the 'unthinkability' of such an event produces its rhetoric opposite: 'a proliferation of discourses about vulnerability and insecurity' (2006: 3). Precarity as an analytic starting point would automatically pigeonhole the study as one of workplace and household domains, giving the text a distinctly 'economic' flair. The 'feeling of exposure' to fluctuations in global markets and 'increased vulnerability' to regimes of political and economic violence associated with precarity (Clifford 2012:426) are modalities of indeterminacy that are 'less the exception than the condition of our times' (Tsing 2015: 2) – or, in Benjamin's words, the vulnerability felt in a state of emergency is no longer the exception, but the rule (Benjamin 1999: 248). As such, arguments on precarity do resonate with the task of detailing vertiginous life. For one thing, facets of temporality are apparent, yet not always foregrounded, in the precarity literature. Allison, for instance, has noted that 'the precarious lack [of] handrails for anchoring the future' from an uncertain present means that 'everyday efforts don't align with a teleology of progressive betterment'. In her writing on a campaign to stop the construction of a trash incinerator in Baltimore, Ahmann (2018) digs into the relationship between precarity and temporal distortion by way of slow violence and time manipulation. Arguing for a theory of moral punctuation where people endeavour to 'halt time' and make an 'event out of nothing' (2018: 166), Ahmann supposes time to be a medium of violence, harbouring purpose-built temporalities of resistance and refusal (on the eventedness of repetition and associated affects, see Bandak (2019)).

Vertigo, though, goes further than precarity in accounting for life on the edge, seeping like a noxious gas into the cracks where vulnerability lurks. A more holistic take on a pervading atmosphere of precariousness and vulnerability, vertigo asks existential questions, permeates material relations and skews temporalities. As an aesthetic of crisis, vertigo is a central motif of the prevalent mood at a time of seemingly interminable social upheaval. Vertigo offers an alternative reading of vulnerability and intense affective strife against a backdrop of economic crisis and struggles with global systems of dispossession.

NOTE

1. The references to research on crisis and pre-crisis Greece are merely representative. It is not my intention to provide a full review of the literature here.

REFERENCES

Adorjan, Michael, Tony Christensen, Benjamin Kelly and Dorothy Pawluch. 2012. 'Stockholm Syndrome as Vernacular Resource'. *Sociological Quarterly* 53: 454–74.

Agamben, Giorgio. 2011. *Nudities*. Stanford: Stanford University Press.

Ahmann, Chloe. 2018. 'It's Exhausting to Create an Event out of Nothing: Slow Violence and the Manipulation of Time'. *Cultural Anthropology* 33(1): 142–71.

Allison, Anne. 2013. *Precarious Japan*. Durham, NC: Duke University Press.

———. 2016. 'Precarity'. *Cultural Anthropology*. Retrieved 17 March 2021 from https://journal.culanth.org/index.php/ca/precarity-commentary-by-anne-allison.

Anderson, Paul, and Andreas Bandak. n.d. 'Urgency and Imminence: The Politics of the Very Near Future' (working title, under review).

Argenti, Nicolas. 2017. 'Introduction: The Presence of the Past in the Era of the Nation-State'. *Social Analysis* 61(1): 1–25.

Argenti, Nicolas, and Daniel M. Knight. 2015. 'Sun, Wind, and the Rebirth of Extractive Economies: Renewable Energy Investment and Metanarratives of Crisis in Greece'. *Journal of the Royal Anthropological Institute* 21(4): 781–802.

Argenti, Nicolas, and Katharina Schramm (eds). 2010. *Remembering Violence: Anthropological Perspectives on Intergenerational Transmission*. Oxford: Berghahn Books.

Argyrou, Vassos. 1996. *Tradition and Modernity in the Mediterranean: The Wedding as Symbolic Struggle*. Cambridge: Cambridge University Press.

Avieli, Nir, and Tsahala Sermoneta. 2020. 'Maasai on the Phone: Materiality, Tourism, and the Extraordinary in Zanzibar'. *Humanities and Social Sciences Communications* 7(117): 1–10.

Azoulay, Ariella. 2013. 'When a Demolished House Becomes a Public Square', in Ann Stoler (ed.), *Imperial Debris: On Ruins and Ruination*. Durham, NC: Duke University Press, pp. 194–225.

Bakhtin, Mikhail. 1981. *The Dialogic Imagination*. Austin: University of Texas Press.

Bandak, Andreas. 2019. 'Repetition and Uncanny Temporalities: Armenians and the Recurrence of Genocide in the Levant'. *History and Anthropology* 30(2): 190–211.

Bandak, Andreas, and Simon Coleman. 2019. 'Different Repetitions: Anthropological Engagements with Figures of Return, Recurrence and Redundancy'. *History and Anthropology* 30(2): 119–32.

Battaglia, Debbora. 2005. 'Insiders' Voices in Outerspace', in Debbora Battaglia (ed.), *E.T. Culture: Anthropology in Outerspaces*. Durham, NC: Duke University Press, pp. 1–37.

———. 2017. 'Aeroponic Gardens and Their Magic: Plants/Persons/Ethics in Suspension'. *History and Anthropology* 28(3): 263–92.

Bear, Laura. 2015. *Navigating Austerity: Currents of Debt on a South Asian River*. Stanford: Stanford University Press.

Benjamin, Walter. 1999. *Illuminations*. London: Pimlico Press.

Berlant, Lauren. 2011. *Cruel Optimism*. Durham, NC: Duke University Press.

Böhme, Gernot. 2017. *The Aesthetics of Atmospheres*, translated by Jean-Paul Thibaud. Abingdon: Routledge.

Brown, Keith, and Dimitrios Theodossopoulos. 2004. '"Others" Others: Talking about Stereotypes and Constructions of Otherness in Southeast Europe'. *History and Anthropology* 15(1): 3–14.

Bryant, Rebecca. 2010. *The Past in Pieces: Belonging in the New Cyprus*. Philadelphia: University of Pennsylvania Press.

———. 2014. 'History's Remainders: On Time and Objects after Conflict in Cyprus'. *American Ethnologist* 41(4): 681–97.

———. 2016. 'On Critical Times: Return, Repetition, and the Uncanny Present'. *History and Anthropology* 27(1): 19–31.

Bryant, Rebecca, and Daniel M. Knight. 2019. *The Anthropology of the Future*. Cambridge: Cambridge University Press.

Buck-Morss, Susan. 1991. *The Dialectics of Seeing Walter Benjamin and the Arcades Project*. Cambridge, MA: MIT Press.

Cabot, Heath. 2014. *On the Doorstep of Europe: Asylum and Citizenship in Greece*. Philadelphia: University of Pennsylvania Press.

———. 2016. '"Contagious" Solidarity: Reconfiguring Care and Citizenship in Greece's Social Clinics'. *Social Anthropology* 24(2): 152–66.

———. 2019. 'The Business of Anthropology and the European Refugee Regime'. *American Ethnologist* 46(3): 261–75.

Caillois, Roger. 2001. *Man, Play and Games*. Urbana: University of Illinois Press.

Campbell, John. 1964. *Honour, Family and Patronage: A Study of Institutions and Moral Values in a Greek Mountain Community*. Oxford: Oxford University Press.

Caruth, Cathy. 1991. 'Introduction: Psychoanalysis, Culture and Trauma'. *American Imago* 48(2): 417–24.

Chalari, Athanasia, and Panagiota Serifi. 2018. 'The "Crisis Generation": The Effect of the Greek Crisis on Youth Identity Formation'. *GreeSE* papers, no. 123. Hellenic Observatory, European Institute, London School of Economics and Political Science.

Choy, Timothy, and Jerry Zee. 2015. 'Condition-Suspension'. *Cultural Anthropology* 30(2): 210–23.

Clifford, James. 2012. 'Feeling Historical'. *Cultural Anthropology* 27(3): 417–26.

Clogg, Richard. 1992. *A Concise History of Greece*. Cambridge: Cambridge University Press.

Clough, Paul. 2014. *Morality and Economic Growth in Rural West Africa: Indigenous Accumulation in Hausaland*. Oxford: Berghahn Books.

Collins, Jane. 2012. 'Theorizing Wisconsin's 2011 Protests: Community-Based Unionism Confronts Accumulation by Dispossession'. *American Ethnologist* 39(1): 6–20.

Dalsheim, Joyce. 2015. 'There Will Always Be a Gaza War: Duration, Abduction and Intractable Conflict'. *Anthropology Today* 31(1): 8–11.

Danforth, Loring, and Riki van Boeschoten. 2012. *Children of the Greek Civil War: Refugees and the Politics of Memory*. Chicago: University of Chicago Press.

Das, Veena. 1995. *Critical Events: An Anthropological Perspective on Contemporary India*. Oxford: Oxford University Press.

Davey, Ryan. 2020. 'Snakes and Ladders: Legal Coercion, Housing Precarity and Home-Making Aspirations in England'. *Journal of the Royal Anthropological Institute* 26(1): 12–29.

Davies, Thom. 2019. 'Slow Violence and Toxic Geographies: "Out of Sight" to Whom?' *Environment and Planning C: Politics and Space* 1–19.

Davis, Elizabeth. 2015. '"We've Toiled without End": Publicity, Crisis, and the Suicide "Epidemic" in Greece'. *Comparative Studies in Society and History* 57(4): 1007–36.

De Martino, Ernesto. 2012 [1956]. 'Crisis of Presence and Religious Reintegration', prefaced and translated by Tobia Farnetti and Charles Stewart. *HAU: Journal of Ethnographic Theory* 2(2): 431–50.

Dole, Christopher, Robert Hayashi, Andrew Poe, Austin Sarat and Boris Wolfson (eds). 2015. *The Time of Catastrophe: Multidisciplinary Approaches to the Age of Catastrophe*. Abingdon: Routledge.

Driessen, Miriam. 2019. *Tales of Hope, Tastes of Bitterness: Chinese Road Builders in Ethiopia*. Hong Kong: Hong Kong University Press.

Du Boulay, Juliet. 1974. *Portrait of a Greek Mountain Village*. Oxford: Clarendon Press.

Dubisch, Jill. 1995. *In a Different Place: Pilgrimage, Gender and Politics at a Greek Island Shrine*. Princeton: Princeton University Press.

Dzenovska, Dace. 2018. 'Emptiness and Its Futures: Staying and Leaving as Tactics of Life in Latvia'. *Focaal: Journal of Global and Historical Anthropology* 80: 16–29.

———. 2019. 'The Timespace of Emptiness', in Rebecca Bryant and Daniel M. Knight (eds), *Orientations to the Future*. *American Ethnologist* website, 8 March. Retrieved 22 February 2021 from http://americanethnologist.org/features/collections/orientations-to-the-future/the-timespace-of-emptiness.

———. 2020. 'Emptiness: Capitalism without People in the Latvian Countryside'. *American Ethnologist* 47(1): 10–26.

Dzenovska, Dace, and Daniel M. Knight. 2020. 'Emptiness'. *Cultural Anthropology*, Theorizing the Contemporary. Retrieved 17 March 2021 from https://culanth.org/fieldsights/series/emptiness.

Eriksen, Thomas Hylland. 2016a. *Overheating: An Anthropology of Accelerated Change*. London: Pluto.

———. 2016b. 'Overheating: The World since 1991'. *History and Anthropology* 27(5): 469–87.

Farnetti, Tobia, and Charles Stewart. 2012. 'Translators' Preface: An Introduction to "Crisis of Presence and Religious Reintegration" by Ernesto De Martino'. *HAU: Journal of Ethnographic Theory* 2(2): 431–33.

Fassin, Didier. 2007. 'Humanitarianism as a Politics of Life'. *Public Culture* 19(3): 499–520.

———. 2010. *Humanitarian Reason: A Moral History of the Present*. Berkeley: University of California Press.

Fassin, Didier, and Richard Rechtman. 2007. *The Empire of Trauma: An Inquiry into the Condition of Victimhood*. Princeton: Princeton University Press.

Faubion, James D. 1993. *Modern Greek Lessons: A Primer in Historical Constructivism*. Princeton: Princeton University Press.

———. 2019. 'On Parabiopolitical Reason'. *Anthropological Theory* 19(2): 219–37.

Feldman, Allen. 2015. *Archives of the Insensible: Of War, Photopolitics, and Dead Memory*. Chicago: Chicago University Press.

Franquesa, Jaume. 2018. *Power Struggles: Dignity, Value, and the Renewable Energy Frontier in Spain*. Bloomington: Indiana University Press.

Frederiksen, Martin. 2013. *Young Men, Time, and Boredom in the Republic of Georgia*. Philadelphia: Temple University Press.

Friedl, Ernestine. 1976. 'Kinship, Class, and Selective Migration', in John Peristiany (ed.), *Mediterranean Family Structures*. Cambridge: Cambridge University Press, pp. 363–87.

Geissler, Paul. W. 2013. 'Public Secrets in Public Health: Knowing Not to Know While Making Scientific Knowledge'. *American Ethnologist* 40(1): 12–34.

Gille, Zsuzsa. 2020. 'Emptiness, Vacancy and Waste'. *Cultural Anthropology*, Theorizing the Contemporary. Retrieved 17 March 2021 from https://culanth.org/fieldsights/emptiness-vacancy-and-waste.

Gilmore, David. 1987. *Aggression and Community: Paradoxes of Andalusian Culture*. New Haven: Yale University Press.

Goddard, Victoria. 1996. *Gender, Family and Work in Naples*. Oxford: Berg.

———. 2006. 'This Is History: Nation and Experience in Times of Crisis – Argentina 2001'. *History and Anthropology* 17(3): 267–86.

Goodkin, Richard E. 1987. 'Film and Fiction: Hitchcock's Vertigo and Proust's "Vertigo"'. *MLN* 102(5): 1171–81.

Gordillo, Gaston. 2013. 'The Void: Invisible Ruins on the Edges of Empire', in Ann Stoler (ed.), *Imperial Debris: On Ruins and Ruination*. Durham, NC: Duke University Press, pp. 227–51.

———. 2014. *Rubble: The Afterlife of Destruction*. Durham, NC: Duke University Press.

Gordon, Lewis G. 2015. 'Disaster, Ruin, and Permanent Catastrophe', in Christopher Dole, Robert Hayashi, Andrew Poe, Austin Sarat and Boris Wolfson (eds), *The Time of Catastrophe: Multidisciplinary Approaches to the Age of Catastrophe*. Abingdon: Routledge, pp. 125–42.

Graham, Dee. 1994. *Loving to Survive: Sexual Terror, Men's Violence and Women's Lives*. New York: New York University Press.

Green, Jim. 2009. *Colleen Stan, The Simple Gifts of Life*. Bloomington: iUniverse.

Greenhouse, Carol. 2019. 'Times Like the Present: Political Rupture and the Heat of the Moment', in Martin Holbraad, Bruce Kapferer and Julia Sauma (eds), *Ruptures: Anthropologies of Discontinuity in Times of Turmoil*. London: UCL Press, pp. 70–92.

Griffiths, Melanie. 2014. 'Out of Time: The Temporal Uncertainties of Refused Asylum Seekers and Immigration Detainees'. *Journal of Ethnic and Migration Studies* 40(12): 1991–2009.

Gros, Stéphane, Kamala Russell and William F. Stafford Jr. 2019. 'Introduction: Topology as Method'. *Cultural Anthropology*, Theorizing the Contemporary. Retrieved 22 February 2021 from https://culanth.org/fieldsights/series/topology-as-method.

Gupta, Akhil. 2015. 'Suspension'. *Cultural Anthropology*, Theorizing the Contemporary. Retrieved 17 March 2021 from https://culanth.org/fieldsights/suspension.

Gutiérrez Garza, Ana. 2018. 'The Temporality of Illegality: Experiences of Undocumented Latin American Migrants in London'. *Focaal: Journal of Global and Historical Anthropology* 81: 86–98.

Guyer, Jane. 2007. 'Prophecy and the Near Future: Thoughts on Macroeconomic, Evangelical, and Punctuated Time'. *American Ethnologist* 34(3): 409–21.

Hage, Ghassan. 2009. 'Waiting out the Crisis: On Stuckedness and Governmentality', in Ghassan Hage (ed.), *Waiting*. Melbourne: Melbourne University Press, pp. 97–106.

Han, Clara. 2012. *Life in Debt: Times of Care and Violence in Neoliberal Chile*. Berkley: University of California Press.

———. 2018. 'Precarity, Precariousness, and Vulnerability'. *Annual Review of Anthropology* 47: 331–43.

Hart, Laurie K. 1992. *Time, Religion, and Social Experience in Rural Greece*. Lanham: Rowman & Littlefield.

Harvey, David. 2005. *A Brief History of Neoliberalism*. Oxford: Oxford University Press.

Heemskerk, Marieke. 2003. 'Scenarios in Anthropology: Reflections on Possible Futures of the Suriname Maroons'. *Futures* 35(9): 931–49.

Heidegger, Martin. 1972. 'Summary on a Seminar on the Lecture "Time and Being"', in *On Time and Being*. New York: Harper & Row, pp. 25–54.

———. 1993. *Being and Time*. Berkeley: University of California Press.

Heinlein, Robert A. 2012 [1941]. 'Elsewhen', in Robert A. Heinlein. *Assignment in Eternity*. New York: Baen, pp 79–114.

Henig, David. 2020. *Remaking Muslim Lives: Everyday Islam in Postwar Bosnia and Herzegovina*. Champaign: University of Illinois Press.

Hermez, Sami. 2012. 'The War Is Going to Ignite: On the Anticipation of Violence in Lebanon'. *Political and Legal Anthropology Review* 35(2): 327–44.

———. 2017. *War Is Coming: Between Past and Future Violence in Lebanon*. Philadelphia: University of Pennsylvania Press.

Herzfeld, Michael. 1980. 'Honour and Shame: Problems in the Comparative Analysis of Moral Systems'. *Man* 15: 339–51.

———. 1985. *The Poetics of Manhood: Contest and Identity in a Cretan Mountain Village*. Princeton: Princeton University Press.

———. 1987. *Anthropology through the Looking-Glass: Critical Ethnography in the Margins of Europe*. Cambridge: Cambridge University Press.

———. 1992. *The Social Production of Indifference: Exploring the Symbolic Roots of Western Bureaucracy*. Oxford: Berg.

———. 2002. 'The Absent Presence: Discourses of Crypto-Colonialism'. *South Atlantic Quarterly* 101(4): 899–926.

———. 2004. *Cultural Intimacy: Social Poetics and the Real Life of States, Societies, and Institutions*. London: Routledge.

———. 2016. 'The Hypocrisy of European Moralism: Greece and the Politics of Cultural Aggression – Parts 1 & 2'. *Anthropology Today* 32(1): 10–13 and 32(2): 10–13.

High, Casey, Ann Kelly and Jonathan Mair (eds). 2012. *The Anthropology of Ignorance: An Ethnographic Approach*. New York: Palgrave Macmillan.

Hirsch, Eric, and Charles Stewart. 2005. 'Introduction: Ethnographies of Historicity'. *History and Anthropology* 16(3): 261–74.

Hirschon, Renée. 1989. *Heirs of the Greek Catastrophe: The Social Life of Asia Minor Refugees in Piraeus*. Oxford: Berghahn Books.

Hodges, Matt. 2008. 'Rethinking Time's Arrow: Bergson, Deleuze and the Anthropology of Time'. *Anthropological Theory* 8(4): 399–429.

Holbraad, Martin., Bruce Kapferer and Julia Sauma (eds). 2019. *Ruptures: Anthropologies of Discontinuity in Times of Turmoil*. London: UCL Press.

Howe, Cymene. 2014. 'Anthropocenic Ecoauthority: The Winds of Oaxaca'. *Anthropological Quarterly* 87(2): 381–404.

Hromadžić, Azra. 2020. 'Populated Emptiness'. *Cultural Anthropology*, Theorizing the Contemporary. Retrieved 17 March 2021 from https://culanth.org/fieldsights/populated-emptiness.

Irvine, Richard. 2020. *An Anthropology of Deep Time*. Cambridge: Cambridge University Press.

Jackson, Michael. 1998. *Minima Ethnography*. Chicago: University of Chicago Press.

Jenkins, Janis Hunter. 1991. 'Anthropology, Expressed Emotion, and Schizophrenia'. *Ethos* 19(4): 387–431.

Just, Roger. 1991. *Women in Athenian Law and Life*. London: Routledge.

Kar, Sohini. 2018. *Financializing Poverty: Labor and Risk in Indian Microfinance*. Stanford: Stanford University Press.

Kasmir, Sharryn. 2018. 'Precarity'. *The Cambridge Encyclopedia of Anthropology*. Retrieved 17 March 2021 from https://www.anthroencyclopedia.com/entry/precarity.

Kenny, Michael. 1996. '*Trauma*, Time, Illness, and Culture: An Anthropological Approach to *Traumatic* Memory', in Paul Antze and Michael Lambek (eds), *Tense Past: Cultural Essays in Trauma and Memory*. New York: Routledge, pp. 151–72.

Kermode, Frank. 2000. *The Sense of an Ending: Studies in the Theory of Fiction*. Oxford: Oxford University Press.

Kidron, Carol. 2020. 'Emancipatory Voice and the Recursivity of Authentic Silence: Holocaust Descendant Accounts of the Dialectic between Silence and Voice'. *History and Anthropology*. DOI: 10.1080/02757206.2020.1726907.

Kierkegaard, Søren. 1980. *The Concept of Anxiety: A Simple Psychologically Oriented Deliberation in the View of the Dogmatic Problem of Hereditary Sin*. New York: Liveright.

———. 2012. *Fear and Trembling*. Milton Keynes: Merchant Books.

Kirtsoglou, Elisabeth. 2004. *For the Love of Women: Gender, Identity and Same-Sex Relationships in a Greek Provincial Town*. London: Routledge.

———. 2010. 'Introduction: Rhetoric and the Workings of Power – the Social Contract in Crisis'. *Social Analysis* 54(1): 1–14.

Kirtsoglou, Elisabeth, and Giorgos Tsimouris. 2018. 'Migration, Crisis, Liberalism: The Cultural and Racial Politics of Islamophobia and "Radical Alterity" in Modern Greece'. *Ethnic and Racial Studies* 41(10): 1874–92.

Klein, Naomi. 2007. *The Shock Doctrine: The Rise of Disaster Capitalism*. London: Penguin.

Knight, Daniel M. 2012a. 'Cultural Proximity: Crisis, Time and Social Memory in Central Greece'. *History and Anthropology* 23(3): 349–74.

———. 2012b. 'Turn of the Screw: Narratives of History and Economy in the Greek Crisis'. *Journal of Mediterranean Studies* 21(1): 53–76.

———. 2015. *History, Time, and Economic Crisis in Central Greece*. New York: Palgrave Macmillan.

———. 2016. 'Temporal Vertigo and Time Vortices on Greece's Central Plain'. *Cambridge Journal of Anthropology* 34(1): 32–44.

———. 2017a. 'Energy Talk, Temporality, and Belonging in Austerity Greece'. *Anthropological Quarterly* 90(1): 167–91.

———. 2017b. 'Fossilized Futures: Topologies and Topographies of Crisis Experience in Central Greece'. *Social Analysis* 61(1): 26–40.

———. 2017c. 'The Green Economy as Sustainable Alternative?' *Anthropology Today* 33(5): 28–31.

———. 2017d. 'Anxiety and Cosmopolitan Futures: Brexit and Scotland'. *American Ethnologist* 44(2): 237–42.

———. 2018. 'The Desire for Disinheritance in Austerity Greece'. *Focaal: Journal of Global and Historical Anthropology* 80: 30–42.

———. 2019a. 'Time of Crisis: Permanence as Orientation', in Rebecca Bryant and Daniel M. Knight (eds), *Orientations to the Future. American Ethnologist* website, 8

March. Retrieved 22 Feburary 2021 from http://americanethnologist.org/features/
collections/orientations-to-the-future/time-of-crisis-permanence-as-orientation.

———. 2019b. 'Perceptions of Balkan Belonging in Postdictatorship Greece', in David
Montgomery (ed.), *Everyday Life in the Balkans*. Bloomington: Indiana University
Press, pp 188–98.

———. 2020. 'Sun Grab: Failing Futures in Greece'. *Cultural Anthropology*, Theorizing the Contemporary. Retrieved 21 February 2021 from https://culanth.org/
fieldsights/sun-grab-failing-futures-in-greece.

Knight, Daniel M., and Charles Stewart. 2016. 'Ethnographies of Austerity: Temporality,
Crisis and Affect in Southern Europe'. *History and Anthropology* 27(1): 1–18.

Kole, William J. 2006. 'Neighbors Say They Saw Captive Girl Alone Outside'. North
Jersey.com. Retrieved 4 January 2020 from https://eu.northjersey.com/.

Koselleck, Reinhart. 2002. *The Practice of Conceptual History: Timing History, Spacing
Concepts*. Stanford: Stanford University Press.

Kozaitis, Kathryn. 2020. *Indebted: An Ethnography of Despair and Resilience in Greece's
Second City*. Oxford: Oxford University Press.

Lepselter, Susan. 2016. *The Resonance of Unseen Things: Poetics, Power, Captivity, and
UFOs in the American Uncanny*. Ann Arbor: University of Michigan Press.

———. 2019. 'Take Me up, I Want to Go: Captivity, Disorientation and Affect in the
Neurosphere'. *History and Anthropology* 30(5): 533–39.

Lisón-Tolosana, Carmelo. 1966. *Belmonte de los Caballeros: A Sociological Study of a
Spanish Town*. Oxford: Clarendon Press.

Lynteris, Christos. 2019. *Human Extinction and the Pandemic Imaginary*. Abingdon:
Routledge.

———. 2020. 'Emptiness and COVID-19 Cartography'. *Cultural Anthropology*, Theorizing the Contemporary. Retrieved 17 March 2021 from https://culanth.org/
fieldsights/emptiness-and-covid-19-cartography.

MacGaffey, Janet. 1987. *Entrepreneurs and Parasites: The Struggle for Indigenous Capitalism in Zaire*. Cambridge: Cambridge University Press.

———. 1991. *The Real Economy of Zaire: The Contribution of Smuggling and Other Un-
official Activities to National Wealth*. Philadelphia: University of Pennsylvania Press.

Makkai, Katalin (ed.). 2013. *Vertigo*. Abingdon: Routledge.

Manley, Gabriela. 2019a. 'Scotland's Post-referenda Futures'. *Anthropology Today* 35(4):
13–17.

———. 2019b. 'A Scottish Kind of Conspiracy'. *Anthropology News* 60(4): 49–52.

———. 2020. 'Emptiness and Futures'. *Cultural Anthropology*, Theorizing the Contemporary. Retrieved 17 March 2021 from https://culanth.org/fieldsights/empti
ness-and-futures.

Markowitz, Fran. 2018. 'Betwixt and Between in Beer Sheva: Consumption and Chronotopes in the Negev', in Italo Pardo and Giuliana Prato (eds), *The Palgrave Handbook
of Urban Ethnography*. New York: Palgrave Macmillan, pp. 153–68.

Masco, Joseph. 2006. *The Nuclear Borderlands: The Manhattan Project in Post-Cold War
New Mexico*. Princeton: Princeton University Press.

———. 2015. 'The Age of Fallout'. *History of the Present* 5(2): 137–68.

May, Rollo. 2015. *The Meaning of Anxiety*. New York: Penguin.

McLean, Stuart. 2017. *Fictionalizing Anthropology: Encounters and Fabulations at the
Edges of the Human*. Minneapolis: University of Minnesota Press.

Merriam-Webster.com Dictionary, s.v. "vertiginous". Retrieved 9 March 2021 from https://www.merriam-webster.com/dictionary/vertiginous.

Molé, Noelle. 2010. 'Precarious Subjects: Anticipating Neoliberalism in Northern Italy's Workplace'. *American Anthropologist* 112(1): 38–53.

Moss, Stephen. 2000. 'Falling for Vertigo by W.G. Sebald'. *The Guardian*, 20 January. Retrieved 22 February 2021 from https://www.theguardian.com/books/2000/jan/20/wgsebald.

Muehlebach, Andrea. 2013. 'On Precariousness and the Ethical Imagination: The Year 2012 in Sociocultural Anthropology'. *American Anthropologist* 115(2): 297–311.

Muehlebach, Andrea, and Nitzan Shoshan. 2012. 'Introduction to Special Collection on Post-Fordist Affect'. *Anthropological Quarterly* 85(2): 317–43.

Namnyak, M., N. Tufton, R. Szekely, M. Toal, S. Worboys and E.L. Sampson. 2008. 'Stockholm Syndrome: Psychiatric Diagnosis or Urban Myth?' *Acta Psychiatrica Scandanavica* 117: 4–11.

Narotzky, Susana. 2016. 'Between Inequality and Injustice: Dignity as a Motive for Mobilization during the Crisis'. *History and Anthropology* 27(1): 74–92.

Navaro-Yashin, Yael. 2012. *The Make-Believe Space: Affective Geography in a Postwar Polity*. Durham, NC: Duke University Press.

Neilson, Brett, and Ned Rossiter. 2005. 'Precarity as a Political Concept, or, Fordism as Exception'. *Theory, Culture and Society* 25(7–8): 51–72.

Nelissen, Catherine, and Pauline Coullet. 2016. *Book Analysis: Nausea*. London: Bright Summaries.

Nietzsche, Friedrich. 1974. *The Gay Science: With a Prelude in Rhymes and an Appendix of Songs*. New York: Vintage.

Nixon, Rob. 2011. *Slow Violence and the Environmentalism of the Poor*. Cambridge, MA: Harvard University Press.

O'Neill, Kevin Lewis. 2019. 'On the Aesthetics of Captivity'. *History and Anthropology* 30(5): 540–45.

O'Neill, Kevin Lewis, and Jatin Dua. 2019. 'A Forum on Captivity'. *History and Anthropology* 30(5): 491–96.

O'Neill, Kevin Lewis, and Benjamin Fogarty-Valenzuela. 2020. *Art of Captivity/Arte del Cautiverio*. Toronto: University of Toronto Press.

Oustinova-Stjepanovic, Galina. 2020. 'Introduction: Futile Political Gestures'. *Anthropological Theory Commons*. Retrieved 16 August 2021 from https://www.at-commons.com/2020/08/23/introduction-futile-political-gestures/.

Papadogiannis, Giannis. 2017. 'To Sindromo tis Stokholmis, i Ellada kai ta capital controls pou den airontai'. *I Kathimerini*, 27 March. Retrieved 22 February 2021 from https://www.kathimerini.gr/902027/article/oikonomia/ellhnikh-oikonomia/to-syndromo-ths-stokxolmhs-h-ellada-kai-ta-capital-controls-poy-den-airontai.

Papanikolaou, Dimitris. 2011. Archive Trouble. *Cultural Anthropology*, Hot Spots. Retrieved 17 March 2021 from https://culanth.org/fieldsights/archive-trouble.

———. 2021. *Greek Weird Wave: A Cinema of Biopolitics*. Edinburgh: Edinburgh University Press.

Peristiany, John (ed.). 1965. *Honour and Shame: The Values of Mediterranean Society*. London: Weidenfeld & Nicolson.

Pilevsky, Philip. 1989. *Captive Continent: The Stockholm Syndrome in European-Soviet Relations*. Westport: Praeger.

Pippin, Robert B. 2017. *The Philosophical Hitchcock: 'Vertigo' and the Anxieties of Unknowingness*. Chicago: University of Chicago Press.

Pipyrou, Stavroula. 2014a. 'Cutting *Bella Figura*: Irony, Crisis, and Secondhand Clothes in South Italy'. *American Ethnologist* 41(3): 532–46.

———. 2014b. 'Narrating Death: Affective Reworking of Suicide in Rural Greece'. *Social Anthropology* 22(2): 189–99.

———. 2020. 'Displaced Children, Silence, and the Violence of Humanitarianism in Cold War Italy'. *Anthropological Quarterly* 93(3): 161–92.

Pipyrou, Stavroula, and Antonio Sorge. n.d. 'Everyday Axioms of Violence' (working title).

Povinelli, Elizabeth. 2011. *Economies of Abandonment: Social Belonging and Endurance in Late Liberalism*. Durham, NC: Duke University Press.

Proust, Marcel. 1992. *In Search of Lost Time*. New York: Random House.

Psathas, Dimitris. 1944. *Cheimonas tou '41*. Athens: Maris.

Rakopoulos, Theodoros. 2016. 'Solidarity: The Egalitarian Tensions of a Bridge Concept'. *Social Anthropology* 24(2): 142–51.

Rao, Vyjayanthi. 2013. 'The Future in Ruins', in Ann Stoler (ed.), *Imperial Debris: On Ruins and Ruination*. Durham, NC: Duke University Press, pp. 287–322.

Rapport, Nigel. 2012. *Anyone: The Cosmopolitan Subject of Anthropology*. New York: Berghahn Books.

———. 2018. 'Cosmopolitan Politesse: Goodness, Justice, Civil Society'. *Journal of Legal Anthropology* 2(1): 92–99.

———. 2019. 'A Cosmopolitan Orientation to the Future as Human Birthright', in Rebecca Bryant and Daniel M. Knight (eds), *Orientations to the Future. American Ethnologist* website, 8 March. Retrieved 22 February 2021 from http://american ethnologist.org/features/collections/orientations-to-the-future/a-cosmopolitan-orientation-to-the-future-as-human-birthright.

Reed, Adam. 2003. *Papua New Guinea's Last Place: Experiences of Constraint in a Postcolonial Prison*. Oxford: Berghahn Books.

Ringel, Felix. 2014. 'Post-industrial Times and the Unexpected: Endurance and Sustainability in Germany's Fastest Shrinking City'. *Journal of the Royal Anthropological Institute* 20(S1): 52–70.

———. 2018. *Back to the Postindustrial Future: An Ethnography of Germany's Fastest Shrinking City*. New York: Berghahn Books.

———. 2020. 'Coronavirus: How the Pandemic Has Changed Our Perception of Time'. *The Conversation*, 28 May. Retrieved 17 March 2021 from https://theconversation .com/coronavirus-how-the-pandemic-has-changed-our-perception-of-time-139240.

Roitman, Janet. 2014. *Anti-crisis*. Durham, NC: Duke University Press.

Rosenberg, Daniel, and Anthony Grafton. 2010. *Cartographies of Time: A History of the Timeline*. New York: Princeton Architectural Press.

Rozakou, Katerina. 2017. 'Nonrecording the "European Refugee Crisis" in Greece: Navigating through Irregular Bureaucracy'. *Focaal: Journal of Global and Historical Anthropology* 77: 36–49.

———. 2019. '"How Did You Get in?" Research Access and Sovereign Power during the "Migration Crisis" in Greece'. *Social Anthropology* 27(S1): 68–83.

Runia, Eelco. 2010. 'Into Cleanness Leaping: The Vertiginous Urge to Commit History'. *History and Theory: Studies in the Philosophy of History* 49(1): 1–20.

———. 2014. *Moved by the Past: Discontinuity and Historical Mutation*. New York: Columbia University Press.

Sartre, Jean-Paul. 1965 [1938]. *Nausea*. London: Penguin.

Scanlan, Padraic X. 2019. 'Emancipation and Captivity in the British Empire'. *History and Anthropology* 30(5): 503–8.

Schatzki, Theodore. 2010. *The Timespace of Human Activity: On Performance, Society, and History as Indeterminate Teleological Events*. Lanham: Lexington Books.

Scheele, Judith. 2019. 'Saharan Prisons'. *History and Anthropology* 30(5): 509–14.

Scheper-Hughes, Nancy. 2007. 'Violence and the Politics of Remorse: Lessons from South Africa', in João Biehl, Byron Good and Arthur Kleinman (eds), *Subjectivity: Ethnographic Investigations*. Berkeley: University of California Press, pp. 179–234.

Schneider-Mayerson, Matthew. 2015. *Peak Oil: Apocalyptic Environmentalism and Libertarian Political Culture*. Chicago: University of Chicago Press.

Schuster, Caroline. 2015. *Social Collateral: Women and Microfinance in Paraguay's Smuggling Economy*. Berkeley: University of California Press.

Scranton, Roy. 2017. *Learning to Die in the Anthropocene: Reflections on the End of a Civilization*. San Francisco: City Lights.

Sebald, W.G. 1990. *Vertigo*. London: Vintage.

Serres, Michel. 1995. *Genesis*, translated by Geneviève James and James Nielson. Ann Arbor: University of Michigan Press.

———. 2014. *Times of Crisis: What the Financial Crisis Revealed and How to Reinvent our Lives and Future*. London: Bloomsbury.

Serres, Michel, and Bruno Latour. 1995. *Conversations on Science, Culture, and Time*. Ann Arbor: University of Michigan Press.

Shevchenko, Olga. 2009. *Crisis and the Everyday in Postsocialist Moscow*. Bloomington: Indiana University Press.

Shir-Vertesh, Dafna, and Fran Markowitz. 2015. 'Between War and Peace: Israel Day by Day'. *Ethnologie Française* 45(2): 209–21.

Smith, Richard. 2016. 'The Virtues of Unknowing'. *Journal of Philosophy of Education* 50(2): 272–84.

Spanos, William V. 1978. 'The Un-naming of the Beasts: The Postmodernity of Sartre's "La Nausee"'. *Criticism* (20)3: 223–80.

Standing, Guy. 2011. *The Precariat: The New Dangerous Class*. London: Bloomsbury.

Stewart, Charles. 1991. *Demons and the Devil: Moral Imagination in Modern Greek Culture*. Princeton: Princeton University Press.

———. 2003. 'Dreams of Treasure: Temporality, Historicization, and the Unconscious'. *Anthropological Theory* 3(4): 481–500.

———. 2012. *Dreaming and Historical Consciousness in Island Greece*. Cambridge, MA: Harvard University Press.

———. 2017. 'Uncanny History: Temporal Topology in the Post-Ottoman World'. *Social Analysis* 61(1): 129–42.

Stewart, Kathleen. 2005. 'Trauma Time: A Still Life', in Daniel Rosenberg and Susan Harding (eds), *Histories of the Future*. Durham, NC: Duke University Press, pp. 321–40.

Stoler, Ann Laura. 2008. 'Imperial Debris: Reflections on Ruins and Ruination'. *Cultural Anthropology* 23(2): 191–219.

———. 2013. 'Introduction "The Rot Remains": From Ruins to Ruination', in Ann Laura Stoler (ed.), *Imperial Debris: On Ruins and Ruination*. Durham, NC: Duke University Press, pp. 1–38.

Sullivan, Harry Stack. 1953. *Conceptions of Modern Psychiatry*. New York: W.W. Norton.

Sutton, David. 1998. *Memories Cast in Stone: The Relevance of the Past in Everyday Life*. Oxford: Berg.

———. 2003. 'Poked by the "Foreign Finger" in Greece: Conspiracy Theory or the Hermeneutics of Suspicion?', in Keith Brown and Yannis Hamilakis (eds), *The Usable Past: Greek Metahistories*. Lanham: Lexington Books, pp. 191–210.

Theodossopoulos, Dimitrios. 2013. 'Infuriated with the Infuriated? Blaming Tactics and Discontent about the Greek Financial Crisis'. *Current Anthropology* 54(2): 200–21.

———. 2014. 'On De-pathologizing Resistance'. *History and Anthropology* 25(4): 415–30.

Ticktin, Miriam. 2017. 'A World without Innocence'. *American Ethnologist* 44(4): 577–90.

Trouillot, Michel-Rolph. 1995. *Silencing the Past: Power and the Production of History*. Boston, MA: Beacon Press.

Tsing, Anna Lowenhaupt. 2005. *Friction: An Ethnography of Global Connection*. Princeton: Princeton University Press.

———. 2015. *The Mushroom at the End of the World: On the Possibility of Life in Capitalist Ruins*. Princeton: Princeton University Press.

Turner, Victor. 1981. 'Social Dramas and Stories about Them', in W.J.T. Mitchell (ed.), *On Narrative*. Chicago: University of Chicago Press, pp. 137–64.

Valentine, David, Valerie A. Olson and Debbora Battaglia. 2012. 'Extreme: Limits and Horizons in the Once and Future Cosmos'. *Anthropological Quarterly* 85(4): 1007–26.

Vigh, Henrik. 2008. 'Crisis and Chronicity: Anthropological Perspectives on Continuous Conflict and Decline'. *Ethnos* 73(1): 5–24.

Weszkalnys, Gisa. 2015. 'Geology, Potentiality, Speculation: On the Indeterminacy of "First Oil"'. *Cultural Anthropology* 30(4): 611–39.

Wilde, Matt. 2017. 'Embryonic Alternatives amid London's Housing Crisis'. *Anthropology Today* 33(5): 16–19.

Williams, Raymond. 2001 [1961]. *Long Revolution*. Peterborough: Broadview Press.

Wolf-Meyer, Matthew. 2019. *Theory for the World to Come: Speculative Fiction and Apocalyptic Anthropology*. Minneapolis: University of Minnesota Press.

Zerubavel, Eviatar. 2003. *Time Maps: Collective Memory and the Social Shape of the Past*. Chicago: University of Chicago Press.

Žižek, Slavoj. 2014. *Event: Philosophy in Transit*. London: Penguin.

INDEX

www.ingramcontent.com/pod-product-compliance
Lightning Source LLC
Chambersburg PA
CBHW070627030426
42337CB00020B/3942